CASE STUDY RESEARCH
IN SOFTWARE
ENGINEERING

CASE STUDY RESEARCH IN SOFTWARE ENGINEERING
Guidelines and Examples

PER RUNESON
Lund University, Sweden

MARTIN HÖST
Lund University, Sweden

AUSTEN RAINER
University of Hertfordshire, UK

BJÖRN REGNELL
Lund University, Sweden

A JOHN WILEY & SONS, INC., PUBLICATION

Library of Congress Cataloging-in-Publication Data:

Case study research in software engineering : guidelines and examples /
Per Runeson ... [et al.]. – 1st ed.
      p. cm.
   Includes bibliographical references and index.
   ISBN 978-1-118-10435-4 (hardback)
  1. Computer software–Development–Case studies.   I. Per Runeson.
   QA76.76.D47C37 2012
   005.1–dc23
                                                    2011031429

ISBN: 9781118104354

10 9 8 7 6 5 4 3 2 1

CONTENTS

FOREWORD

This book is very timely given the increasing interest in case study research within the software engineering community and the realization by many that research that uses a case study approach provides us with a good understanding of what actually happens in the real world. What use is our research if we do not actually understand what is really happening and cannot provide useful insights into organizations targeting their practical needs?

Doing case study research in software engineering and ensuring that the research is thorough is not easy. Although there is a long history of case study research in the social sciences, it has been difficult to translate their research guidelines into the software engineering domain. This book will help both experienced and novice case study researchers improve their research methodology. The authors provide comprehensive examples of case study research they, and others, have conducted. They also critique the examples. This is very useful for researchers wanting to undertake case study research and will help them to avoid some of the problems already experienced by the authors and other researchers.

In case study research, we choose to study some phenomenon within its real-life setting. Our "unit of analysis" may be some aspect of a software engineering project, a software engineering methodology and its use within an organization, a software engineering section of an organization, or the whole or a particular part of a new or ongoing development or maintenance project. The unit of analysis will vary depending on the research question; the authors provide us with a number of case studies where the chosen unit of analysis varies according to the research question.

Yes, much of the data can be subjective, but I do not agree with the view that case studies in software engineering are somewhat suspect, lacking in rigor, and somehow not as good as other research methods. Properly done case studies can provide much useful information, both for the researchers and the organization involved. The authors, who are all well known for their case study research in software engineering, make a very telling comment regarding one of their research papers that used a case study methodology. They tell us that the paper was rejected by journal reviewers due to "the subjective nature of their data." Such a comment from a reviewer or an editor illustrates the timeliness of this book and a very real need within the software engineering community.

Case studies provide us with research results from real-world projects; these results would be difficult to achieve with any other research method. While surveys and experiments can supply useful information, I do not believe that there is any substitute for a case study when we want to find out what is happening in real projects or when methodologies and so on are implemented within a specific environment. Not only is this type of research interesting for researchers, but it is also imperative that organizations understand what is happening so that they can make informed decisions regarding what works well and what does not work, within their own particular environment.

Case studies can be very time consuming for both the researchers involved and the organizations concerned, and we cannot generalize from a single case as we do not have enough data for statistical analysis. To generalize, we need replications that use exactly the same protocol as was used for the original case. Hence, it is important to carefully develop and use a case study protocol, to accurately describe the context of the case, and to make the protocol available to other researchers. Context is very important when we are trying to answer a particular software engineering research question as we cannot begin to understand what is happening in a project or is an organization without carefully considering the context of the case we are investigating. The research question(s), proposition(s), and any hypotheses must be explicitly stated. Replications are important so that we can understand how much context influences our results. If we replicate some case study research and get the same results as the research we replicate, that is an important result; these results deserve to be published so that generalizations regarding the particular research question(s) can be made. Owing to my innate cynicism, I can see an exact replication, which yields the same results as the prior research, being rejected by journal and conference reviewers. They will say that the research does not provide anything new, even though the result is important and does add to our body of knowledge, thus making generalizations from case study research even more difficult.

In the first part of this book, readers will find useful advice covering all aspects of case study research in chapters that include discussion on case study design, data collection, data analysis and interpretation, the reporting of case studies, scaling up case study research, and using case studies; the second part of the book comprises useful, informative, and comprehensive examples of actual case study research. All in all, this book provides the means to help us all do better case study research.

DR. JUNE M. VERNER

Conjoint Professor of Software Engineering, CSE, University of New South Wales, Sydney, Australia
Marie Curie Fellow, Keele University, Staffordshire, UK

PREFACE

The authors' first contact with case study research and qualitative analysis was around the turn of the millennium. For Rainer, the journey started when entering his PhD program in 1995, and guidance was given by an earlier edition of Yin's book on case studies [216] from social sciences and Benbasat et al's paper [19] from information systems. For Runeson, Höst, and Regnell, the journey began by studying the first edition of Robson's book [161] and by inviting a sociologist, the late Dr. Peter Arvidson, to give a seminar on "sociologic research methodology," which was a first step of our journey toward using these "fuzzy" tools for research.

Our experience of adapting and applying case study methodology from other disciplines to software engineering has motivated us to write this book. We intend to provide comprehensive guidance for researchers and students conducting case studies, for reviewers of case study manuscripts, and for readers of case study papers; and we do so to help these groups of people in their efforts to better understand and improve software engineering practice. The nature of case study research means that it is hard to provide precise guidelines, so we complement our guidelines with a range of examples; examples of not only "good practice" but also of mistakes that we have made and from which we hope others can learn. Hence, we provide examples that the reader may learn from and adapt to their situations.

The book is constituted of two main parts: methodology and examples. Part I begins with Chapter 1 dealing with motivation and a historical background to case studies in software engineering. Chapter 2 defines terms in the field of empirical research, which we use throughout the book, and sets case study research into the context of other research methods. Chapter 3 elaborates the design of a case study and planning for data collection. Chapter 4 describes the process of data collection and validation. In Chapter 5, issues on data analysis are treated, as well as the validity issues for the analysis and the whole study. Reporting case studies to different audiences is discussed in Chapter 6. Chapter 7 describes issues on scaling up to large case studies and Chapter 8 discusses different uses of case studies. In Part II of the book, Chapter 9 gives an introduction to the example case studies in Chapters 10–14. These five examples of case studies are intended as illustrations of the presented guidelines in a more concrete way and are taken from research areas on eXtreme programming (XP), project management (PM), quality assurance (QA), requirements management tools (RMT), and requirements engineering and verification and validation (REVV). Finally, the appendices contain checklists for reading and reviewing case study papers, together with examples of documents for the case study process.

We hope that those who design, conduct, and report case studies and those who read the results of case studies may build upon our guidelines and examples, for better understanding of and improving the software engineering practice.

P. RUNESON, M. HÖST, A. RAINER AND B. REGNELL

Lund, Sweden and Hatfield, UK

December, 2011

ACKNOWLEDGMENTS

We are very grateful to Professor June Verner for the support she has given us in her Foreword. We are also very grateful to Professor Verner and Professor Barbara Kitchenham for reviewing an earlier version of the book. Both Professors have contributed enormously to the development of the field of software engineering research and we greatly appreciate their constructive feedback.

This book began as an article in the journal of *Empirical Software Engineering* and the first two authors (Runeson and Höst) thank the editor of the journal, Professor Lionel Briand, for his encouragement to prepare and submit the article. The first two authors also thank the International Software Engineering Research Network (ISERN: http://isern.iese.de/Portal/) for contributing to the development and evaluation of the case study checklists that appear in the original article, and that are reproduced here in Appendix A.

We also thank students at Lund University and Blekinge Institute of Technology for reviewing earlier drafts of this book as a part of a course on case study research: Nauman bin Ali, Elizabeth Bjarnason, Markus Borg, Alexander Cedergren, Ronald Jabangwe, Samireh Jalali, Nils Johansson, Christin Lindholm, Jesper Pedersen Notander, and Michael Unterkalmsteiner.

Several people and organizations were involved in making the example case studies possible. We acknowledge their specific contributions below.

The XP study in Chapter 10 was conducted with main contributions from Dr. Daniel Karlström, and this would not have been possible without the people that were available for interviews at ABB, Ericsson, and Vodafone.

For the material in Chapter 11, Austen Rainer thanks IBM Hursley Park, Paul Gibson, John Allan, and all the project members of Project B and Project C for their support during the two case studies; and also the other stakeholders at IBM Hursley

Park who agreed for their projects to be studied. Thanks are also due to Professor Martin Shepperd for supervising Austen's PhD.

The iterative quality assurance study in Chapter 12 was conducted with main contributions from Dr. Carina Andersson, and this would not have been possible without the people that supported the data collection and were available for discussions and validation of the analyses.

Chapter 13 represents Austen Rainer's interpretation of the work carried out by Cei Sanderson, while supervising Cei's Masters of Research degree at the University of Hertfordshire. Austen also thanks all the employees at 1Spatial for their cooperation and assistance during the Knowledge Transfer Project (KTP). KTP was funded by a grant (grant number: KTP000933) from the UK's Technology Strategy Board.

For the material in Chapter 14, Björn Regnell and Per Runeson thank Dr. Annabella Loconsole, Dr. Giedre Sabaliauskaite, Michael Unterkalmsteiner, Markus Borg, Elizabeth Bjarnason, Emelie Engström, Dr. Tony Gorschek, and Dr. Robert Feldt for collaboration in the study. The study project is led by Björn Regnell, with Tony Gorschek as vice leader and Per Runeson as manager of the research program EASE, to which the presented study belongs. The researchers of this project are very grateful to the anonymous interviewees for their dedicated participation in this study.

Per Runeson's work with case studies and this book were partially funded by the Swedish Research Council under grants 622-2004-552 and 622-2007-8028 for a senior researcher position in software engineering. Austen Rainer's work on this book was partially funded by a grant from the UK's Royal Academy of Engineering International Travel Grant scheme (grant number: ITG10-279) and from Lund University, Department of Computer Science. Martin Höst's and Björn Regnell's work was partly funded by the Industrial Excellence Center EASE—Embedded Applications Software Engineering (http://ease.cs.lth.se).

We are most thankful to our families for their support in the preparation of this book and helping us find the time to write it: Kristina, Jesper, Malin, Lovisa, and Hampus; Anna, Tilde, and Gustav; Clare, Samuel, and Maisie; Susanne, Rasmus, and Felix. They are closer to our hearts than case study research.

P. RUNESON, M. HÖST, A. RAINER AND B. REGNELL

PART I

CASE STUDY METHODOLOGY

CHAPTER 1

INTRODUCTION

1.1 WHAT IS A CASE STUDY?

The term "case study" appears every now and then in the title of software engineering research papers. These papers have in common that they study a specific case, in contrast to a sample from a specified population. However, the presented studies range from very ambitious and well-organized studies in the field of operations (*in vivo*) to small toy examples in a university lab (*in vitro*) that claim to be case studies. This variation creates confusion, which should be addressed by increased knowledge about case study methodology.

Case study is a commonly used research strategy in areas such as psychology, sociology, political science, social work, business, and community planning (e.g., [162, 196, 217]). In these areas, case studies are conducted with the objectives of not only increasing knowledge (e.g., knowledge about individuals, groups, and organizations and about social, political, and related phenomena) but also bringing about change in the phenomenon being studied (e.g. improving education or social care). Software engineering research has similar high-level objectives, that is, to better understand how and why software engineering should be undertaken and, with this knowledge, to seek to improve the software engineering process and the resultant software products.

There are different taxonomies used to classify research in software engineering. The term case study is used in parallel with terms like field study and observational study, each focusing on a particular aspect of the research methodology. For example,

Case Study Research in Software Engineering: Guidelines and Examples, First Edition.
Per Runeson, Martin Höst, Austen Rainer, and Björn Regnell.
© 2012 John Wiley & Sons, Inc. Published 2012 by John Wiley & Sons, Inc.

Lethbridge et al. use the term *field studies* as the most general term [118], while Easterbrook et al. call *case studies* one of the five "classes of research methods" [47]. Zelkowitz and Wallace propose a terminology that is somewhat different from what is used in other fields, and categorize project monitoring, case study, and field study as *observational methods* [218]. Studies involving change are sometimes denoted *action research* [119, 162, pp. 215–220]. This plethora of terms causes confusion and problems when trying to aggregate multiple empirical studies and to reuse research methodology guidelines from other fields of research.

Yin defines case study as

> an empirical enquiry that investigates a contemporary phenomenon within its real-life context, especially when the boundaries between phenomenon and context are not clearly evident. [217, p. 13]

This fits particularly well in software engineering. Experimentation in software engineering has clearly shown that there are many factors impacting on the outcome of a software engineering activity, for example, when trying to replicate studies [182]. One of Kitchenham et al.'s [105] preliminary guidelines for empirical research in software engineering states

> Be sure to specify as much of the industrial context as possible. In particular, clearly define the entities, attributes, and measures that are capturing the contextual information.

On the subject of observational studies, which would include case studies, Kitchenham et al. write

> There is an immense variety to be found in development procedures, organizational culture, and products. This breadth implies that empirical studies based on observing or measuring some aspect of software development in a particular company must report a great deal of contextual information if any results and their implications are to be properly understood. Researchers need to identify the particular factors that might affect the generality and utility of the conclusions. [105, p. 723]

Case studies offer an approach that does not require a strict boundary between the object of study and its environment. Case studies do not generate the same results on, for example, causal relationships, as controlled experiments do, but they provide a deeper understanding of the phenomena under study. As they are different from analytical and controlled empirical studies, case studies have been criticized for being of less value, being impossible to generalize from, being biased by researchers, and so on. This critique can be met by applying proper research methodology practices and by reconsidering that knowledge is more than statistical significance [56, 115, 128]. However, the research community has to learn more about the case study methodology in order to conduct, report, review, and judge it properly.

1.2 A BRIEF HISTORY OF CASE STUDIES IN SOFTWARE ENGINEERING

The term *case study* first appeared in software engineering journal papers in the late 1970s. At that time, a case study was typically a *demonstration case*, that is, a case that demonstrated the implementation of some software technology or programming concept.

In the mid- to late-1980s, papers started to report case studies of a broader range of software development phenomena, for example, Alexander and Potter's [3] study of formal specifications and rapid prototying. For these types of papers, the term *case study* refers to a self-experienced and self-reported investigation. Throughout the 1990s the scale of these "self investigations" increased and there were, for example, a series of papers reporting case studies of software process improvement in large and multinational organizations such as Boeing, Hughes, Motorola, NASA, and Siemens.

Case studies based on the external and independent observation of a software engineering activity first appeared in the late 1980s, for example, Boehm and Ross's [23, p. 902] "extensive case study" of the introduction of new information systems into a large industrial corporation in an emerging nation. These case studies, however, did not direct attention at case study methodology that is, at the design, conduct, and reporting of the case study.

The first case study papers that explicitly report the study methodology were published in 1988: Curtis et al.'s [37] field study of software design activities and Swanson and Beath's [199] multiple case study of software maintenance. Given the status of case study research in software engineering at the time, it is not surprising that Swanson and Beath were actually researchers in a school of management in the United States, and were not *software engineering* researchers. Swanson and Beath use their multiple case studies to illustrate a number of challenges that arise when conducting case studies research, and they also present methodological lessons. Their paper therefore appears to be the first of its kind in the software engineering research community that explicitly discusses the challenge of designing, conducting, and reporting case study research.

During the 1990s, both demonstration studies and genuine case studies (as we define them here) were published, although only in small numbers. Glass et al. analyzed software engineering publications in six major software engineering journals for the period 1995–1999 and found that only 2.2% of these publications reported case studies [61]. Much more recently, a sample of papers from Sjøberg et al.'s large systematic review of *experimental* studies in software engineering [195] were analyzed by Holt [72]. She classified 12% of the sample as case studies. This compares to 1.9% of papers classified as formal experiments in the Sjøberg study. But differences in the design of these reviews make it hard to properly compare the reviews and draw firm conclusions.

The first recommendations, by *software engineering researchers*, regarding case study methodology were published in the mid-1990s [109]. However, these recommendations focus primarily on the use of quantitative data. In the late 1990s, Seaman published guidelines on qualitative research [176]. Then, in the early twenty-first century, a broader set of guidelines on empirical research were published by Kitchenham et al. [105]. Sim et al. arranged a workshop on the topic, which was summarized in *Empirical Software Engineering* [189], Wohlin et al. provided a brief introduction to case studies among other empirical methods [214], and Dittrich et al. edited a special issue of *Information and Software Technology* on qualitative software engineering research [43]. A wide range of aspects of empirical research issues for software engineering are addressed in a book edited by Shull et al. [186]. But the first comprehensive guides to case study research in software engineering were not published until 2009, by Runeson and Höst [170] and Verner et al. [208]. Runeson and Höst's paper was published in the peer-reviewed journal *Empirical Software Engineering* and provides the foundation for this book.

1.3   WHY A BOOK ON CASE STUDIES OF SOFTWARE ENGINEERING?

Case study methodology handbooks are superfluously available in, for example, social sciences [162, 196, 217], which have also been used in software engineering. In the field of information systems (IS) research, the case study methodology is also much more mature than in software engineering. However, IS case studies mostly focus on the information system in its *usage context* and less on the *development and evolution* of information systems. Example sources on case study methodology in IS include Benbasat et al. who provide a brief overview of case study research in information systems [19]. Lee analyzes IS case studies from a positivistic perspective [115] and Klein and Myers do the same from an interpretive perspective [111].

It is relevant to raise the question: what is specific for software engineering that motivates specialized research methodology? In addition to the specifics of the examples, the characteristics of software engineering objects of study are different from social sciences and also to some extent from information systems. The study objects in software engineering have the following properties:

- They are private corporations or units of public agencies *developing* software rather than public agencies or private corporations *using* software systems.
- They are *project*-oriented rather than *line*- or *function*-oriented organizations.
- The studied work is an *advanced engineering work* conducted by highly educated people, rather than a *routine work* [60].
- There is an aim to improve the engineering practices, which implies that there is a component of design research [71] (i.e. prescriptive work).

Sjøberg et al. [194] write that in the typical software engineering situation *actors* apply *technologies* in the performance of *activities* on an existing or planned *software-related* product or interim products. So, for example, requirements analysts (the actors) use requirements engineering tools (the technologies) during requirements elicitation (an activity) to produce a requirements specification (an interim software-related product). Like Pfleeger [139], we use a broad definition of *technology*: any method, technique, tool, procedure, or paradigm used in software development or maintenance. Sjøberg et al.'s use of the term *actor* is not restricted to mean individual people, but can refer to levels of human behavior. For example, Curtis et al. [37] identified five layers of behavior: the individual, the team, the project, the organization, and the business mileu.

There is a very wide range of activities in software engineering, such as development, operation, and maintenance of software and related artifacts as well as the management of these activities. A frequent aim of software engineering research is to investigate how this development, operation, and maintenance is conducted, and also managed, by software engineers and other stakeholders under different conditions. With such a wide range of activities, and a wide range of software products being developed, there is a very diverse range of skills and experience needed by the actors undertaking these activities.

Software engineering is also distinctive in the *combination* of *diverse* topics that make up the discipline. Glass et al. [60] describe software engineering as an intellectually intensive, nonroutine activity, and Walz et al. [212] describe software engineering as a multiagent cognitive activity. Table 1.1 provides an indication of the topics in the computing field, and therefore the expertise needed by practitioners and researchers.

Many of the interim products are produced either intentionally by the actors (e.g., the minutes of meetings) or automatically by technology (e.g., updates to a version of control system). Therefore, one of the distinctive aspects of software engineering is the raw data that are naturally, and often automatically, generated by the activities and technologies.

There are clear overlaps with other disciplines, such as psychology, management, business, and engineering, but software engineering brings these other disciplines together in a unique way, a way that needs to be studied with research methods tailored to the specifics of the discipline.

Case studies investigate phenomena in their real-world settings, for example, new technologies, communication in global software development, project risk and failure factors, and so on. Hence, the researcher needs to consider not only the practical requirements and constraints from the researcher's perspective, but also the objectives and resource commitments of the stakeholders who are likely to be participating in, or supporting, the case study. Also, practitioners may want to intervene in future projects – that is, change the way things are done in future projects – on the basis of the outcomes from the case studies, and often software engineering managers are interested in *technology* interventions, such as adopting a new technology. This includes both software process improvement (SPI) work [201] and design of solutions [71]. There are, therefore, distinctive practical constraints on case study research in software engineering.

In addition, the software engineering research community has a pragmatic and result-oriented view on research methodology, rather than a philosophical stand, as noticed by Seaman [176]. The community does not pay any larger attention to the inherent conflict between the positivistic foundation for experiments and the interpretive foundation for case studies. This conflict has caused life-long battles in other fields of research. As empirical software engineering has evolved from empirical studies in

TABLE 1.1   Topics in Computing (from Glass et al. [59]).

Problem-solving concepts	Real-time
Algorithms	Edutainment
Mathematics/computational science	
Methodologies	*Systems/software management concepts*
Artificial intelligence	Project/product management
	Process management
Computer Concepts	Measurement/metrics
Computer/hardware principles/	Personnel issues
architecture	Acquisition of software
Intercomputer communication	
Operating systems	*Organizational concepts*
Machine/assembler-level	Organizational structure
data/instructions	Strategy
	Alignment
System/software concepts	Organizational learning/knowledge
System architecture/engineering	management
Software life cycle/engineering	Technology transfer
Programming languages	Change management
Methods/techniques	Information technology implementation
Tools	Information technology usage/operation
Product quality	Management of "computing" function
Human–computer interaction	IT Impact
System security	Computing/information as a business
	Legal/ethical/cultural/
Data/information concepts	
Data/file structures	*Societal concepts*
Database/warehouse/mart organization	Cultural implications
Information retrieval	Legal implications
Data analysis	Ethical implications
Data security	Political implications
Problem domain-specific concepts	*Disciplinary issues*
Scientific/engineering	"Computing" research
Information systems	"Computing" curriculum/teaching
Systems programming	

a natural science context, experimentation and quantitative studies have been considered of higher value compared to case studies and qualitative studies. However, we can observe a slowly growing acceptance for the the case study methodology as a basis for high-quality research, in its contribution to understanding and change in the complex industrial environment of software engineering.

Existing methodology guidelines specifically addressing case studies in software engineering include several publications as presented in Section 1.2 [43, 109, 170,

176, 186, 189, 208, 214]. Still, a comprehensive handbook on *case study research in software engineering* is missing, and that is what this book offers, with *guidelines and examples*.

1.4 CONCLUSION

The term "case study" is used for a broad range of studies in software engineering. There is a need to clarify and unify the understanding of what is meant by a case study, and how a good case study is conducted and reported. There exist several guidelines in other fields of research, but we see a need for guidelines, tailored to the field of software engineering, which we provide in this book.

CHAPTER 2

BACKGROUND AND DEFINITION OF CONCEPTS

2.1 INTRODUCTION

In this chapter, we lay out the general foundation for case study research in software engineering. We characterize the case study strategy and compare it with other empirical research strategies, primarily survey, experiment, and action research. Aspects of empirical research strategies are elaborated, for example, their primary purpose, whether they have a fixed or flexible design, whether data are quantitative or qualitative, and the roles which triangulation and replication play. We discuss, on the basis of different sources within and outside software engineering, what constitutes an exemplary case study and summarize criteria or good case study research. We set out a scheme to help decide when case study is a feasible research strategy, and we define a general research process for case studies, which is used throughout the book.

2.2 RESEARCH STRATEGIES

Let us start with three different general definitions of the term case study, one by Robson [162], one by Yin [217], both in the social science field, and one definition by Benbasat et al. [19] in the information systems field.

Case Study Research in Software Engineering: Guidelines and Examples, First Edition.
Per Runeson, Martin Höst, Austen Rainer, and Björn Regnell.
© 2012 John Wiley & Sons, Inc. Published 2012 by John Wiley & Sons, Inc.

Robson. Case study is a strategy for doing research that involves an empirical investigation of a particular contemporary phenomenon within its context using multiple sources of evidence.

Yin. Case study is an empirical inquiry that investigates a contemporary phenomenon within its real-life context, especially when the boundaries between the phenomenon and its context are not clearly evident.

Benbasat. A case study examines a phenomenon in its natural setting, employing multiple methods of data collection to gather information from one or a few entities (people, groups, or organization). The boundaries of the phenomenon are not clearly evident at the outset of the research and no experimental control or manipulation is used.

The three definitions agree on that case study is an empirical method aimed at *investigating contemporary phenomena in their context.* Robson calls it a research strategy and stresses the use of *multiple sources of evidence,* Yin denotes it an inquiry and remarks that *the boundary between the phenomenon and its context may be unclear,* while Benbasat et al. make the definitions somewhat more specific, mentioning *information gathering from few entities* (people, groups, and organizations) and the *lack of experimental control.* The three definitions together emphasize important characteristics of case studies.

We derive from these general definitions, specifically for software engineering, the conclusion that

Case study in software engineering is an empirical enquiry that draws on multiple sources of evidence to investigate one instance (or a small number of instances) of a contemporary software engineering phenomenon within its real-life context, especially when the boundary between phenomenon and context cannot be clearly specified.

There are three other major research strategies that are related to case studies, survey, experiment, and action research:

Survey is the "collection of standardized information from a specific population, or some sample from one, usually, but not necessarily by means of a questionnaire or interview" [162]. Surveys provide an overview rather than depth in the studied field.

Experiment or controlled experiment is characterized by "measuring the effects of manipulating one variable on another variable" [162] and that "subjects are assigned to treatments by random" [215]. The effect of one specific variable is studied in experiments. Quasi-experiments are similar to controlled experiments, except that subjects are not randomly assigned to treatments [32]. Quasi-experiments conducted in an industry setting may have many characteristics in common with case studies.

Action research with its purpose to "influence or change some aspect of whatever is the focus of the research" [162] is closely related to case study. In some definitions, a case study is purely observational while action research is focused on and involved in the change process. In software process improvement [44, 75] and technology transfer studies [64], the research method has clear characteristics of action research, although it is sometimes referred to as an "iterative case study" [7]. In IS, where action research is widely used, there is a discussion on finding the balance between action and research, see for example, Avison et al. [10] and Baskerville and Wood-Harper [16]. We prefer including action research in the wider notion of case study, and for the research part, these guidelines in this book apply as well. For the action part, guidelines on software process improvement may be useful [201], as well as literature on design science [71].

Easterbrook et al. [47] also count *ethnographic studies* among the major research strategies. We prefer to consider ethnographic studies as a specialized type of case studies with focus on cultural practices [47] or long duration studies with large amounts of participant-observer data [111]. Zelkowitz and Wallace define four different "observational methods" in software engineering [218]: *project monitoring, case study, assertion*, and *field study*. The guidelines in this book apply to all these, except assertion that we do not consider a proper research method. We also prefer to see *project monitoring* as part of a case study and *field studies* as multiple case studies.

Yin includes archival analysis and history studies, as distinct types of research methods [217, p. 5]. We prefer including the archives and historical data as sources for information in case studies, rather than distinct research methods. Yin also recognizes that multiple strategies may be appropriate for a given study and we hold the same view. For example, a survey may be conducted within a case study to get a broad overview of the studied object, literature search often precedes a case study to identify the foundations for the studied object, and archival analyses may be a part of its data collection. Ethnographic methods, such as interviews and observations, are mostly used for data collection in case studies.

In general, the borderline between the types of study is not always distinct. Robson summarizes his view, which we consider applies also to software engineering research, "Many flexible design studies, although not explicitly labeled as such, can be usefully viewed as case studies" [162, p. 185].

2.3 CHARACTERISTICS OF RESEARCH STRATEGIES

2.3.1 Purpose

Different research strategies serve different purposes; one type of research strategy does not fit all purposes. We distinguish between the following four general types of purposes for research, tailored from Robson's classification [162]:

Exploratory – finding out what is happening, seeking new insights, and generating ideas and hypotheses for new research.

Descriptive – portraying the current status of a situation or phenomenon.

Explanatory – seeking an explanation for a situation or a problem, mostly but not necessarily, in the form of a causal relationship.

Improving – trying to improve a certain aspect of the studied phenomenon.

Case study strategy was originally used primarily for exploratory purposes, and some researchers still limit case studies to this purpose, as discussed by Flyvbjerg [56]. However, it is also used for descriptive purposes if the generality of the situation or phenomenon is of secondary importance. Case studies may also be used for explanatory purposes, for example, in interrupted time series design (pre- and postevent studies), although the isolation of factors may be a problem. This involves testing of existing theories in confirmatory studies. Finally, as indicated above, case studies in the software engineering discipline often take an improvement approach, similar to action research; see, for example, the iterative case study of quality assurance in Chapter 12.

Klein and Myers define three types of case studies depending on the research perspective: positivist, critical, and interpretive [111]. A *positivist* case study searches evidence for formal propositions, measures variables, tests hypotheses, and draws inferences from a sample to a stated population, which is close to the natural science research model [115] and related to Robson's explanatory category. A *critical* case study aims at social critique and at being emancipatory, that is, identifying different forms of social, cultural, and political domination that may hinder human ability. Improving case studies may have a character of being critical to the current practice and contribute to change. An *interpretive* case study attempts to understand phenomena through the participants' interpretation of their context, which is similar to Robson's exploratory and descriptive types. Software engineering case studies tend to lean toward a positivist perspective, especially for explanatory-type studies. This is related to the pragmatic nature of empirical software engineering research, where the practical implications of a certain practice is more relevant than the questions on abstract philosophical principles.

2.3.2 Control and Data

Conducting research on real-world phenomena implies a constant trade-off between level of control and degree of realism. The realistic situation is often complex and nondeterministic, which hinders the understanding of what is happening, especially for studies with explanatory purposes. On the other hand, increasing the control reduces the degree of realism, sometimes leading to the underlying causal factors and structures being set outside the scope of the study. Case studies are by definition conducted in real-world settings, and thus have a high degree of realism, mostly at the expense of the level of control. Experiments on the other hand mostly isolate a certain part of reality, for example, the inspection process [9] for better control of the situation, but at the expense of realism.

TABLE 2.1   Overview of Research Strategy Characteristics

	Experiment	Survey	Case Study	Action Research
Primary objective	Explanatory	Descriptive	Exploratory	Improving
Primary data	Quantitative	Quantitative	Qualitative	Qualitative
Design type	Fixed	Fixed	Flexible	Flexible

The data collected in an empirical study may be *quantitative* or *qualitative*. Quantitative data involve numbers and classes, while qualitative data involve words, descriptions, pictures, diagrams, and so on. Quantitative data are analyzed using statistics, while qualitative data are analyzed using categorization and sorting. Quantitative data are more exact, while qualitative data are 'richer' in what they may express. Case studies tend mostly to be based on qualitative data, but combinations of qualitative and quantitative data often provide better understanding of the studied phenomenon [176], what is sometimes called 'mixed methods' [162].

The research process may be characterized as a *fixed* or *flexible* design according to Anastas and MacDonald [4] and Robson [162]. In a fixed design process, all parameters are defined at the launch of the study, while in a flexible design process key parameters of the study may be changed during the course of the study. Case studies are typically flexible design studies as they may be adjusted to findings during the course of the study. Experiments and surveys are fixed design studies, which cannot be changed once they are launched. Other literature use the terms quantitative and qualitative design studies for fixed and flexible design studies, respectively, [34]. We prefer to adhere to the fixed/flexible terminology since it reduces the risk for confusion that a study with, in its terminology, "qualitative design" may collect both qualitative and quantitative data. Otherwise, it may be unclear whether the term qualitative refers to the data or the design of the study.

Table 2.1 shows an overview of the primary characteristics of the above-discussed research strategies. Note that there may be other secondary characteristics of each of the strategies.

2.3.3 Triangulation

Triangulation is important to increase the precision and strengthen the validity of empirical research. Triangulation means taking multiple perspectives towards the studied object and thus providing a broader picture. The need for triangulation is obvious when relying primarily on qualitative data, which is broader and richer, but less precise than quantitative data. However, it is relevant also for quantitative data, for example, to compensate for measurement or modeling errors. Four different types of triangulation may be applied [196]:

Data (Source) Triangulation – using more than one data source or collecting the same data at different occasions.

Observer Triangulation – using more than one observer in the study.

Methodological Triangulation – combining different types of data collection methods, for example, qualitative and quantitative methods.

Theory Triangulation – using alternative theories or viewpoints.

In an example case study, multiple interviewees may be interviewed (data triangulation) by more than one interviewer (observer triangulation), complemented with data from time and defect reporting systems (methodological and data source triangulation), using two different theories as a basis for the analysis (theory triangulation).

A case study will never provide conclusions of statistical significance. On the contrary, many kinds of evidence, figures, statements, and documents are linked together to support a strong and relevant conclusion. Bratthall and Jørgensen investigate this issue related to a specific software engineering case study [27]. They conclude on the basis of empirical evidence from the case study that "a multiple data source case study is more trustworthy than a comparable single data source case study."

2.3.4 Replication

An important characteristic of a good and trustworthy research, in general, is transparency that enables replication by others. The replications as such should add to the validity of the research findings. This is also true for case study research. However, the type of replication in flexible design studies, based on qualitative data, is very different from fixed design studies, based on quantitative data.

The quantitative replication is based on *sampling logic*, for example, an experiment is replicated with new subjects or artifacts, assuming the subjects and artifacts are sampled from a population. There are many different types of replication in different fields of research, and terminology is not yet defined for software engineering [63]. Whether the replications should be exact or varied is debated. Basili et al. argue that replications should be as exact as possible [14], while Miller argues for learning by variations in replications [129], which is supported by Kitchenham [94].

Replication in qualitative studies follows a different logic. In general, cases are not sampled from a population but selected for a certain purpose. Selecting a replication case is either aimed at finding similar results, confirming earlier findings (literal replication), or aimed at finding contrasting results for predictable reasons (theoretical replication).

Conclusions can be drawn across replicated quantitative studies using meta-analysis [127]. Regarding synthesis of evidence from multiple case studies with qualitative studies, the area is less mature and needs further development [36].

2.3.5 Inductive and Deductive Enquiries

Empirical research may be *inductive*, meaning that theory is induced from the observations. In inductive research, the researcher first observes with an open mind, identifies patterns in the observations, sets up tentative hypotheses, and finally relates them to existing theory or develops new theory (see Figure 2.1a). This is the original principle

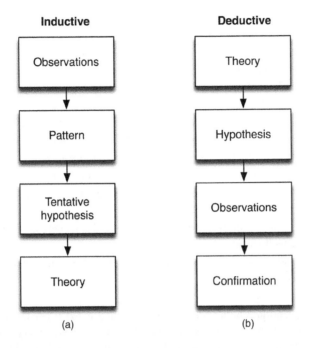

FIGURE 2.1 Inductive (a) and deductive (b) approaches to empirical research.

of grounded theory research [34], although the two founders of the method, Strauss and Glaser, developed it in different directions [205]. The Straussian approach is the most pragmatic of the two, which makes it more feasible to software engineering research.

The *deductive* research starts with existing theory, sets out hypothesis for the research, and finally makes observations (see Figure 2.1b). During the analysis, observations either confirm or reject the hypothesis, which leads to either confirmed or rejected theories.

Case study may have characteristics of both paradigms. An exploratory case study has *inductive* characteristics, while an explanatory case study has *deductive* characteristics.

2.4 WHAT MAKES A GOOD CASE STUDY?

The label "case study" is used for many kinds of studies, ranging from small demonstrations of toy size to full-scale industrial situations. By definition, a case study "investigates a contemporary phenomenon within its real-life context" [217]. However, the size and the context are not sufficient to characterize a good case study.

Yin has speculated on the characteristics of exemplary case studies, and it is worth considering these here as suggestions to further improve the standards of software engineering case studies. The characteristics are as follows [217, pp. 160–165]:

- The study is of a significant topic. The significance of a topic could be determined by, for example, reference to the extant literature on the topic or through consultation with stakeholders and participants in the prospective case study.
- The study must be complete in that
  - the boundary of the case (i.e., the distinction between the phenomenon of interest and its context) is made explicit;
  - there is a comprehensive collection of appropriate evidence;
  - there are no significant constraints on the conduct of the study, for example, the study does not run short of time, budget, or resources.
- The study must consider alternative perspectives on the topic.
- The study must *present* sufficient evidence when reporting the results and disseminating the artifacts of the case study.
- The reports of the study must be engaging to the reader; in other words, the reports are well written.
- The case study must respect the ethical, professional, and legal standards relevant to that study.

Where a replication is being performed, and hence an existing case study protocol is available for reference, it may be easier to design for an exemplary study. Implied within Yin's characteristics are case study design and case study workplan issues, to which we have added the recognition of ethical, professional, and legal standards. Kyburz-Graber [113] summarizes Yin's quality criteria, stating that an exemplary case study should have

- A theoretical basis including research questions is described.
- Triangulation is ensured by using multiple sources of evidence (data collection and interpretation).
- A chain of evidence is designed with traceable reasons and arguments.
- The case study research is fully documented.
- The case study report is compiled through an iterative review and rewriting process.

These criteria cover the foundation for the study, including the theory it is based on and the research questions it is set out to answer. The criteria relate to the data collection and the use of multiple sources of evidence. They address the analysis procedure and its ability to clearly define which evidence backs up the conclusions. They concern the reporting and the overall study process, including requirements on transparency to enable external evaluation of the procedures. All these aspects are important for the quality of the case study, and no single criterion is sufficient to judge the quality of a study.

Perry et al. define similar criteria for a case study [134] in the domain of software engineering, but still they are very general. It is expected that

- A case study has research questions set out from the beginning of the study.
- Collects data in a planned and consistent manner.
- Draws inferences from the data to answer the research question.
- Explores a phenomenon or produces an explanation, description, or causal analysis of the phenomenon.
- Addresses threats to validity in a systematic way.

These characteristics stress the need for planning and order in a case study, which shall not be considered to be in conflict with the flexible nature of case studies. Instead, it is stated to ensure a transparent path from observations to conclusions in the study.

In summary, the key characteristics of a good case study are that

1. it is of flexible type, coping with the complex and dynamic characteristics of real-world phenomena, like software engineering;
2. its conclusions are based on a clear chain of evidence, whether qualitative or quantitative, collected from multiple sources in a planned and consistent manner; and
3. it adds to existing knowledge by being based on previously established theory, if such theory exists, or by building a theory.

2.5 WHEN IS THE CASE STUDY STRATEGY FEASIBLE?

First and foremost, the case study strategy is feasible when studying "a contemporary phenomenon within its real-life context, especially when the boundaries between the phenomenon and context are not clearly evident" [217]. This is valid for many, if not most, research studies in software engineering. The contemporaneousness is a necessity to allow data collection from the case. The fuzzy borderline between the phenomenon and the context may be handled within a case study, and its flexible design principles.

Second, the type of research question is an important criterion for strategy selection. For exploratory research questions, the case study strategy is a perfect match. However, also for descriptive research questions, the case study may be feasible if representativeness of a sampling based study may be sacrificed for better realism in a case study. If representativeness is critical, the survey is a better option. Explanatory research questions may be addressed in case studies, but the evidence is not a statistically significant quantitative analysis of a representative sample, rather a qualitative understanding of how phenomena function in their context. If quantitative evidence is critical, the experiment strategy is the better option. For improving the type of research purposes, the action research strategy is a natural choice, which we consider as a variant of case study research.

Third, case studies may be launched when the degree of control is not a critical issue. The realism achieved in case studies is in stark conflict with the ability to control the situation. Studies that strictly aim at comparing different options under the same

TABLE 2.2   When to Use Different Research Methods?

Criteria	Experiment	Survey	Case Study
Yin criteria [217]			
Contemporaneous event	Yes	Yes	Yes
Type of research question	How, Why	Who, What Where, How many, How much	How, Why
Requires control	Yes	No	No
Fenton and Pfleeger criteria [54]			
Level of control	High		Low
Difficulty of control	Low		High
Level of replication	High		Low
Cost of replication	Low		High

circumstances are not in line with case study strategy, although there are means to use case studies of, for example, tools selection [109]. Experiments are primarily designed for that type of research questions, but normally less realistic, at least for *in vitro* studies.

Yin [217] uses these three criteria, originating from the COSMOS Corporation[1], to determine when a case study is the more suitable research strategy: the degree to which the phenomenon under study is a contemporary phenomenon, the type of research question, and the degree of control required. The criteria of Yin are summarized in the upper part of Table 2.2.

Fenton and Pfleeger [54] identify four factors that affect the choice between experiment and case study: level of control, difficulty of control, level of replication, and cost of replication. The last two factors are not covered by Yin's criteria. When statistical replication is important, experiment is a better choice than case study. However, there are also other types of replication in case study designs, which may provide generalization, also from case studies. The criteria of Fenton and Pfleeger are summarized in the lower part of Table 2.2.

2.6 CASE STUDY RESEARCH PROCESS

When conducting a case study, there are five major process steps to be considered, as defined in Figure 2.2. Each of the steps is elaborated in detail in Chapters 3–6, respectively. Chapters 7 and 8 also relate these steps on matters of scaling up and using case studies.

---

[1]www.cosmoscorp.com

1. *Case study design* – objectives are defined and the case study is planned.

2. *Preparation for data collection* – procedures and protocols for data collection are defined.

3. *Collecting evidence* – data collection procedures are executed on the studied case.

4. *Analysis of collected data* – data analysis procedures are applied to the data.

5. *Reporting* – the study and its conclusions are packaged in feasible formats for reporting.

FIGURE 2.2   Case study process.

This process is almost the same for any kind of empirical study, compare, for example, to the processes proposed by Wohlin et al. [215] and Kitchenham et al. [105]. However, as the case study strategy is a flexible design strategy, there is a significant amount of iteration over the steps [6], which is explicitly modeled on a process by Verner et al. [208]. The data collection and analysis may be conducted incrementally. If insufficient data are collected for the analysis, more data collection may be planned. However, there is a limit to the flexibility; the case study should have specific objectives set out from the beginning. If the objectives change, it is a new case study rather than the existing one, though this is a matter of judgment like all other classifications. Eisenhardt adds two steps between 4 and 5 above in her process for building theories from case study research [48], (a) shaping hypotheses and (b) enfolding literature, while the rest, except for terminological variations, are the same as above.

Hence, the process steps are very general, and form only a framework for presenting the guidelines.

2.7 CONCLUSION

Since the case study strategy originates from different fields of research, it is no surprise that terminology and definitions vary somewhat. In this chapter we define basic concepts for case studies in software engineering, which are used throughout the book. We hope that defining a set of basic concepts can help establish a standard of terminology in the empirical software engineering research community. We also identify characteristics of the case study strategy, to help researchers choose a feasible research strategy for a specific research situation.

CHAPTER 3

DESIGN OF THE CASE STUDY

3.1 INTRODUCTION

Software engineering case studies examine software engineering phenomena in their real-life settings and it is because the phenomena and setting will change during the study that such case studies require a flexible design, in contrast to for example the fixed designs of classic experiments. A flexible design does not mean that there should be no design or, alternatively, that a laissez-faire attitude to the design of the case study is acceptable. It is precisely because the case study researcher expects the phenomenon to change, and in unanticipated ways, that the design should be intended to be flexible enough to accommodate that change. In other words, the researcher should *design for flexibility* while also maintaining rigor and relevance.

The *research design* for the case study can be distinguished from both a *workplan* for the study, and from the legal, professional, and ethical requirements of the study. For example, researchers could develop a sophisticated multiple case study design but not have the time or resources to conduct a study with such a design. Software, and hence software engineering, is becoming increasingly complex with increased costs and resource requirements. Software engineering research must examine these increases in complexity, but this has implications for the costs and resource requirements of the software engineering research itself. Research projects will typically have resource constraints and these constraints may affect the feasibility to study software engineering, particularly large-scale, complex software engineering. Case study researchers should therefore carefully consider the case study workplan, particularly

Case Study Research in Software Engineering: Guidelines and Examples, First Edition.
Per Runeson, Martin Höst, Austen Rainer, and Björn Regnell.
© 2012 John Wiley & Sons, Inc. Published 2012 by John Wiley & Sons, Inc.

where changes in the design of the study may impact the time, resource, effort, and budget available for the study. Similarly, a sophisticated case study design with a feasible workplan may still be inappropriate if the study fails to maintain ethical, professional, or legal standards.

This chapter provides guidance on the design of a case study, and on legal, ethical and professional requirements. The research design for a specific case study is often documented as a case study protocol and this chapter therefore considers case study protocols too. As case studies are research projects, with resource constraints and time limits, the researcher should also carefully *plan* for the case study. This planning should not just cover the explicit stages of a case study (i.e., design, data collection, data analysis, and reporting) but also the necessary preparation for those stages, including training, appropriate agreements and arrangements with participating organizations and individuals, and other administrative activities.

3.2 ELEMENTS OF THE CASE STUDY DESIGN

Researchers have recognized a range of elements that need to be considered in the design of a case study. These elements are summarized in Table 3.1 and considered in more detail below.

3.2.1 Rationale for the Study

The researcher should be clear about the reasons for undertaking the study. For academic research, a typical reason for undertaking a study is to make a novel contribution to the body of knowledge on a subject, for example through the generation of new theory and hypotheses or through the testing of such theories and hypotheses. The opportunity for a novel contribution may be determined by identifying a "gap" in the existing literature on a subject.

In industry, a typical reason for undertaking a study is to make some kind of improvement in the organization or project. For example, practitioners may undertake a study to benchmark some process or technology, to assess a candidate technology (e.g., through an evaluation), or to prepare for a wider scale deployment of a technology by undertaking a pilot study first.

3.2.2 Objective of the Study

The overall objective of a study is a statement of what the researcher, and perhaps the industrial participants, expects to achieve as a result of undertaking that study. Others may use the terms goal, aim or purpose as synonyms or hyponyms for the term objective. The objective is refined into a set of research questions and these are answered through the case study's data collection and analysis.

When a study is being undertaken in collaboration with industry, it can sometimes be difficult to agree on a common set of objectives for the study. One source of difficulty is the potential diversity of stakeholders, for example, in terms of the

TABLE 3.1   Elements of a Research Design.

Element	Example Questions Describing the Element
Rationale	Why is the study being done?
Purpose	What is expected to be achieved with the study?
The case	Overall, what is being studied?
Units of analysis	In more detail, what is being studied?
Theory	What is the theoretical frame of reference?
Research questions	What knowledge will be sought or expected to be discovered?
Propositions	What particular (causal) relationships are to be investigated?
Define concepts and measures	How are entities and attributes being defined and measured?
Methods of data collection	How will data be collected?
Methods of data analysis	How will data be analyzed?
Case selection strategy	How will cases (and units of analyses) be identified and selected?
Data selection strategy	How will data be identified and selected? For example, who will be interviewed? What electronic data sources are available for use in the study? What nonelectronic, naturally occurring data sources are available for use in the study?
Replication strategy	Is the study intended to literally replicate a previous study, or theoretically replicate a previous study; or is there no intention to replicate?
Quality assurance, validity and reliability	How will the data collected be checked for quality? How will the analysis be checked for quality?

different goals and problems for each stakeholder. This diversity, together with the availability of only a finite amount of resource and time, can lead to political interactions between the stakeholders (this political activity is not necessarily malicious) for which the case study researcher does not have the appropriate knowledge, experience, or the authority to resolve. There may also of course be professional and personal conflicts between the sponsor, who may be a senior line manager, and other participants and stakeholders in the case study. It can therefore be difficult for the case study researcher to prioritize the stakeholder goals and problems, and to address them, during the case study. There can be further difficulties. A sponsor may commit to the case study on the basis of high-level aims, but it may be very difficult to translate these high-level aims into specific research objectives for the case study. Also, the very nature of research (e.g., that it is an enquiry into an unknown) means that the outcomes from the case study may be quite different from those originally anticipated and, as a result, hard to align with the sponsor's original high-level aims. And of course, there can simply be tension between the goals of practitioners (e.g., practical action with commercial value) and those of researchers (e.g., the pursuit of knowledge for its own sake).

Example 3.1:   The objective of the eXtreme programming (XP) study was to investigate how an Agile process can coexist with a stage–gate management organization. One of the objectives of the project management (PM) study was to better understand what actually happens on software projects as they progress over time. Another objective of the PM study was to better understand the factors affecting time-to-market and how time-to-market could therefore be reduced. The objective of the quality assurance (QA) study was to find quantitative prediction models and procedures for defect data. There were several objectives to the requirements management tool (RMT) study, for example, to learn how to better evaluate software tools. For the REVV study, a long-term objective was to improve productivity through the alignment of requirements engineering (RE) and validation and verification (VV). Further details on these examples are available in Chapters 10–14.

3.2.3 Cases and Units of Analyses

In software engineering, the case may be anything that is a contemporary software engineering phenomenon in its real-life setting (as we have modified Yin's [217] definition in Section 2.2). Software projects, as an approach to organizing software engineering, are used throughout the global software industry, and measures of the success and failure of software projects are used as indicators of the state of that industry. Software projects are therefore an obvious candidate as an object of study in a case study. The study of an entire software project as it progresses over time is however extremely challenging and, as a result, researchers tend to focus on some aspect or aspects of a software project for their case studies.

Example 3.2:   Damian and Chisan [39] conducted a 30-month longitudinal study and they focused on the impact of improved requirements engineering on productivity, risk management, and product quality. Curtis et al. [37] conducted an interview-based study of the software design activities in 17 software projects.

Alternative candidates for cases include the individual, a group of people, a process, a product, a policy, a role in the organization, an event, a technology, and so on. With the emergence of open source software, the evolution of the software is a common object of case study. Given our definition of a case study, investigations of "toy programs" or similar are of course excluded due to their lack of real-life context. Such investigations may make valuable pilot studies, for example to "test" aspects of the research design, in preparation for subsequent case studies.

Researchers make a distinction between a case and the unit or units of analysis within that case. Yin [217] distinguishes between *holistic case studies*, where the case is studied as a whole, and *embedded case studies* where multiple units of analysis are studied within a case, see Figure 3.1.

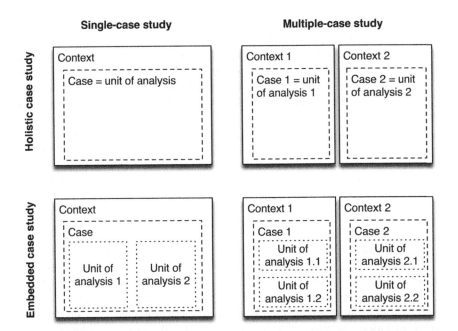

FIGURE 3.1   Holistic case study (top row), embedded case study (bottom row), single case study (left column), and multiple case study (right column). Adapted from Yin [217].

For Yin [217], the holistic design is more appropriate when there are no logical subunits to the case, and therefore no obvious additional units of analyses. The holistic design is also appropriate where the theoretical framework supporting the study is itself holistic in nature. Within software engineering, examples of phenomena that are typically more suited to the holistic design might be the case study of an individual developer, or of unit testing, or perhaps of a design review or code inspection. By their nature, holistic designs take a broad perspective on the case. One implication is that the study may not be able to examine sufficient detail in the case and may therefore miss important issues. Also, where cases are being investigated over an extended period of time, or where the case is inherently complex, the holistic design may over time become inappropriate to the case under study. Under these situations an embedded case study design becomes much more appropriate because, by its nature, such a design anticipates the need to collect, analyze, and report on complex detail in the case. As there may be more instances of each of the embedded units of analysis, in contrast to the small number of holistic cases, the researcher can sometimes use data collection techniques (e.g., surveys) and data analysis techniques (e.g., statistics) more suited to samples and populations.

Example 3.3:   Fenton and Ohlsson [53] report on the study of two major consecutive releases of a large legacy project at Ericsson Telecom AB. They refer to their study as a "case study" and they are explicit that they make "no claims about the generalization of these results" [53, p. 811]. They collected various metrics from 140 modules of the first release studied and 246 modules of the second release. They also collected data on the number of faults, traced to unique modules, for four nonoverlapping phases: function test, system test, the first 26 weeks of site testing, and the first year of operation after site tests. Although Fenton and Ohlsson refer to their study as a "case study", using the terminology of this book Fenton and Ohlsson's study could be characterized as a single *embedded* case study, with an overall case (the organization), two units of analyses (the two releases) and then various subunits of analyses (e.g., the four nonoverlapping phases). Alternatively, the study could be treated as a multiple embedded case study, with two cases (the two releases) and various units of analyses within each case (e.g., the four nonoverlapping phases). Another strength of the case study is that the authors investigated 14 formal hypotheses derived from previous work and theory. Andersson and Runeson [6] have subsequently replicated this study.

One risk with embedded designs however is that the researcher remains focuses on the subunits of the case and does not direct sufficient attention at the case overall. Within software engineering, examples of phenomena more suited to embedded case study design might be the case study of a software project, a software product line, or of organizational software process improvements. In these examples, the scale, duration, and complexity of the phenomena would suggest the likelihood of multiple units of analyses within each case. In situations where there is no established theoretical framework, and where the researcher is therefore undertaking an exploratory case study, an embedded case study design may be a more appropriate approach.

Example 3.4: In the RMT case study, the researcher examined a number of distinct activities, for example, the selection of a methodology for evaluation; the identification and selection of RMTs to evaluate; the evaluation of those tools; the deployment of the adopted tool; and the postdeployment evaluation of the RMT. As each of these activities is distinct from the others, each of these activities could constitute a unit of analysis in itself. In addition, there would be the overall unit of analysis that was the overall evaluation project. As a result, an embedded case study design be more appropriate. See Chapter 13 for more information.

Researchers also make a distinction between single case studies and multiple case studies. This refers to the context of the case, see Figure 3.1. Two or more cases within different contexts make up a multiple case study. Each case may then be holistic or embedded.

Whether to define a study consisting of two cases as holistic or embedded depends on other aspects of the research design, for example, the objectives of the research, the research questions and propositions, and the basis of replication and generalization. Benbasat et al. comment on a specific case study: "Even though this study appeared to be a single case, embedded unit analysis, it could be considered a multiple case design, due to the centralized nature of the sites" [19]. Therefore, the decision as to whether a study is holistic or embedded depends on the chosen perspective.

Example 3.5: In the XP case study, two projects are studied in two different companies in two different application domains, both using Agile practices [85]. The projects may be considered two units of analysis in an embedded case study if the context is software companies in general and the research goal is to study Agile practices. On the contrary, if the context is considered to be the specific company or application domain, the two projects would be better studied as two separate holistic cases. See Chapter 10 for more detail.

Example 3.6: In the PM case studies at IBM, the general research questions were: *What happens on a software project?* and *How can one reduce time-to-market?.* Given the substance of the research questions, it makes sense for each software project to constitute a case in its own right, but with the potential for a range of units of analyses within each case, resulting in two embedded case studies. See Chapter 11 for more detail.

3.2.4 Theoretical Framework

Using theories to underpin the case study research is not well established in the software engineering field, as concluded in a systematic review on the topic by Hannay et al. [68] and by Shull and Feldman [184]. However, defining the theoretical frame of reference of the study makes the context of the case study research clear, and helps both those conducting the research and those reviewing its results. As theories are underdeveloped in software engineering, the frame of reference may alternatively be expressed in terms of related work which the study builds upon, the viewpoint taken in the research and the background of the researchers. Grounded theory case studies naturally have no specified theory at the beginning of the study [34].

Verner et al. [208] recommend that a comprehensive literature review is conducted earlier in the research project, to form a solid foundation for the subsequent study. A comprehensive literature review would identify areas for additional contributions to knowledge as well as provide (part of) the justification for the study. The literature review would also provide input to the definition of research questions, propositions, and concepts and their measures, as well as insights into how previous researchers have designed and conducted studies of the subject. Systematic literature reviews (SLR) and systematic mapping studies (SMS) [97, 136] are being adopted in software engineering research as two methods for undertaking comprehensive literature reviews. SLR synthesize empirical data in a field of interest while SMS provide an overview of the presence and absence of research in a field of interest.

Example 3.7: Petersen and Wohlin [137] extended a systematic literature review by Dybå and Dingsøyr [46] to derive the theoretical framework for their case study of agile and incremental development practices. Based on advantages and issues identified in the primary studies in the literature review, they formed research questions and propositions for the case study.

The limited theory development in software engineering research also means that theoretical generalization (also know as analytical generalization) will be hard to sustain. But, conversely, statistical generalization is also hard to sustain because is it extremely difficult to know the population (e.g., of developers, or projects, of software artifacts) from which one draws a sample, and it is also hard to randomly sample from the population. Hence, there is an urgent need to develop theories in software engineering to fully utilize the strengths of case study research.

Example 3.8: No explicit theories are referenced in the XP case study, however, the approaches investigated in those studies are based on existing methods that have, to some extent, been previously investigated by other researchers. Earlier studies therefore influenced the designs of the studies. Study QA was partly a replication, which means that the original study formed a frame of reference from which theories on, for example, the Pareto principle and fault persistence between test phases were used when hypotheses were defined. See Chapters 10 and 12 for more detail.

3.2.5 Research Questions

Research questions are statements about the knowledge that is being sought, or is expected to be discovered, during the case study. The discovery or attainment of this knowledge demonstrates that the case study has achieved its intended objectives.

As the case study progresses, it is likely that the research questions will be refined, probably several times, as the researcher better appreciates the knowledge he or she seeks [7]. The refinement of the research questions implies that the overall objectives of the case study are also being refined. The nature of case study research means of course that research questions will commonly of the "why" and "how" types of question.

A case may be based on a *software engineering theory*. Sjøberg et al., describe a framework for theories including constructs of interest, relations between constructs, explanations to the relations, and scope of the theory [193]. Alternatively, for exploratory and descriptive case studies, where there is an absence of established theory, the researcher may simply be asking questions such as: *What is going on here?* as a prelude to then asking questions like: *Why is this behavior occurring?* or *How has a particular outcome come about?*. Verner et al. [208] state that research questions should be precise and unambiguous, achievable with the case study being planned, and not better suited to investigation through other scientific means.

Robson [162, p. 54] states that there is no automatic, infallible way of generating research questions and he draws on the work of Campbell et al. [31] to emphasize that the generation of innovative research questions is not a single act or decision.

Research questions may be organized into a hierarchy of more general and more specific research questions as the researcher decomposes the objectives of the case study into more specific research questions. A research question may be related to a *hypothesis*, that is a supposed explanation for an aspect of the phenomenon under study. Hypotheses may alternatively be generated from the case study for further research.

3.2.6 Propositions and Hypotheses

Propositions are predictions about the world that may be deduced logically from theory, and hypotheses are generated from propositions [179]. Yin [217] implies that propositions are more specific "implementations" of research questions, providing further detail and structure to the inquiry. Yin also recognizes however that some case studies have legitimate reasons not to have propositions, for example, where a subject is under exploration and for which there is little if any established theoretical frameworks. In these situations, propositions could be *outputs* from the study rather than elements of the design of the study. Verner et al. [208] recommend that propositions should be grouped with their corresponding research questions. Other researchers (such as Shanks [179]) however do not recognize research questions in their model of case studies, instead proceeding from theory to propositions to hypotheses and then hypotheses testing, that is applying a deductive approach.

Robson [162] believes that hypotheses can provide a useful bridge between the research question and the design of the enquiry. For Verner et al. [208], a hypothesis "...is an empirically testable statement that is generated from propositions..." A proposition could generate several hypotheses. Because hypotheses are empirically testable statements, the researcher must operationalize the concepts expressed in the propositions. Consequently, one particularly valuable benefit of generating hypotheses is that, through this process, the researcher better defines the concepts and measures to be used in the study [208].

Example 3.9: Verner et al. [208] provide examples of the relationship between research questions, propositions, and hypotheses. A sample of these examples are presented in Table 3.2 for illustration. For research proposition RP1.1 the proposition is expressed in terms of an IF... THEN... prediction. By contrast, research proposition RP2.1 is simply presented as a statement. For research proposition RP1.1, a corresponding hypothesis is also presented. The example hypothesis does not present a causal statement. The two research questions where derived from a more general

TABLE 3.2 Grouping Research Questions, Propositions and Hypotheses (from Verner et al. [208])

Research Question	Proposition with Accompanying Hypotheses
RQ1: How do motivational factors encourage longevity in clinical expert systems?	RP1.1: IF there are motivational factors THEN users will continue to use the clinical expert system. H1.1: Motivating factors are highly correlated with the continued use of a clinical laboratory expert system.
RQ2: How do long-lasting clinical laboratory expert systems support maintenance in order to adapt to changes over time?	RP2.1: Long-lasting clinical expert systems are easy to maintain.

research question: *Why do most medical expert systems fail shortly after their intro-duction, while some clinical laboratory expert systems last for longer than five years and continue to form an important part of a user's job?*

3.2.7 Concepts

The concepts being used in the research questions, propositions and hypotheses need to be defined and, where appropriate, measures for those concepts also need to be defined. Some concepts may not be measurable directly and it will be necessary to identify and define surrogate measures. Fenton and Pfleeger [54] provide detailed advice and examples on developing and using measures in software engineering and software engineering research. van Solingen specifically provides guidance on the Goal Question Metric (GQM) [206].

3.2.8 Methods of Data Collection

The principal decisions on methods for data collection are defined at design time for the case study, although detailed decisions on data collection procedures are taken later. There may of course be unexpected opportunities for collecting data that emerge during the conduct of the case study. Verner et al. [208] present three principles for data collection:

- Use multiple sources of data.
- Create a case study database.
- Validate data and maintain a chain of evidence.

Methods of data collection will of course be influenced by the sources of data expected to be available. For example, if the researchers intend to gather information from software engineers, then interviews, focus groups, and questionnaire surveys are obvious methods of data collection; and for example, the researchers would then define procedures for undertaking appropriate interviews. One potentially distinctive aspect of the phenomenon of software engineering is that data is often automatically collected as part of the software engineering activity, for example, through fault reporting databases, version control systems, emails, automatic test suites, and so on. For example, in their study of the relationship between faults and failures, Fenton and Ohlsson [53] write:

> In the case study system described in this paper, the data-collection activity is con-sidered to be a part of routine configuration management and quality assurance. [53, p. 812–813]

Lethbridge et al. [118] define three categories of methods: direct (e.g., interviews), indirect (e.g., tool instrumentation), and independent (e.g., documentation analysis). These are further elaborated in Chapter 4. A broad distinction can also be made be-tween quantitative data and qualitative data, although there may be the opportunity to treat some structured qualitative information as simple quantitative data. Seaman [176] points out that the distinction between qualitative and quantitative data is not the same as the distinction between subjective and objective data and that, for example, quantitative data can be subjective and conversely qualitative data can be objective.

Example 3.10: In the XP case study, the data was primarily collected using interviews, supplemented with some quantitative defect metrics. In the QA case study, defect metrics from a company was the major data source. In the two PM case studies at IBM, data was collected primarily from the minutes of project status meetings. These meetings occurred with a weekly or fortnightly frequency. The minutes were supplemented with several interviews for each case, a feedback workshop for each case, and access to other documentation. See Chapters 10–12 for more detail.

3.2.9 Methods of Data Analysis

The quantity and type of data being collected will influence the kinds of analysis subsequently performed on the collected data. During the development of the research design of the study, it may be premature to know which particular analytical techniques will be used, but the researcher should be able to anticipate the kinds of techniques. The nature of case studies, including the volume and the variety of data collected during case studies, means that researchers will need to design their study to handle large, complex, diverse data sets. Due to the complexity and importance of data analysis in case studies, we defer a detailed discussion of these issues to Chapter 5.

3.2.10 Case Selection

In case studies, the case and the units of analysis should be selected intentionally. This is in contrast to surveys and experiments, where subjects are sampled from a population to which the results are intended to be generalized. The purpose of the selection may be to study a case that is expected to be "typical", "critical", "revelatory", or "unique" in some respect [217, pp. 40–42], and the case is selected accordingly. Flyvbjerg defines four variants of information-oriented case study selections [56]:

Extreme/deviant. To obtain information on unusual cases, which can be especially problematic or especially good in a more closely defined sense.

Maximum variation. To obtain information about the significance of various circumstances for case process and outcome (e.g., three to four cases that are very different on one dimension: size, form of organization, location, budget).

Critical. To achieve information that permits logical deductions of the type, "If this is (not) valid for this case, then it applies to all (no) cases."

Paradigmatic. To develop a metaphor or establish a school for the domain that the case concerns.

In a comparative case study, the units of analysis must be selected to have the variation in properties that the study intends to compare.

In practice, however, many cases in software engineering research are selected based on availability [19], which is similar for software engineering experiments [195]. Also, it can be hard to know beforehand whether a case will be typical, revelatory, and so on. For example, many software projects overrun their budget and schedule but this is of course not expected at the beginning of the project. If a researcher is intending to proactively study a software project, rather than retrospectively study it, the researcher cannot know at the commencement of the project, and of the case study of that project, whether the project will complete on budget and within schedule. Therefore, for some phenomena of interest it can be very hard to select upfront cases that are extreme, or conversely that are typical.

Case selection is particularly important when replicating case studies. A case study may be *literally replicated*, that is the case is selected to predict similar results, or it is *theoretically replicated*, that is the case is selected to predict contrasting results for predictable reasons [217]. With limited theory development in software engineering, theoretical replication will be harder to achieve. But with so much variation in software engineering, it can also be extremely hard to design for literal replication.

Example 3.11: For the XP and QA studies, all of the companies involved in the studies were selected based on existing relationships with the respective researchers. The units of analysis were selected to fit the respective purpose of each case study.

As the study progresses it may be necessary to remove or add cases depending on practical constraints and the objectives of the research. For example, it might become clear that a case is inappropriate for the research objective and should, as a result, be dropped from the study. As another example, pragmatic constraints may require the reduction in number of cases. During the identification of cases, a useful strategy may be to identify backup or contingency cases that could be subsequently studied if needed. Of course if the researcher starts to investigate a case later than planned, valuable data may have been lost.

Example 3.12: For the PM case studies at IBM Hursley Park, there was a limited amount of effort available (one full-time PhD student) and there was also a need to ensure that the case studies were completed in time to allow the completion of the doctoral studies. With these constraints, software projects with a planned maximum duration of 12 months or less were considered as cases, implying 18 software projects were considered as candidates for case study. Several software projects were initially selected for study with others identified as candidates for further study. Due to practical constraints, the number of software projects that continued to be studied declined during the project. Overall

- Two case studies were completed (cases B and C).
- Two further cases were started but not completed due to practical constraints (cases A and G).
- Three cases had some data collected but this data has not been analyzed (cases H, K, and M).
- Four cases had no data collected but data was available (cases I, L, and N1 and N2).
- Four cases were deferred (cases D, E, F, and J).
- One case did not respond to the approach from the researcher (case O).
- Two cases were considered but were not approached as there was by that time a sufficient number of cases (cases P and Q).

This example also indicates that case selection may not occur only at the beginning of the study and is another reason why it is important to have a flexible case study design.

3.2.11 Selection of Data

The methods of data collection are distinct from the source of the data, although the two are related. For example, deciding to collect data through interviews obviously implies that data will be collected from people, but there is also a need to be clear about the appropriate people to interview. It is important to ensure that there is sufficient *coverage* of sources of data as this will support triangulation of data and therefore enhance the reliability and validity of the findings of the study. One "dimension" of coverage is to ensure that a sufficiently representative selection of people is interviewed. A second "dimension" of coverage is time, for example, to ensure that data is collected regularly throughout the period of time over which the phenomenon of interest is studied.

Example 3.13: In the IBM case studies, Project B included a wide range of 'functional areas' such as the build team, a defect screen team, design and code teams, early market support, service, testing and project management. There were also a number of other projects and business units at IBM Hursley Park and within the wider IBM Corporation with which the project interacted. There was therefore a potentially very wide range of different stakeholders that could, and perhaps should, have been interviewed. Eight interviews were conducted for the case study, and the interviewees were drawn from a small range of 'functional areas', primarily the project management team. In addition, the interviews were all conducted in the first half of the case study. The validity of the case study is therefore potentially weakened by the limited coverage across time and stakeholders. To some degree, this limitation was compensated for by the regular collection of meeting minutes and the conduct of a feedback workshop with the Project Leader and his Assistant after the completion of the project. See Chapter 11 for more details.

3.2.12   Data Definition and Data Storage

Concepts, and measures for the concepts, have been briefly considered in Section 3.2.7. The data collected on these measures will need to be stored in a structured way for preprocessing, analysis, and sharing among researchers. Kitchenham et al. [99] have proposed a method for specifying models of software data sets.

As already noted, case studies collect a large, complex, diverse body of data and it is important to ensure that this data is stored in a structured way to ensure ease of retrieval, completeness of data set, and ability to share data with coresearchers; as well as to support triangulation and the development and maintenance of a chain of evidence. A further complication is that several distinct items of data, particularly qualitative data, could be held in the same physical or electronic document. For example, an interview transcript could provide many specific quotes, with each quote being relevant to more than one hypothesis, proposition or research question. This can complicate the maintenance of a chain of evidence.

The nature of quantitative data—that it is already structured—makes it easier to store and access quantitative data, for example, as an Excel^{TM}document, or an Oracle^{TM}database. There may also be physical artifacts (e.g., tape recordings, hard copies of documents) separate from the electronic artifacts, so the challenges of data storage are more than having a network-accessible file structure.

Shull et al. [185] have introduced the experimentation knowledge-sharing model (EKSM), which is intended to help researchers share their explicit and tacit knowledge of empirical studies. The EKSM comprises iterations through four phases: socialization, externalization, combination, and internalization. The model is intended to augment *laboratory packages* to help researchers disseminate artifacts from their studies, and also to help the replication of studies. The EKSM would also seem appropriate for sharing information among a family of studies. Shull et al. illustrate the application of the EKSM using two replications of perspective-based reading (PBR) experiments.

The PROMISE Group (http://promisedata.org/repository/) are promoting the development of publicly accessible archives of data to support secondary analyses and meta-analyses in software engineering. As such, PROMISE is concerned with sharing data across research groups once it has been collected (and possibly analyzed) whereas our focus here is on indexing and sharing data within a research group during the case study. Nevertheless, the experiences and lessons learned by PROMISE could benefit individual case studies.

3.2.13   Quality Control and Assurance

Validity and reliability can rarely be retrospectively attained in a case study, and the researcher should therefore consider the quality of the case study during all stages of the case study. In the design stage, the researcher should monitor and evaluate various aspects of the case study design in order to ensure that rigor and relevance of case study findings and artifacts are being established from the outset.

There are several methods for assuring the quality of the case study design. These include the following:

1. Have the draft case study design reviewed by peers external to the project.
2. Conduct a pilot study to evaluate the case study design.
3. Invite independent observers to observe design activities in the case study, for example, observers attend meetings that review the case study design, or that review the selection of cases. Such observers are likely to have to commit to confidentiality, and so on.
4. Review the actual progress of the case study against the planned progress to determine if there are any significant differences. Recall that the researcher should expect changes in a case study, and where a difference or discrepancy has occurred this may demonstrate a weakness in the study; or alternatively the change could provide a fortuitous opportunity, for example, a change in the case provides an opportunity to compare differences in the case.

The researcher should also try to anticipate how to maintain quality, validity and reliability in the subsequent stages of the project. For example, once an interview has been recorded and transcribed, asking the interviewee to review and comment on the transcription helps to ensure that the interview data provides a fair representation of the interviewee's opinions. As another example, having two or more researchers code the transcript helps to ensure consistency of coding during the initial analyses activities.

Validity and reliability are considered in more depth in Section 5.4 and checklists to be applied for quality assurance of each study phase are provided in Appendix A.

3.2.14 Maintaining the Case Study Protocol

A case study *protocol* defines the detailed procedures for collection and analysis of the raw data, sometimes called *field procedures*. The case study protocol is a continuously changing document. For example, the protocol is updated either as a result of proactive decisions by the researchers to change the case study or, alternatively, the protocol is updated in response to changes in the case being studied or its context.

There are several reasons for keeping an updated version of a case study protocol. First, an updated protocol serves as a guide when conducting the data collection, and in that way prevents the researcher from failing to collect data that were planned to be collected. Second, the processes of formulating the protocol makes the research concrete in the planning phase, which may help the researcher to decide what data sources to use and what questions to ask. Third, other researchers and relevant people may review the protocol in order to give feedback. Feedback on the protocol can, for example, lower the risk of missing relevant data sources, interview questions, or roles to interview. As another example, the feedback can also help to clarify the relationship between the research questions and the data being collected, for example, the research questions and the interview questions. Finally, an updated protocol can serve as a log or diary where all design decisions, data collection, and analysis can be recorded together with records of changes to design, collection, and analysis and a rationale for those changes. This helps to ensure that a flexible case study remains a rigorous case study. Also, the protocol can be an important source of information when the case study is subsequently reported, to demonstrate quality assurance or to support a replication by other researchers. In order to keep track of changes during the research project, the protocol should be kept under some form of version control.

Brereton et al. [28] propose a template for a case study protocol comprising the following nine sections: background, design, case selection, case study procedures and roles, data collection, analysis, plan validity, study limitations, and reporting. The protocol is summarized in Table 3.3. As the proposal shows, the protocol is quite detailed to support a well-structured research approach.

It may not be appropriate to publish a case study protocol in its entirety for ethical, legal, or professional reasons. It should however be possible to publish parts of the protocol.

Example 3.14:   In the XP case study, the interview instruments have been published. In the QA case study, a logbook was maintained, and this logbook documented iterations to the case study. A condensed version, which shows seven case study cycles indicating the evolutionary characteristic of the case study, is published by Andersson and Runeson [7] and also presented in Chapter 10. For the PM case studies, electronic and handwritten journals were maintained however these have not been published.

Bouwman and Faber [24] also provide an example of a case study protocol. This protocol contains information on the criteria for selecting cases, a research framework, an interview protocol and interview form, units of research and observation, a code of conduct, template letters of introduction, and a database structure for storing information on the cases. In addition to a research *design*, the document also recognizes pragmatic and legal criteria. The authors write

> There is no limitation for the cases to be Dutch or European, apart from the available budget. However if we are going to discuss international cases we have to pay attention to the different (regulatory, cultural, economical, etc.) setting. Moreover, there is limited space for travel expenses in the project budget. [24, p. 11]

3.2.15 Reporting and Disseminating the Case Study

The reporting of the findings of the case study, together with dissemination of the case study protocol, artifacts of the study, and experiences of doing the study are essential to a successful case study. As with data collection and data analysis, reporting and dissemination should be considered at a high level in the case study design, with the low-level details considered as the case study progresses and the time comes to report on the case study. Similarly, the researcher should also plan for reporting and dissemination, for example, making time and effort available for those activities.

TABLE 3.3   Outline of Case Study Protocol According to Brereton et al. [28]

	Section	Content
1.	Background	(a) Identify previous research on the topic.
		(b) Define the main research question being addressed by this study.
		(c) Identify any additional research questions that will be addressed.
2.	Design	(a) Identify whether single case or multiple case and embedded or holistic designs will be used, and show the logical links between these and the research questions.
		(b) Describe the object of study (e.g., a new testing procedure; a new feature in a browser).
		(c) Identify any propositions or subquestions derived from each research question and the measures to be used to investigate the propositions.
3.	Selection	(a) Criteria for case selection.
4.	Procedures	(a) Procedures governing field procedures.
	and roles	(b) Roles of case study research team members.
5.	Data	(a) Identify the data to be collected.
	collection	(b) Define a data collection plan.
		(c) Define how the data will be stored.
6.	Analysis	(a) Identify the criteria for interpreting case study findings.
		(b) Identify which data elements are used to address which research question/subquestion/proposition and how the data elements will be combined to answer the question.
		(c) Consider the range of possible outcomes and identify alternative explanations of the outcomes, and identify any information that is needed to distinguish between these.
		(d) The analysis should take place as the case study task progresses.
7.	Plan validity	(a) General: check plan against Höst and Runeson's [73] checklist items for the design and the data collection plan (also in Appendix A of this book).
		(b) Construct validity—show that the correct operational measures are planned for the concepts being studied. Tactics for ensuring this include using multiple sources of evidence, establishing chains of evidence, expert reviews of draft protocols and reports.
		(c) Internal validity—show a causal relationship between outcomes and intervention/treatment (for explanatory or causal studies only).
		(d) External validity—identify the domain to which study finding can be generalized. Tactics include using theory for single-case studies and using multiple-case studies to investigate outcomes in different contexts.
8.	Study limitations	Specify residual validity issues including potential conflicts of interest (i.e., issues that are inherent in the problem, rather than arising from the plan).
9.	Reporting	Identify target audience, relationship to larger studies [217].
10.	Schedule	Give time estimates for all of the major steps: planning, data collection, data analysis, reporting. Note data collection and data analysis are not expected to be sequential stages.
11.	Appendices	(a) Validation: report results of checking plan against Höst and Runeson's [73] checklist items (also in Appendix A of this book).
		(b) Divergences: update while conducting the study by noting any divergences from the above steps.

Considering the reporting and dissemination of the case study in the design stage can be hard to do particularly if the study is exploratory or there is a lack of existing, relevant theoretical frameworks. Where a replication is being performed, and hence an existing case study protocol is available for reference, designing for the reporting and dissemination of the case study may be much easier. We discuss these issues in more detail in Chapter 6.

3.3   LEGAL, ETHICAL, AND PROFESSIONAL ISSUES

In 2001, Hall and Flynn [66] reported the conduct of a survey to investigate the awareness of research ethics among academic computer science and software engineering researchers in the United Kingdom. They contacted all 97 heads of departments of computer science in the United Kingdom, with follow-up reminders, receiving 44 responses. Only 16 of the 44 (36%) respondents considered monitoring the ethical considerations of software engineering research to be very important, with other respondents stating that they did not have feelings either way (39%), that monitoring was not important (18%), or that they didn't know (7%). Hall and Flynn also reported some striking comments from respondents:

> I find this questionnaire very worrying because the idea of having to seek ethical approval threatens academic freedom.

> (Seeking ethical approval) has never arisen and I don't know why this is an issue.

> No one is responsible for the ethical approval of CS research.

The survey was conducted over a decade ago and reported as part of a Special Issue on ethical issues in the journal *Empirical Software Engineering* [191]. We are not aware of any more recent survey in the field of software engineering research but even if the survey results are out-of-date, the survey together with the Special Issue highlight the importance of ethical issues to the conduct of software engineering research.

It is essential that the case study researcher takes account of legal, professional and ethical issues in the design, conduct and reporting of his or her research. In many countries, government funding for research requires that research involving human subjects must be reviewed by an appropriate ethics committee to ensure compliance with relevant ethical guidelines and standards [191]. There can also be pragmatic reasons: maintaining legal, professional, and ethical standards helps to develop and maintain trust with human subjects and organizations, and this trust will help the research to go more smoothly [191]. But also, an unethical and disreputable study can undermine the overall reputation of the discipline of software engineering research. There is also of course the basic motivation of humans: that they want to be treated respectfully [191].

Example 3.15: The Special Issue on ethical issues in the journal *Empirical Software Engineering* [191] provides several cases illustrating ethical issues, with each of these cases complemented by independent commentaries. Three of the cases are briefly summarized below. A fourth case, based on Becker–Kornstaedt's work [18], is discussed in the main text.

- The implications of divulging the identity of companies involved in a previous study to a current study. The identity of the companies involved in the previous study were in the public domain, as a result of academic publications, however extent of formal and informal contact between the researcher and participants in the current study led to difficult situations where participants were asking about details of the companies involved in the previous study. The case is presented by Seaman [177] with a supporting commentary by Gotterbarn [65].
- A research group was developing software for a company and also, with the knowledge of the company, was using that software to perform some research. In some cases, it is hard to distinguish between the research activities, which required ethics approval, and the development activities, which did not require such approval. The case is presented by Lethbridge [117] with a supporting commentary by Sieber [187].
- Open source software is, by definition, in the public domain however the developers of open source software did not develop the software with the intention or awareness that it would be subject to wide-spread investigation by researchers. This raises issues about informed consent, as well as other ethical principles recognized by Singer and Vinson [192]. The case is presented by El Emam [49] with a supporting commentary by Vinson [209].

Even though a research study first and foremost is built on trust between the researcher and the participants and stakeholders involved with the case [8], explicit measures must be taken to prevent problems. In software engineering, case studies often include dealing with confidential information in an organization. If it is not made clear at the beginning of the study how this kind of information is handled, and who is responsible for deciding and accepting what information to publish, there may be problems later on. Key ethical factors include

- Informed consent.
- Review board approval.
- Confidentiality.
- Handling of sensitive results.
- Inducements.
- Feedback.

Subjects and organizations must explicitly agree to participate in the case study, that is give informed consent. In some countries, this is even legally required. It

TABLE 3.4   Example Content for a Consent Agreement (from Singer and Vinson [192])

Items Included in the Consent Agreement
Names of researchers and contact information.
Purpose of the study.
Procedures used in the study, that is a short description of what the participant should do during the study and what steps the researcher will carry out during these activities.
A text clearly stating that the participation is voluntary, and that collected data will be anonymous.
A list of known risks.
A list of benefits for the participants, in this case for example experience from using a new technique and feedback effectiveness.
A description of how confidentiality will be assured. This includes a description of how collected material will be coded and identified in the study.
Information about approvals from review board.
Date and signatures from participant and researchers.

may be tempting for the researcher to collect data, for example, through indirect or independent data collection methods, without asking for consent. However, there are very good reasons for why ethical standards must be maintained in software engineering research.

Legislation of research ethics differs between countries and continents. In many countries it is mandatory to have the study proposal reviewed and accepted with respect to ethical issues [176] by a review board or a similar function at a university. In other countries, there are no such rules. Even if there are no such rules, it is recommended that the case study protocol is reviewed by colleagues to help avoid pitfalls.

Consent agreements are preferably handled through a form or contract between the researchers and the individual participant [162]. Table 3.4 summarizes the kinds of information used by authors of the current book in an empirical study.

If the researchers intend to use the data for other, not yet defined purposes, this should be signed separately to allow participants to choose if their contribution is for the current study only, or for possible future studies.

Example 3.16:   For the REVV study, a contract was drawn up between the university and each of the companies involved in the study. In addition to the formal agreement between the university and the individual companies, a consent letter was also prepared for individual employees in the respective companies. The letter informed the individual employee about the study and allowed that individual to decide for themselves whether to participate in the study. A template for the letter is presented in Appendix E.

The inducements for individuals and organizations to participate in a case study vary, but there are often incentives, however tangible or intangible. It is preferable to make the inducements explicit, that is specify what the incentives are for the

TABLE 3.5   Examples of Ethical Dilemmas (from Becker-Kornstaedt [18])

#	Dilemma
1.	An employee knowingly misled a superior, to protect themselves, in the presence of the researcher and the researcher knew the employee was misleading the superior.
2.	A mandatory process was not followed by a team.
3.	Resolving inconsistencies in accounts of a situation would reveal the identify of individual employees.
4.	A superior unexpectedly joins a sensitive group interview with employees.
5.	Analysis by the researcher could reveal the identify of employees in a poorly performing department.
6.	Toward the completion of some research, a superior wanted to distribute the findings more broadly in the organization, to help improve the organization, but this would reveal weaknesses in the studied department.
7.	Information is provided privately, for example, upon completion of the formal part of an interview.

participants. Thereby the inducements' role in threatening the validity of the study may also be analyzed.

Becker-Kornstaedt [18] reports her experiences of descriptive process modeling in industry, discussing seven examples of ethical dilemmas and suggesting four techniques for helping to address those dilemmas. Each of these techniques could however introduce additional problems. The seven ethnical dilemmas are summarized in Table 3.5 and the four techniques are summarized in Table 3.6.

Singer and Vinson [192] reviewed 22 ethical codes, including for example, IEEE-CS/ACM Joint Task Force on Software Engineering Ethics and Professional

TABLE 3.6   Techniques for Managing Ethical Dilemmas (from Becker-Kornstaedt [18])

#	Technique
1.	Manipulate data to reduce the risk to participants, for example, through removing identifying information like names (anonymization), through leaving out information, or through summarizing or aggregating information. But, for example, a process model that is aggregated or summarized may be too abstract to be beneficial to the respective organization.
2.	Develop different research reports for different stakeholders. For example, a high-level process model could be developed for superiors with a more detailed model for participants. But, for example, superiors may gain access to the more detailed models or (as with the first technique) the high-level model for superiors may be too abstract for effective decision making in the organization.
3.	Give participants the right to review findings and withdraw information. But, for example, withdrawing information may weaken the chain of evidence and hence the credibility of the research findings.
4.	Use external parties to conduct some, or all, of the research. But, for example, an external party may not appreciate the sensitivity of certain information.

TABLE 3.7 Ethical Principles and Illustrative Examples (from Singer and Vinson [192])

#	Principles and Description
1.	*Informed consent.* Two of the main populations used for studies in software engineering—students and company employees—are considered vulnerable populations by (at least) the Canadian, Australian, and US government funding agencies.
2.	*Scientific value.* Scientific value comprises two components: the importance of the research topic and the validity of the results. Research in software engineering can be unethical if inappropriate methodologies are used or appropriate methodologies are used inappropriately. In both cases, the research will be flawed, the results will be invalid and the study will have no merit. Put simply, a study with no merit should not be performed.
3.	*Benifiance to humans.* Researchers must seek to maximize benefits of the research to society, organizations and the human subjects while also minimizing the harm that can result from the research. If a company consents to participate in a study the respective employees may have little real choice as to whether they participate. For example, the research may lead to considerable disruption, and hence harm, to the employees.
4.	*Benifiance to organizations.* As with example 3, published research may harm a particular organization, for example, if flaws in the organization are revealed to others. Conversely, however, a researcher may have an oblization to whistle-blow on an organization where that organization may be causing or likely to cause harm to the general public. There may also be difficult decisions to be made between maximizing the benefits to the organization (e.g., by revealing defficiencies in working practices) or harming the employees.
5.	*Confidentiality.* Confidentiality refers to both the anonymity of subjects and organizations, but also the confidentiality of the data itself. Anonymity is harder to maintain in software engineering research, which is conducted in the field where coworkers, and management, will more easily be able to identify individuals.
6.	*Artifacts.* Much research in software engineering is conducted on artifacts of the software process, rather than on or with human subjects directly, for example, cost estimation and source code analysis. There are, for example, issues as to whether consent needs to be sought from the creators of these artifacts and, conversely, whether the analyses of the artifacts would impact the creators and users of the artifacts, for example, by revealing their identity.

Practice, UNESCO's Universal Declaration of Human Rights, and the World Medical Association's Ethnical Principles for Medical Research Involving Human Subjects. From this review, Singer and Vinson abstracted four high-level ethical principles: informed consent, scientific value, beneficence, and confidentiality. They then presented and discussed in detail six contrived examples to illustrate these principles. These examples are summarized in Table 3.7.

Earlier in this chapter, we discussed data storage as an element of case study design. Secure storage of data is also a legal requirement in some countries, for example with the UK's Data Protection Act, and the UK's Information Commissioner's Office (http://www.ico.gov.uk) provides advise on protecting personal data, which includes as examples:

- Only allow your staff access to the information they need to do their job and don't let them share passwords.

- Encrypt any personal information held electronically if it will cause damage or distress if it is lost or stolen.
- Take regular backups of the information on your computer system and keep them in a separate place so that if you lose your computers, you don't lose the information.
- Don't dispose of old computers until all the personal information on them has been securely removed.

The need to store the case study data in a secure and effective way is increased as the number of cases increases, the quantity and diversity of data collected for the cases increases, and as the quantity of personal and also commercially sensitive data increases. Software and IT systems support increasingly easy access and distribution of data, sometimes without the owner of that data being aware that the data is being distributed. Social networking sites are one obvious example. A more subtle example is the user's own media player: recorded interviews in MP3 format could automatically but accidentaly be indexed as music files.

3.4 CONCLUSION

In this chapter, we have considered in detail the design of a case study in terms of a range of elements of that design. It is increasingly common to document the design for a specific case study as a case study protocol, and to update that protocol as the case study progresses. The chapter therefore considered the maintenance of case study protocols. The chapter also briefly considered legal, ethical, and professional standards and requirements of research, as these requirements place obligations on the researcher in the design and conduct of her or his study.

CHAPTER 4

DATA COLLECTION

4.1 INTRODUCTION

For software engineering case studies, it is common for a large amount of raw data to be collected, and this data will then need to be refined, for example, transcribed and then coded. Further, many alternative sources of data exist which may inform the study. It is important therefore to carefully select the data sources, and to organize the raw and refined data in a structured way so that it is possible to find appropriate data, for example, during analysis. Organizing the raw data not only makes it easier to subsequently refine the data, and then to analyze it, but it also helps the researcher to assure the quality of the study by ensuring that data is not lost or overlooked through disorganization.

In Section 4.2 different types of data source are discussed. Sections 4.3–4.7 then review five methods of data collection commonly used in software engineering case studies: interviews, focus groups, observations, archival data, and metrics.

4.2 DIFFERENT TYPES OF DATA SOURCE

4.2.1 Classification of Data Sources

According to Lethbridge et al. [118], data collection techniques can be divided into three degrees:

Case Study Research in Software Engineering: Guidelines and Examples, First Edition.
Per Runeson, Martin Höst, Austen Rainer, and Björn Regnell.
© 2012 John Wiley & Sons, Inc. Published 2012 by John Wiley & Sons, Inc.

First degree. These are direct methods, where the researcher is in direct contact with the interviewees and collect data in real time. This is the case with, for example, interviews [162, pp. 277–282], focus groups [162, pp. 284–289], Delphi surveys [38], and observations with "think aloud" and protocol analysis [133].

Second degree. These are indirect methods where the researcher directly collects raw data without actually interacting with the interviewees during the data collection. This approach is, for example, taken in Software Project Telemetry [78] where the usage of software engineering tools is automatically monitored, and observed through video recording.

Third degree. These are methods where the researcher independently analyses work artifacts that are already available. This approach is used when, for example, requirements specifications and failure reports are analyzed, or when data from organizational databases such as time accounting is analyzed.

First-degree methods tend to be more expensive to apply than second or third-degree methods, because the latter two methods require significant effort both from the researcher and the subjects. An advantage of first- and second-degree methods is that it is easier for the researcher to control what data is collected, how it is collected, in what form the data is collected, the context in which the data is collected, and so on. Third-degree methods are mostly less expensive, but they do not offer the same control to the researcher. This means that the researcher does not have the same control over the quality of the data. In many cases the researcher must, to some extent, base the details of the data collection on what data is available. For third-degree methods it should also be noted that the data has been collected and recorded for another purpose than that of the research study, contrary to general metrics guidelines [206]. Where third-degree methods are used, it may be much harder for the researcher to determine whether the requirements on data validity and completeness were the same when the data was collected as they are in the research study.

Example 4.1: In studies XP and REVV, data is collected mainly through interviews, that is a first-degree method. The RMT study involves ranking features of the tool, which the researchers later analyzed. These rankings are a second-order method. In study QA stored data in the form of defect reporting metrics were used as a major source of data, that is, a third-degree method. All studies also included one or several feedback steps where the organizations gave feedback on the results, that is, a first-degree data collection method. These data were complemented with second- or third-degree data, for example, process models were used in studies XP and QA.

Example 4.2: Abdullah and Verner [2] use only third-degree data for their case study on project failures. The case went to the High Court of Justice in London and all the court material from the court case (witness statements, etc.) is available online. There was considerable press discussion around the case, in publications such as the *London Financial Times, Computerworld, IT Today,* and so on, where various people were interviewed, both before the case went to court and while the case was being heard. This material constitutes the data for the case study, see Abdullah and Verner [2] for a complete list of references.

4.2.2 Data Source Selection

It is important to carefully decide which data to collect and how to collect the data. In the beginning of a study it is often hard to decide exactly what data to collect, because there are so many activities in the research taking place at the same time. At the time when the objectives of the study are being decided and the detailed research questions of the study are being defined it is impossible to know everything about the studied case. But as the case study progresses and the researcher learns more about the case, the research develops a greater appreciation of what data is desirable, what data is available, and what data is feasible to collect and subsequently analyze. This is one reason why a flexible design for case studies is necessary: so that the researcher can adapt the data collection as the study progresses.

It is advantageous to use several data sources, and several types of data source, in order to limit the effects of one interpretation of one single data source. This is referred to as data triangulation (see Section 2.3.3). Using Lethbridge et al.'s [118] three degrees of data collection techniques, as discussed above, is an effective way of ensuring that complementary information is collected in the study. For example, if a researcher uses only meeting minutes as the source of data, and does not talk to people who were present at the meeting, the researcher cannot judge the completeness and correctness of the minutes, or the degree to which the minutes represent the different views of meeting attendees. Independent confirmation of the content of the minutes by attendees can help improve the researcher's confidence in the validity of the data.

If the same conclusion can be drawn from several sources of information, this conclusion is stronger than a conclusion based on a single source. In a case study it is also important to take into account the perspectives of different roles, and to investigate differences, for example, between different projects and products. This can be understood as a variant of observer triangulation, where different perspectives are represented (see Section 2.3.3). Conclusions may be drawn by analyzing differences between data from different sources. For example, if managers and engineers have different opinions on a topic, that may explain conflicts of interest within an organization, or if meeting minutes tell a different story than interviews, that could reveal a culture of hiding problems.

As discussed above, it is in many cases hard to know at the start of the study exactly which sources of data to use in the study. Consequently, the researchers may need to collect data before they know whether and how that data will be useful. Also, the researchers may not know, at the start of the study, about all of the data that could be collected and, therefore, the researchers are likely to have to iteratively add data sources as the study progresses. An example of iterative data collection using two interview iterations can be found in Karlsson et al. [82].

4.3 INTERVIEWS

Data collection through interviews is one of the most frequently used and most important sources of data in case studies in software engineering. Almost all case studies involve some kind of interviews, either for primary data collection or as validation of other kinds of data. The reason for this is simply that much of the knowledge that is of interest is not available anywhere else than in the minds of the people working in the case being investigated. Even if the researcher studies documents that are available, he or she often wants to know something about the quality of the documents, to what extent they really were used, or to what extent interviewees agree with the contents in them, and so on.

An interview can be carried out in many different ways, but essentially a researcher talks to an interviewee and asks questions that the interviewee attempts to answer. There is, however, much variation on the conduct of interviews. Questions can be more or less specific, interviews can last for more or less time, interview sessions can be more or less structured, and so on.

4.3.1 Planning Interviews

The dialogue between the researcher and the interviewees is guided by a set of interview questions. The interview questions are based on the topic of interest in the case study, in particular the formulated research questions. In most cases, however, interview questions are not formulated in the same way as the research questions because the research question itself could be too hard for the interviewee to answer. Consequently, interview questions are often derived from the research questions.

Interview questions may be *open*, that is, allowing and inviting a broad range of answers and issues from the interviewee, or *closed*, offering a limited set of alternative answers. An open question may be phrased "Please tell me about your experiences of software testing?", while a closed question may be phrased "Of the following, which testing phases do you have experience: (a) unit testing, (b) integration testing, and (c) system testing?". The advantage of open questions is that the answers are not as limited in scope as the more closed questions. The advantage of the closed questions is that it is easier to analyze the results. If questions are closed this also implies that the interviewee gives more consistent answers because the range of answers is more directed and constrained by the questions than with open questions. With open questions it is more likely that the interviewee will give information about a wider range of topics. The diversity of answers will partly be a reflection of the specific perspective taken by the interviewee, for example as a result of that interviewee's role in the case being studied.

Interviews may be divided into *unstructured*, *semistructured*, and *fully structured* interviews [162, pp. 277–282]. The different types of interviews are summarized in Table 4.1.

In an unstructured interview, the interview questions are formulated in an open way as general concerns and interests from the researcher. In this case the interview

TABLE 4.1 Overview of Interview Types

	Unstructured	Semistructured	Fully Structured
Typical foci	How individuals qualitatively experience the phenomenon	How individuals qualitatively and quantitatively experience the phenomenon	Researcher seeks to find relations between constructs
Interview questions	Interview guide with areas to focus on	Mix of open and closed questions	Closed questions
Objective	Exploratory	Descriptive and explanatory	Descriptive and explanatory

conversation will develop based on the interest of the interviewee and the researcher. This type of interviews is most feasible for exploratory studies, where only little is preconceived about the outcome of the interviews.

In a semistructured interview, questions are planned, but they are not necessarily asked in the same order as they are listed. The development of the conversation in the interview can influence the order in which the different questions are presented to the interviewee, and the researcher can use the list of questions to be certain that all questions are raised with the interviewee at some point in the interview. Additionally, semistructured interviews allow for improvization and exploration of the issues raised in the conversation. Semistructured interviews are common in software engineering case studies.

In a fully structured interview all questions are planned in detail in advance and all questions are asked in the same order as in the plan. For these types of interview it is most likely that most questions will be closed, and in many ways a fully structured interview is similar to a questionnaire-based survey.

During the planning phase of a case study it is decided whom to interview. Due to the qualitative nature of the case study it is recommended to select interviewees based on differences instead of trying to replicate similarities, as discussed in Chapter 3. This means that it is good to try to involve different roles, personalities, and so on, in the interview. The number of interviewees has to be decided during the study. One criterion for when sufficient interviews are conducted is "saturation", that is, when no new information or viewpoint is gained from new subjects [34].

When the interview questions have been formulated they can be piloted in a first set of interviews. In this step it can be certified that the questions, for example, are understandable for the interviewee and that it is probable they will result in useful answers in forthcoming interviews. Pilot interviews are conducted as traditional in-terviews, although extra attention is given to understand how well formulated the questions are. It is, for example, possible to ask the interviewee specifically about how understandable questions are and how easy or hard it is to answer them.

4.3.2 The Interview Session

An interview session may be divided into a number of phases. First the researcher presents the objectives of the interview and the case study, and explains how the data from the interview will be used. During this step the researcher can also get permission to record the interview. Then a set of introductory questions are typically asked about the background of the subject, the organization, project, and so on. These questions are often relatively simple to answer. After this introduction, both the interviewer and the interviewed person hopefully feel comfortable with the situation and are ready for other questions.

The main interview questions, which take up the largest part of the interview, then follow on from the introduction. If the interview contains personal and maybe sensitive questions, for example concerning political issues in the organization, opinions about colleagues, why things went wrong, or questions related to the interviewees own competence [74] or conflicts, and so on, special care must be taken. In this situation it is important that the interviewee is ensured confidentiality and that the interviewee trusts the interviewer. It is not recommended to start the interview with these questions or to introduce them before a climate of trust has been obtained.

The major findings should be summarized by the researcher toward the end of the interview, in order to confirm that the interviewee's opinions have been properly understand, to identify and misunderstandings, and to gather further feedback either on the questions and their answers, or on the structure and nature of the interview itself.

Different types of questions can be asked in different order according to three general principles, as outlined in Figure 4.1. The *funnel* model begins with open questions and moves toward more specific questions. The *pyramid* model begins with specific ones, and opens the questions during the course of the interview. The *timeglass* model can be seen as a mixture of the other two alternatives and begins with open questions, straightens the structure in the middle, and opens up again toward the end of the interview. It is necessary to think through the interview session and

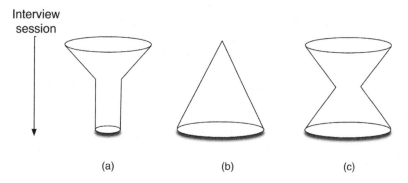

FIGURE 4.1 General principles for interview sessions: (a) funnel, (b) pyramid, and (c) timeglass.

decide which model to choose instead of just asking the questions in random order. However, it is not possible to say that any of the models is best in all situations.

During the interview session the role of the researcher is to ask questions to the interviewee and to listen to the answers, and to follow up answers with additional questions when this is necessary. During this process the researcher should try to find a good balance between asking questions, listening to the interviewee's answers, and monitoring what questions have been answered. It is, of course, important to steer the interview and ensure that all important topics are covered. However, as case study research is a flexible research form and interviews often are semistructured or even unstructured, the structure and flow of the interview should not be overly restricted by the researcher. In some cases questions can be postponed to a follow-up interview session. In some cases it is an advantage to be two persons that carry out the interview. Then one person can ask the questions and focus on the dialogue with the interviewee, and the other one can focus more on what questions have been discussed and what questions that remain to be discussed during the interview.

A typical error common with inexperienced researchers is to ask leading questions, which may result in receiving answers that are inaccurate. Another error is to interrupt the interviewee, or not to give the interviewee enough time to think about answers. The researcher must sometimes allow some time of silence that gives the interviewee the possibility to think about an answer. It may be tempting to "help" the interviewee by proposing an answer. In these situations, the researcher should be careful not to bias the answer provided by the interviewee.

Where it is convenient to do so, and the interviewee agrees, the researcher should record the interview, for example, as an MP3 audio recording. This is because even if notes are taken during the interviews, it is hard to record all details, and it is almost impossible to know what is important to record during the interview. It may be possible to have a dedicated and trained scribe to record sufficient detail of the interview in real time, but even then a recording should be made as a backup [74].

4.3.3 Postinterview Activities

After the interview session there is often a need to conduct a number of activities before the analysis can be started.

When the interview has been recorded it needs to be transcribed into text before it is analyzed. This is a time consuming task, but in many cases new insights are made during the transcription, and it is therefore not recommended that this task is conducted by anyone else than the researchers involved during the interview process.

It may be advantageous to have the transcripts reviewed by the interview subject. This provides the opportunity for the interviewee to correct, clarify or expand on the answers he or she gave in the interview itself. The review also provides an opportunity for the researcher to ask for clarification and expansion of particular answers.

Example 4.3: Interviews were conducted in study XP. The researchers had an initial hypothesis about potential problems of combining agile methods with a traditional stage–gate model. However no details about this were known and the hypotheses were not detailed with respect to this. Hence a semistructured approach was chosen, which supports the combination of exploratory and explanatory type of case study. An interview guide was developed, based on knowledge of agile and stage–gate models, together with the hypotheses of the study. The interviews were semistructured, where the structure was given in terms of topics, which we wanted to cover and approximate time budget for each topic, as for example described by Klein and Myers [111, Appendix A].

Relevant people to interview were identified in cooperation with the involved organizations. All interviewed persons were promised that only anonymous data would be presented externally and internally in the organization. Two researchers conducted most of the interviews together, which were audio recorded, and later transcribed. The interviewers also took notes on what they spontaneously found relevant.

4.4 FOCUS GROUPS

In interview-based data collection, the researcher normally asks a series of questions to one person. In a focus group, data collection is conducted with several people at the same time in a session resembling an interview [112, 162].

This type of data collection technique is often very useful in qualitative research and it has some strengths as listed by Kontio et al. [112]:

- Discovery of new insights due to different backgrounds and the nature of the group setting.
- Aided recall in the sense that people are able to confirm (or reject) facts that would have been hidden in an individual interview.
- Cost-efficiency due to the fact that several people are "interviewed" at the same time.
- Depth due to the nature of a discussion compared to, for example, a questionnaire.
- Business benefit to the participants since they are able to both network and compare their own ways of working to the other participants.

According to Robson [162] another advantage is that there is a natural quality control in this kind of session. Participants tend to provide checks and react to extreme views that they do not agree with, and group dynamics help in focusing on the most important topics [162, Box 9.5]. There is also a chance that people who normally are reluctant to be interviewed alone since they feel they have nothing to say may participate in this kind of research.

Example 4.4: Lehtola et al. [116] conducted a study on requirements prioritization practices, based on focus group sessions. Four participants from two companies took part in discussion around five topics, scheduled for half an hour each:

- Current requirements prioritization practices in the companies.
- Problems that companies have with their current practices.

- Factors that have, or should have, an effect on priority decisions.
- Sources for priority information.
- Development phases in which requirements are prioritized.

The focus group discussions were followed up with two in-depth interviews and one prioritization session was monitored through observations.

Example 4.5: Runeson conducted a study on unit testing practices across several companies using focus group discussions [167]. The focus group was composed of 17 representatives from 12 companies. The focus group discussions were organized around three themes:

- What is unit testing?
- What are the participants? Strengths regarding unit testing?
- What are the participants? Problems regarding unit testing?

Being open across so many companies requires trust, which in this case was established in a software process improvement network (SPIN) [169]. The focus group discussions were followed up by a questionnaire, created from the focus group results.

There are however weaknesses to focus groups, as for example described by Kontio et al. [112] and Robson [162]. For example, if the group dynamics do not work it may be hard to moderate the session. It requires that the moderator has significant experience of both the subject area and moderating group discussions. While these sessions can be recorded it may be difficult to identify who said what, and be clear on what was said (because people talk over each other). So the researcher should think carefully about how to take notes during these kinds of sessions. It is also possible that secrecy inhibits participants from providing information that they would provide in a normal interview. Here the researcher has to try to anticipate if the questions concern material that may be sensitive in advance. In some cases it is possible to formulate nondisclosure agreements between participants before the meeting. However, if material are sensitive and secret, writing a formal agreement may not solve this problem.

People will maybe have "hidden agendas," and emphasize answers for other reasons than providing data. They may for example want to make a good impression on a potential business partner if they are also participating in the session. The researcher can try to anticipate the risk of this in advance and try to monitor this during the session.

Social acceptability in terms of what points are made during the discussion, may affect the participants so they will not provide honest and complete answers to the questions in a group setting. Again, the researcher can try to anticipate the risk of this in advance and try to monitor this during the session.

It should also be noted that there is limited time at a meeting and that it is not possible to discuss too many topics and too complex topics in detail. This must be considered in the planning phase of the focus group meeting.

4.5 OBSERVATIONS

Observations can be conducted in order to investigate how a certain task is conducted by software engineers. This is a first- or second-degree method according to the classification in Section 4.2. There are many different approaches for observation. One approach is to monitor a group of software engineers with a video recorder and later on analyze the recording. Another alternative is to apply a "think aloud" protocol, where the researcher repeatedly asks questions like "What is your strategy?" and "What are you thinking?" to remind the subjects to think aloud. This can be combined with recording of audio and keystrokes as proposed, for example, by Wallace et al. [210]. Observations in meetings is another type, where meeting attendants interact with each other, and thus generate information about the studied object. An alternative approach is presented by Karahasanović et al. [81] where a tool for sampling is used to obtain data and feedback from the participants. The tool that Karahasanović et al. used is computer based and in regular intervals the participants are asked questions that they answer immediately.

Approaches for observations can be divided into categories, depending on whether the interaction of the researcher is high or low, and whether the awareness of the subjects is high or low, see Table 4.2.

Observations according to category 1 or category 2 are typically conducted in action research or classical ethnographic studies where the researcher is part of the team, and not only seen as a researcher by the other team members. The difference between category 1 and category 2 is that in category 1 the researcher is seen as an "observing participant" by the other subjects, while she is more seen as a "normal participant" in category 2. In category 3, the researcher is seen only as a researcher. The approaches for observation typically include observations with first-degree data collection techniques, such as a "think aloud" protocol as described above. In category 4, the subjects are typically observed with a second-degree technique such as video recording (sometimes called video ethnography).

An advantage of observations is that they may provide a deep understanding of the phenomenon that is studied. Further, it is particularly relevant to use observations, where it is suspected that there is a deviation between an "official" view of matters

TABLE 4.2 Different Approaches to Observations

	High Awareness of Being Observed	Low Awareness of Being Observed
High degree of interaction by the researcher	Category 1	Category 2
Low degree of interaction by the researcher	Category 3	Category 4

and the "real" situation [161]. It should however be noted that observations produce a substantial amount of data that makes the analysis time-consuming.

Example 4.6: Sharp et al. [180] use observations in a study of agile development practices. The observer spent one week with an XP team, taking part in everyday activities, including pair programming, that is, an approach like Case 1 above. Data collected consisted of field notes, audio recordings of meetings and discussions, photographs and copies of artifacts.

Example 4.7: Vans et al. [207] observed four professional programmers' comprehension of a program during maintenance tasks, using protocol analysis [133]. The programmers were asked to think aloud, and their comments were video or audio recorded. A comprehension model was derived from theory, which comprises actions and sequences of actions, expected to be conducted during a maintenance task. Think-aloud reports of the programmers were transcribed, and mapped to the comprehension model.

4.6 ARCHIVAL DATA

Archival data refers to data that is available in archives. Examples include

- Meeting minutes, such as regular project-level status meetings or sprint reviews.
- Technical documents from different development phases, like requirements specifications, test specifications, and source code.
- Management documents, like project plans.
- Organizational charts, both for the line organization and the project organization.
- Financial records.
- Reports summarizing previously collected measurements, for example, status of system testing over time.

Benbasat et al. [16] and Yin [217] distinguish between documentation and archival records, while we treat them together and see the borderline rather between qualitative data (minutes, documents, charts) and quantitative data (records, metrics), the latter discussed in Section 4.7. Some archival data, such as meeting minutes, could contain a mixture of qualitative and quantitative data, and the researcher may need to separate out these different kinds of data in an appropriate way so that they can be analyzed using appropriate analysis techniques.

Archival data is a third-degree type of data that can be collected in a case study. For this type of data, a configuration management tool is an important source in software development projects, since it enables the collection different versions of files and documents.

As for other third-degree data sources it is important to keep in mind that the documents were not originally developed with the objective to provide data for research in a case study. A document may, for example, include parts that are mandatory according to an organizational template but of lower interest for the project, which may affect the quality of that part. Alternatively, the document may exclude data relevant to a study, for example for political or confidentiality reasons. Where data is missing, the archival data collection and analysis must be combined with other data collection and analysis techniques, for example, questionnaires, in order to obtain missing historical factual data [55]. It is of course hard for the researcher to assess the quality of the data, although some information can be obtained by investigating the purpose of the original data collection, and by interviewing relevant people in the organization. Given that archival data is naturally generated by some activity or activities in the case being studied, the researcher has the opportunity to assess the data before making a decision on which parts of the data, if any, would be relevant and valid for the study. A particularly valuable type of archival data is regular meetings for a project, for example, project status meetings held every week. Provided the data is of sufficient quality and contains appropriate content, this type of data can provide a record of changes over time in the case being studied.

Example 4.8: In study QA, archival data was a major source of information. Three different projects from one organization were studied. One of the projects was conducted prior to the study, which meant that the data from this project was analyzed in retrospect. Process models were studied as well as project specifications and reports.

Example 4.9: In the PM study, the researcher gathered copies of the meeting minutes for the highest level status meeting of the two projects. For Project B, these meetings occurred every week with 49 meetings occurring over the duration of the project. For Project C, these meetings occurred initially every fortnight and then every week, with 37 meetings occurring over the duration of the project. The minutes for Project B were much more structured and detailed than the minutes for Project C, containing a rich mixture of structured qualitative data, narrative data, and quantitative data. By contract, Project C contained mainly narrative data, with a small amount of structured data. Despite the differences in the structure and content of the minutes for the two projects, both sets of minutes provided valuable raw data to the respective case studies. This archival data became the primary source of data for the two case studies, but were complemented by interviews, feedback workshops and other types of archival data. Manual and semiautomated searches were used to code the data in the minutes. For both sets of minutes, some qualitative data was coded and then counted to provide simple metrics for use in nonparametric statistical tests. Further information is provided in Chapter 11.

4.7 METRICS

The above mentioned data collection techniques are mostly focused on qualitative data. However, quantitative data is also important in a case study. Software measurement is the process of representing software entities, like processes, products, and resources, in quantitative numbers [54]. Collected data can either be defined and collected for the purpose of the case study, or already available data can be used in a case study. The first case gives, of course, most flexibility and the data that is most suitable for the research questions under investigation.

There is always a risk that you collect too much data that you do not really need. In the definition phase when it is decided what data to collect it is very tempting to define metrics that "maybe are of interest", in order to avoid ending up in a situation where you miss data in the analysis phase that you would like to have but have not collected. However, there are many problems that arise from collecting too much data. If too much data is collected there is for example a risk that people who need to spend effort on collecting the data start to question that the data is really useful and that you will actually use it, which may affect the quality of the data. It is an advantage if the definition of what data to collect can be based on a goal-oriented measurement technique, such as the Goal Question Metric method (GQM) [15, 206]. In GQM, goals are first formulated, and the questions are refined based on these goals, and after that metrics are derived based on the questions. This means that metrics are derived based on goals that are formulated for the measurement activity, and thus that relevant metrics are collected. It also implies that the researcher can control the quality of the collected data and that no unnecessary data is collected.

In many cases it turns out that metrics that the researcher is attempting to find is not available, and instead another metric must be chosen. For example, if a researcher wants to measure how long time different people have been working on different tasks, he or she may use data from a time reporting system that is not classifying tasks in exactly the same way. It may also be that the researcher want to measure something that is hard to define like experience and decides to use, for example, number of years in the company.

Examples of already available data are effort data from older projects, sales figures of products, metrics of product quality in terms of failures, and so on. This kind of data may, for example, be available in a metrics database in an organization. When this kind of data is used it should be noticed that all the problems are apparent that otherwise are solved with a goal-oriented measurement approach. The researcher can neither control nor assess the quality of the data, since it was collected for another purpose, and as for other forms of archival analysis there is a risk of missing important data.

Example 4.10: The archival data in study QA was mainly in the form of metrics collected from defect reporting and configuration management systems but also from project specifications. Examples of metrics that were collected are number of faults in modules, size of modules and duration for different test phases. In study XP, defect metrics were used as complementary data for triangulation purposes.

Metrics may also be collected for the sole purpose of the case study. For example, Oručević-Alagić and Höst [132] collected proprietary and open source versions of a software system from an archive and calculated metrics for the different versions. Based on that it was possible to investigate where in the architecture changes were made and how different attributes were changed when transferring from proprietary to open source.

4.8 CONCLUSION

Software engineering is a complex activity that naturally produces a variety of types of output, for example, source code, design documentation, meeting minutes. To properly study software engineering the case study researcher must consider a wide range of types of data collection that either gather the naturally produced data or that generate new data. In this chapter, we have reviewed five main types of data collection: interviews, focus groups, observation, archival analysis and metrics. Each of these types of data collection help the researcher gather different kinds of data, and a case study would often use more than one type of data collection. The researcher should therefore carefully select the types of data collection to use. Also, because case studies of software engineering often produce large amounts of raw data, which are then refined, the researcher must ensure that the raw and refined data is well organized, in order to help assure the quality of the data and to help the subsequent analysis.

CHAPTER 5

DATA ANALYSIS AND INTERPRETATION

5.1 INTRODUCTION

Once data has been collected the focus shifts to analysis of data. It can be said that in this phase, data is used to understand what actually has happened in the studied case, and where the researcher understands the details of the case and seeks patterns in the data. This means that there inevitably is some analysis going on also in the data collection phase where the data is studied, and for example when data from an interview is transcribed. The understandings in the earlier phases are of course also valid and important, but this chapter is more focusing on the separate phase that starts after the data has been collected.

Data analysis is conducted differently for quantitative and qualitative data. Sections 5.2–5.5 describe how to analyze qualitative data and how to assess the validity of this type of analysis. In Section 5.6, a short introduction to quantitative analysis methods is given. Since quantitative analysis is covered extensively in textbooks on statistical analysis, and case study research to a large extent relies on qualitative data, this section is kept short.

Case Study Research in Software Engineering: Guidelines and Examples, First Edition.
Per Runeson, Martin Höst, Austen Rainer, and Björn Regnell.
© 2012 John Wiley & Sons, Inc. Published 2012 by John Wiley & Sons, Inc.

5.2   ANALYSIS OF DATA IN FLEXIBLE RESEARCH

5.2.1   Introduction

As case study research is a flexible research method, qualitative data analysis methods are commonly used [176]. The basic objective of the analysis is, as in any other analysis, to derive conclusions from the data, keeping a clear chain of evidence. The chain of evidence means that a reader should be able to follow the derivation of results and conclusions from the collected data [217]. This implies that sufficient information from each step of the study and important decision taken by the researcher must be presented.

Analysis of qualitative research is characterized by having analysis carried out in parallel with the data collection. This is necessary since the analysis can reveal the need for collecting additional data. This is one reason why systematic analysis techniques are needed. Since it is constantly ongoing it is necessary to know exactly what was found out when in the analysis. Being systematic is one condition needed in order to present a chain of evidence.

During the analysis new insights may be found that you did not expect when the data was collected. In order to investigate these insights, new data must often be collected, and instrumentation such as interview questionnaires must be updated. As new findings affect the analysis, data collection techniques can be constantly updated, while at the same time being required to maintain a chain of evidence. This means that it is an important challenge for the researcher to be systematic, and to be able to communicate the chain of evidence for readers of the results.

Analysis of this kind of data is, as described above, characterized by iterations, which means that it is necessary not only to go from data collection to analysis, but also from data analysis to data collection. The same can be said for the relation between reporting and analysis. It may be necessary to go from reporting back to analysis or back to data collection. This is illustrated on a high level in Figure 5.1, which shows the main steps in analysis, that is, the steps between data collection and reporting.

Qualitative analysis is conducted in a series of steps, based on Robson's guidelines [162, p. 459], that may be iterated. First the data is coded, which means that parts of the text is given a code representing a certain theme, area, construct, and so on. One code is usually assigned to many pieces of text, and one piece of text can be assigned more than one code. Codes can form a hierarchy of codes and subcodes. The coded material can be combined with comments and reflections by the researcher (i.e., memos). When this has been done, the researcher can walk through the material to identify a first set of hypotheses. This can, for example, be phrases that are similar in different parts of the material, patterns in the data, differences between sub-groups of subjects, and so on. The identified hypotheses can then be used when further data collection is conducted in the field, that is, resulting in an iterative approach where data collection and analysis is conducted in parallel. During the iterative process a small set of generalizations can be formulated, eventually resulting in a formalized body of knowledge, which is the final result of the research. This is, as pointed out

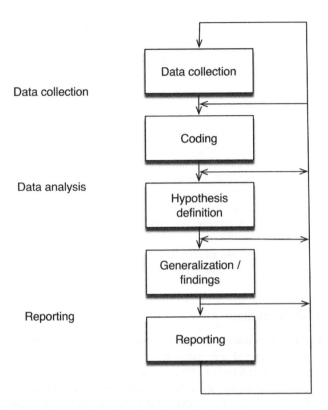

Data collection

Data analysis

Reporting

FIGURE 5.1 Main steps of data analysis.

above, not a simple sequence of steps. Instead, they are executed iteratively and they affect each other.

The activity where hypotheses are identified requires some more information. This is not a simple step that can be carried out by following a detailed, "mechanical," approach. Instead, it requires the ability to generalize, and think innovatively, and so on from the researcher. In quantitative analysis on the other hand, the majority of the innovative and analytical work of the researcher is in the planning phase (i.e., deciding design, statistical tests, etc.). There is, of course, also a need for innovative work in the analysis of quantitative data, but it is not as clear as in the design phase. In qualitative analysis there are major needs for innovative and analytical work in both phases.

In order to reduce bias by individual researchers, the analysis benefits from being conducted by multiple researchers. The preliminary results from each individual researcher are then merged into a common analysis result. Keeping track of, and reporting, the cooperation scheme helps increasing the validity of the study. Not only the validity with respect to researcher bias is improved by working in group. As with any other challenging task, it is also possible to be more innovative in the analysis if more than one researcher are involved.

This analysis process is sometimes referred to as grounded theory analysis [34]. The term is then used in a more "generic sense to denote theoretical constructs derived from qualitative analysis of data." [34, p. 1], compared to the original definition [205]. Applied to software engineering Kasurinen et al. define the steps of grounded theory analysis [87]:

> The grounded theory method contains three data analysis steps: open coding, where categories and their related codes are extracted from the data; axial coding, where connections between the categories and codes are identified; and selective coding, where the core category is identified and described.
>
> The process started with "seed categories" [48] that contained essential stakeholders and known phenomena based on the literature. Seaman [176] notes that the initial set of codes (seed categories) comes from the goals of the study, the research questions, and predefined variables of interest.

This is similar to the process described above, although we refrain from using the term "grounded theory" to frequently, due to its dual definition [205].

5.2.2 Level of Formalism

A structured approach is important in qualitative analysis. This means, for example, in all cases that a preplanned approach for analysis must be applied, decisions taken by the researcher must be recorded, all versions of instrumentation must be kept, links between data, codes, and memos must be explicitly recorded and documented, and so on. However, the analysis can be conducted at different levels of formalism. Robson [162] mentions the following approaches:

Immersion approaches. These are the least structured approaches, with very low level of structure, more reliant on intuition and interpretive skills of the researcher. These approaches may be hard to combine with requirements on keeping and communicating a chain of evidence.

Editing approaches. These approaches include few *a priori* codes, that is, codes are defined based on findings of the researcher during the analysis.

Template approaches. These approaches are more formal and include more *a priori* based on research questions.

Quasi-statistical approaches. These approaches are much formalized and include, for example, calculation of frequencies of words and phrases.

In our experience, editing approaches and template approaches are suitable in software engineering case studies. It is hard to present and obtain a clear chain of evidence in informal immersion approaches. It is also hard to interpret the result of, for example, frequencies of words in documents and interviews. In our experience, editing approaches and template-based approaches are commonly used approaches in software engineering case studies. For example, the XP study presented in Example 5.1 applied an editing approach.

It is of course possible to analyze data with the other two techniques in software engineering research as in all other research, but editing approaches and template-based approaches are suitable in a case when more is known beforehand than in an immersion approach, and data is not suited for quasi-statistical analysis. Section 5.3 is therefore focused on template approaches and editing approaches.

Example 5.1: Study XP used an editing approach. The analysis started with a set of codes (see Section 10.5), which was extended and modified during the analysis. For example, the code "communication" was split into four codes: "horizontal communication", "vertical communication," "internal communication" and, "external communication".

5.2.3 Relation to Hypotheses

When working with hypotheses, there are two different parts to data analysis. Hypothesis *generating* techniques can be used for exploratory purposes, and hypothesis *confirmation* techniques [176] can be used for explanatory purposes.

Hypothesis generation is intended to find hypotheses from the data. When using these kinds of techniques, there should not be too many hypotheses defined before the analysis is conducted. Instead the researcher should try to be unbiased and open for whatever hypotheses are to be found in the data. The results of these techniques are the hypotheses as such. Examples of hypotheses generating techniques are "constant comparisons" and "cross-case analysis" [176].

Hypothesis confirmation techniques denote techniques that can be used to confirm that a hypothesis is supported, for example, through analysis of more data. Triangulation and replication are examples of approaches for hypothesis confirmation [176]. Negative case analysis tries to find alternative explanations that reject the hypotheses. These basic types of techniques are used iteratively and in combination. First hypotheses are generated and then they are confirmed. Hypothesis generation may take place within one cycle of a case study, or with data from one unit of analysis, and hypothesis confirmation may be done with data from another cycle or unit of analysis, see Chapter 12.

5.3 PROCESS FOR QUALITATIVE DATA ANALYSIS

5.3.1 Introduction

It is not possible to give a simple description of how to carry out qualitative analysis in detail. The analysis depends on a number of aspects, like the type of data that has been collected and on the research questions that are investigated. However, there are a few things that are general for all analysis techniques:

- The idea is to identify generalizations in terms of patterns, sequences, relationships, and so on from the data. This is done by working with the data, for example, by summarizing, coding, categorizing, and commenting it.

- The analysis is carried out as an iterative process. This means, as described in Section 5.2, that you go through the material several times and each time identify or adjust codings, categories, and so on.

- It is important to be systematic and to document each step of the research. This makes it possible to describe a "chain of evidence" for the reader, without which there is no way for the reader to understand that the conclusions are trustworthy.

5.3.2 Steps in the Analysis

As a starting point there is a set of data in form of, for example, interview transcripts, documents from the organization, and meeting minutes, which has been collected by the researchers based on the formulated research questions. It is possible to have data in other forms than text, but for this discussion it is assumed that it is in text format.

As a first step, the material is typically studied in detail by the researchers. Even if the material has already been studied during interviews, document selection, and transcription, it is probably necessary to read the texts again.

One alternative now is to formulate a set of codes that are of interest for the research. It is often beneficial to do this formulation as a group activity if there is more than one researcher. Since the objective of the research is captured in the research questions, it is natural to formulate the codes based on these. Also, other material like referenced literature and identified theories and models in the area are used as a basis for codes.

The next step after this would then be to read all the texts and mark where the codes fit to the contents. During this process it is often clear that some codes must be reformulated, maybe split into more codes, and so on. It is also possible to formulate completely new codes, if you see that this is necessary. This is one part of the analysis, where it is obvious that the process is iterative. If you formulate new codes or change codes you must go back and recode the material.

After this the next step is to use the coded material in order to draw conclusions. This can be done in several ways. One thing that can be done is to compare the text for different codes. For example, if there is one type of statement that is common for all codes of one type but not for another, even if it could be expected also for the other type, then that can be investigated closer.

Different codes can also be compared. For example, if one code relates to the role of the interviewee and another code relates to the interviewee's experience of a certain event, then the experience of different roles can be compared.

In some cases it can be fruitful to summarize what has been found in a report consisting of different sections. This is referred to as "Developing a case description" by Yin [217]. This can, for example, be done by first defining which sections to present, then to identify which codes that are relevant for each section, and then by reading the whole material and looking at the codings in order to identify relevant material.

Again it should be noted that the process is iterative, and there is always the possibility to go back and adapt and change codes, sections, notes, and so on. It is also possible to go back and interview interviewees again, and to identify new interviewees if that is necessary.

Below two examples are presented. Example 5.2 is a basic hypothetical example provided to illustrate how analysis of interview data can be carried out. Example 5.3 presents shortly how the analysis was conducted in the XP case, which is further described in Chapter 10.

Example 5.2: This hypothetical example of a case study on software inspections has research questions about how different participant perceive aspects like effectiveness, and how inspections contribute to the learning in an organization. The researcher may have a hypothesis that faults found during inspections affect the learning of the organization and that they affect what process changes are considered in the future.

Interviews where participants in inspections are interviewed directly after inspections are an important source of data in this study. Examples of interview questions are "Tell me more about the project and the inspection you participated in," and "What kind of faults were found?" After the interviews the answers are transcribed into a text and stored in a spreadsheet with one sentence per row in one column, and other columns with ID of interviewee and codes.

Example codes are as follows:

View. For text about the interviewee's view on the suitability of inspections.

Fault type. For text about what kind of faults that were found.

Learning. For text about what the interviewee learned during the inspection.

During the coding, sentences like "In this project I think it was a good idea to inspect several of the documents" and "It took too much time to find a meeting date" could be coded with the *view*-code.

Sentences like "Some of the faults that were found would be hard to find because they concern timing of different real-time processes," and "This type of fault should not have been discussed so long at the meeting" could be classified with the *fault type*-code.

Examples of sentences that could be coded with the *learning*-code are "I think that we need to spend more time on timing issues with this type of software in the future" and "I will probably be able to avoid timing faults in the future because of what I saw in the inspection." The latter sentence could also be coded with the *fault type*-code.

When the text has been coded the analysis can continue in a number of ways. One alternative is to compare the text that has been coded with the *view*-code for different roles. Then it can be investigated if for example managers and developers, or code developers and testers, have different views on inspections.

Another alternative would be to focus on one aspects, for example, how inspections and learning affect how development is carried out in the future. In this case it would be possible to read all text that is coded with the *learning*-code and/or the *fault type*-code and summarize what has been said about this topic.

When doing the analysis, it is in some cases better to manually read all the texts from beginning to the end and to be aware whether the text is coded with the codes of interest or not, than to first sort the text based on the codes. There is a risk that the sentences become too much out of their context if the text is sorted. However, sorting can in other cases be very useful in order to find the areas of interest, or to understand how much is said about each subject. In Example 5.2, codes are given to individual sentences, which means that reading the whole text from the beginning to the end may be seen as the best option in that case.

During this process it is necessary to consider if more interviews need to be collected, and if codes and codings must be reconsidered. In Example 5.2 there may, for example, be very different answers concerning what faults affect learning. Then it may be necessary to conduct more interviews about that. It may also be that some persons say that own faults found in testing are more important for learning than faults found in inspection. That may even be a reason to go back and change the research questions and interview questions, and complement already conducted interviews.

Example 5.3:   In study XP, analysis was conducted in a series of steps that were iterated. In the data collection phase a number of interviews had been recorded. As said in Example 5.1, the analysis was conducted by editing the text. The following steps were iterated:

- The interviews were transcribed into text files. In these text files it was possible to mark quotes that were seen as interesting for the study.
- The quotes were coded. The following codes were used: project model, communication, planning, follow-up, quality, technical issues, and attitudes.
- The quotes were grouped based on the codes.
- A set of results were formulated as texts on individual subjects based on the groups that were relevant for the subject. That means that one result can be related to more than one group and one group can be related to more than one result.

The results were sent to the participants who were able to comment on them, before the final set of conclusions were formulated. The analysis is focused on building an explanation of the case, and based on this formulating the results. For further details, see Chapter 10.

5.3.3   Techniques

During the process outlined above there are a number of techniques and activities that may be useful. Yin [217] identifies the following specific techniques:

Pattern matching.   With this approach an empirically observed pattern is compared with a predicate pattern. When they agree it supports that the pattern is true. Pattern matching can be based on rival explanations. If you have a number of cases with the same outcome, it is possible to formulate a set of rival explanations for this outcome. Then it is possible to investigate the cases and determine which of the explanations that describe the cases in the best way. A simple example from software engineering could be if you have a number of cases where the introduction of a specific inspection technique has been successful. Then different explanations could be formulated, for example one that is based on the motivation of staff, and one that has to do with the structure of the code. If you then see that the code was structured in very different ways, some possibly easy to inspect and some possibly harder to inspect, while the motivation was seen as very similar in all cases, this would indicate that the explanation based on motivation is most likely to be correct.

Explanation building. In this kind of analysis, patterns are identified based on cause–effect relationships and underlying explanations are sought. For example, it may be possible to identify and explain a relationship between the architectural structure of a system and the tendency of letting faults slip from test phases to the operational phases in a certain type of projects.

Time-series analysis. A time series denotes a set of events happening over time. Time-series analysis in this kind of analysis denotes analyzing what happens over time in a case, such as analyzing what happens in different phases of a fault in a fault management system.

Logic models. Analysis can be carried out based on logical models explaining more complex series of cause–effect relationships. Theoretical predictions of related events can be compared to empirical observations. An example of this could be to first derive explanations of cause-effect relationships in project management and then compare these to empirical data from real projects.

Cross-case synthesis. This type of analysis can be conducted if a multiple case study has been conducted. In that case, the different cases can be compared.

These techniques can be used to decide how to do the analysis in a certain case study. As a general advice it can be said that even if it in many cases is good not to make the analysis too complicated, it is important to discuss the analysis carefully before it starts. The choice of analysis affects the possibility to draw interesting conclusions from the data, and there is, as described above, a need to be creative also in the evaluation phase of the analysis.

Example 5.4: Seaman and Basili studied the role of discussions in inspection meetings [178]. They observed 23 inspection meetings and conducted additional semistructured interviews, and describe their analysis:

> Initial qualitative analysis of the data began about halfway through data collection. The first analysis was similar to the 'constant comparison method' described by Glaser and Strauss [58] and the comparison method suggested by Eisenhardt in [48]. The method consisted of a case-by-case (meeting-by-meeting) comparison in order to reveal patterns among the characteristics of inspection meetings. The goal of this initial analysis was to suggest possible relationships between variables. These suggested relationships would then be further explored quantitatively where appropriate.

Example 5.5: Racheva et al. conducted a cross-case study on requirements prioritization on agile projects. They applied a grounded theory approach to their analysis. However, they started the work with four precise research questions, that helped focusing the analysis, which they describe as follows:

> We first read the interview transcripts and attached a coding word to a portion of the text – a phrase or a paragraph. The coding words were selected to reflect the relevance of the respective portion of the interview text to a specific part of the studied phenomenon. This could be a concept (e.g. 'value', 'method'), or an activity (e.g. 'estimation'). Some of the codes were a logical continuation of the composition of the interviews as standard aspects of the process were discussed, e.g. 'size of the team', or 'decision-maker'. Other categories and, respectively, codes emerged during the coding process as a result of observations we didn't anticipate and concerning concepts and aspects of the process we haven't explicitly addressed in the questionnaire. Those are for example 'problems that the developers encountered during the process', 'feeling about the way of work', or 'trade-off quality – schedule'. We clustered all pieces of text that relate to the same code in order to analyze it in a consistent and systematic way.

5.3.4 Tool support

Qualitative analysis means to a large extent to work with text in the form of interview transcripts, project documents like project plans, product documents like requirements specifications and QA documents, and meeting minutes. The analysis involves working with the text as described above, which means that some kind of text-based tool support is necessary.

With this kind of tool it is necessary to be able to edit and annotate text and to work with codings. It is possible to use standard text editors for this. Then you can store the text in one or several documents and edit and add annotations and codes in separate styles and fonts, and so on. It is also possible to use a spreadsheet and have the text in one columns in different cells and add codes and annotations in other columns. The sorting capability of a spreadsheet can be useful in the analysis. If the analyzed text is in one column and the codes are in an other column then it is possible to sort the data in order to see all text that is coded in the same way. It should however be noted that it sometimes can be hard to decide how to code the material if more than one code should be given to one piece of text.

There are also several specific tools available for qualitative analysis. The advantage of this kind of tool is that they are specialized for data analysis and therefore have specific functionalities for coding, annotation, and so on. The drawbacks are its cost and that the researcher has to learn a new tool if he or she is not familiar with it. NVivo[1] and Atlas[2] are examples of commercial tools that are available.

---

[1] http://www.qsrinternational.com.
[2] http://www.atlasti.com.

5.4 VALIDITY

The validity of a study denotes the trustworthiness of the results, and to what extent the results are not biased by the researchers' subjective point of view. It is, of course, too late to consider the validity during the analysis. The validity must be addressed during all phases of the case study. However, the validity is discussed in this section, since it cannot be finally evaluated until the analysis phase.

There are different ways to classify aspects of validity and threats to validity in the literature. In this book we chose a classification scheme that is also used by Yin [217] and similar to what is usually used in controlled experiments in software engineering [215]. Robson [162], for example, refers to the possibility of having a different classification scheme for flexible design studies (e.g., credibility, transferability, dependability, confirmability), while we prefer to operationalize this scheme for flexible design studies, instead of changing the terms. This scheme distinguishes between four aspects of the validity, construct validity, internal validity, external validity, and reliability.

5.4.1 Construct Validity

This aspect of validity reflects to what extent the operational measures that are studied really represent what the researcher has in mind and what is investigated according to the research questions. If, for example, the constructs discussed in the interview questions are not interpreted in the same way by the researcher and the interviewed persons, there is a threat to the construct validity.

5.4.2 Internal Validity

This aspect of validity is of concern when causal relations are examined. When the researcher is investigating whether one factor affects an investigated factor there is a risk that the investigated factor is also affected by a third factor. If the researcher is not aware of the third factor and/or does not know to what extent it affects the investigated factor, there is a threat to the internal validity.

5.4.3 External Validity

This aspect of validity is concerned with to what extent it is possible to generalize the findings, and to what extent the findings are of interest to other people outside the investigated case. During analysis of external validity, the researcher tries to analyze to what extent the findings are of relevance for other cases. There is no population from which a statistically representative sample has been drawn. However, for case studies, the intention is to enable analytical generalization where the results are extended to cases which have common characteristics and hence for which the findings are relevant, that is, defining a theory. The context description in the report, see Section 6.6.4, can help the reader understand the relevance of the study for another situation.

5.4.4 Reliability

This aspect is concerned with to what extent the data and the analysis are dependent on the specific researchers. Hypothetically, if another researcher later on conducted the same study, the result should be the same. Threats to this aspect of validity is, for example, if it is not clear how to code collected data or if questionnaires or interview questions are unclear.

5.5 IMPROVING VALIDITY

It is, as described above, important to consider the validity of the case study from the beginning. The whole purpose of selecting and using a good methodology is to take account of the threats in the analysis. That is, by carefully designing the study, by collecting data in the right way, and by analyzing it in a correct way, the threats will be lowered and the most serious threats can be avoided.

More concrete ways to increase the validity have been listed, for example, by Robson [162] and other authors. Some important approaches are as follows:

Prolonged involvement. If the study is conducted over a long-time period, or there is another type of long-term relation between the researcher and the organization, this means that a trustful relations between the researchers and the organization can be built. This means, among other things, that the researcher will understand how participants interpret terms that are used in the study, and that participants may spend more time providing data.

There are different forms of long relations, such as when a research group have cooperated with an organization for several years in different projects, or when a researcher is employed in the organization where the study takes place. See further on longitudinal studies in Section 7.4.

Prolonged involvement does of course have a positive impact in that people in the studied organization trust the researcher, the researcher can get access to the right data, and so on. However, there may also be a risk that the researcher looses independence or gets biased by being too involved in the organization.

Triangulation. This is an important and often applied approach to increase the validity of a study with respect to all aspects of validity. For example, using data from different sources means that contradictions between different sources can be identified. If more than one researcher is involved in the data collection the risk of being biased by one person is lowered, which can improve the reliability. See further on triangulation in Section 2.3.3.

Peer debriefing. Often it is an advantage to carry out case study research as a group of researchers instead of working alone, since it will lower the risk of being biased by one researcher. Involving a group of researchers can also help in using terms that are understood by participants, since a group of researchers together can know more about the subject and a studied organization than what is possible for a single researcher.

Peer debriefing can be achieved in several ways. One way is to do the research jointly as a team of several researchers. Another way is to involve research colleagues in reviewing documents like the research design.

Member checking. Often it is possible to have material reviewed by the participants of a study. When transcripts of interviews have been developed they can be sent to the interviewee. Then this person can check that you have not misunderstood anything and that what they said still is true and not something they now feel is wrong. In some cases it is also possible to check details about products and organizations which have been mentioned in the interviews but are harder to remember exactly during an interview. This could improve, for example, reliability since the risk of having fault in the transcripts is lowered. It is, of course, also possible for interviewees to review material resulting from the analysis, such as explanations, models, conclusions and recommendations, although they must not agree with the analysis as such.

Negative case analysis. Formulating alternative explanations and theories in the analysis can improve the analysis. This is a normal step in the analysis, which is valuable.

Audit trail. This means keeping track of all data and material in a systematic way. In this kind of research the researcher often has to study and keep track of a large amount of data like development documents and transcripts, and different versions of analysis documents where models are developed and hypotheses and conclusions are formulated. By keeping track of all versions of these is valuable when a chain of evidence is presented. The case study protocol is important with respect to this, and a version control system can be helpful.

All approaches are important and they can help in different ways in different studies depending on the type of case study. For some of the approaches examples of threats they lower are mentioned above. However, since the approaches are broad and generally good practice there is no simple mapping between approach and threat which is true for all studies. This must be considered from case to case.

Example 5.6: In study XP, validity threats were analyzed based on a checklist by Robson [162]. It would also have been possible to analyze threats according to construct validity, internal validity, external validity, and reliability. Countermeasures against threats to validity were then taken. For example, triangulation was achieved in different ways, results were reviewed by case representatives, and potential negative cases were identified by having two researchers working with the same material in parallel. It was also seen as important that sufficient time was spent with the organizations in order to understand it. Even if the case study lasted for a limited time, this threat was lowered by the fact that the researchers had a long-term cooperation with the organizations before the presented case study.

Example 5.7: In study QA, for example, data triangulation was used to check which phase the defect reports originated from. The alignment between the phase reported in the trouble report, and the person's tasks in the project organization was checked. There was a field in the trouble reporting scheme on test phase, for example, system test or function test. This data was compared to the issuer's organizational belonging to the system or function test organization.

5.6 QUANTITATIVE DATA ANALYSIS

For quantitative data, analysis typically includes mathematical and statistical techniques, working with quantitative numbers. All of these activities are relevant in case study research. Some examples of quantitative analyses are as follows:

> *Descriptive statistics.* Descriptive statistics, such as mean values, standard deviations, histograms and scatter plots, are used to get an understanding of the data that has been collected. This is often a natural step before any other methods are applied.
>
> *Development of predictive models.* This type of analysis is conducted in order to describe how a measurement from a later process activity is related to an earlier process measurement. This may involve using correlation analysis and regression analysis.
>
> *Hypothesis testing.* This type of analysis is conducted in order to determine if there is a significant effect of one or several variables (independent variables) on one or several other variables (dependent variables).

Methods for quantitative analysis typically assume a fixed research design. This means that the design is completed before the data collection begins, and it is not possible to change the design when the data collection has started. For example, say that a research study involves measuring the time it takes for an engineer to make changes to a certain type of document with a certain analysis technique. Then, if this has been measured for 10 engineers there are 10 data points. If this was continued with more and more engineers, it would be possible to be more and more precise in an estimate of the mean time it takes to do this kind of change. However, if the design is changed for example by letting the engineers work in pairs in the assignment then it would not be possible to use these data points together with the original 10 data points in order to calculate the mean value, since the measurements are simply not measuring the same thing. It is of course possible to do quantitative calculations also in flexible research, but care must be taken to make sure that the right aspects are calculated, and in many cases changes in design mean that fewer data points can be used in the analysis.

There are some additional concerns when it comes to quantitative data in software engineering. In many studies, people, like engineers, are involved and measurements are made on the work of people. This means in many cases that the number of data points is limited. Quantitative data sets from single cases can therefore be very small, due to the number of respondents or measurement points, which causes special concerns in the analysis.

Another concern is the distribution of data that is collected. In a typical textbook on analysis of quantitative data, many statistical methods assume that data are normally distributed and on an interval or ratio scale. However, in software engineering, quantitative data is in many cases based on subjective opinions (e.g., data from questionnaires) and other kind of data, which is only on an ordinal scale. This means that in many cases it is necessary to use nonparametric statistics [188] instead of parametric statistics.

Quantitative analysis is not covered to any large extent in this book, since it is extensively covered in other texts. For more information about quantitative analysis, refer for example to the following sources:

- Robson [162] presents a general text on research methodology where basic methods for quantitative data analysis are presented.
- Wohlin et al. [215] present guidelines for conducting and analyzing controlled experiments in software engineering. This can be of importance, for example, if hypothesis tests are conducted.
- Montgomery [130] presents descriptions of how to analyze experiments with parametric methods (analysis of variance). This can be of importance, for example, if hypothesis tests are conducted.
- Siegel and Castellan [188] describe how to analyze nonparametric quantitative data.
- Fenton and Pfleeger's [54] comprehensive book on software metrics.

However, many more sources of information exist, such as traditional textbooks on statistics.

Example 5.8:   In study QA the main analyses were conducted with quantitative methods, mainly through analysis of correlation and descriptive statistics, such as scatter plots. In the QA case, the quantitative data acted as a trigger for deeper understanding. Patterns in the data, and lack thereof generated questions in the feedback session. The answers lead to changes in the data analysis, for example, filtering out some data sources, and to identification of real patterns in the data.

Example 5.9:   Briand et al. [30] conducted an industrial case study to assess object-oriented design measures. The analysis was conducted with descriptive statistics, principal component analysis and univariate regression analysis.

In many cases a typical quantitative analysis is combined with a qualitative analysis from, for example, interviews, and a qualitative analysis can be complemented with a quantitative analysis as in Example 5.8.

For example, Kitchenham et al. [100] discuss how the ISO/IEC 15393 [1] international standard gives inappropriate advice for measuring software engineering processes; and when combined with requirements for statistical process control techniques can result in the use of misleading metrics together with the adoption of inappropriate data aggregation and data analysis techniques. Also, Fenton and Pfleeger [54] have written a very comprehensive and insightful book on the design and application of software metrics. Kan [80] has also published a book in this area.

5.7 CONCLUSION

Once a sufficient amount of data has been collected about the case, the focus of the case study can start to shift to the analysis of that data. Given the flexible nature of case studies it is likely that data would continue to be collected even though the analysis has begun. As a wide range of types of data are typically collected in a case study, so the researcher must employ a wide range of data analysis techniques to make sense of that data. A common distinction is made by researchers between quantitative and qualitative types of data, and consequently this chapter has reviewed techniques for analysing both types of data. As quantitative data analysis is extensively covered in other textbooks, this chapter has however focused primarily on qualitative data analysis and has considered: a general process for qualitative data analysis, more specific steps in the analysis, techniques for analysis, tool support, and various aspects of validity and improving validity.

CHAPTER 6

REPORTING AND DISSEMINATION

6.1 INTRODUCTION

A case study cannot be completed successfully without reporting at least the findings of the study. There are however strong arguments for also reporting other aspects of the case study (e.g., the case study protocol) as well as for being prepared to disseminate artifacts collected during the study (while maintaining ethical responsibilities and commercial confidence) such as interview data.

There are a surprising number and diversity of audiences to which the researcher may need to report and disseminate. A consequence is that there are likely to be a surprising number of reports to prepare and publish, with these reports being varied in their content and structure.

Yin [217] considers the reporting activity to be one of the most challenging activities when doing case study research, and also the activity that places the greatest demands on the case study researcher. Indeed, Yin implies that those researchers who do not like composing reports, of various kinds, may want to reconsider whether case study research is an appropriate type of investigation for them.

In this chapter, we focus primarily on case study-specific issues when preparing reports and disseminating artifacts. We recognize, however that a case study can contain other methods of enquiry within it, such as a survey, or archival analysis; and, conversely, that a case study may be part of a larger study. So although this chapter focuses on case study-specific issues, we encourage the reader to also consult

Case Study Research in Software Engineering: Guidelines and Examples, First Edition.
Per Runeson, Martin Höst, Austen Rainer, and Björn Regnell.
© 2012 John Wiley & Sons, Inc. Published 2012 by John Wiley & Sons, Inc.

other sources for guidance on reporting findings and artifacts from other methods of enquiry.

Given the range and diversity of audience, an effective report must carefully consider and address the needs of the specific audience for whom the report is intended. As a simple example, researchers may be interested in the novelty, validity, and theoretical significance of the case study while a policymaker may be interested in the practical actions that should be taken based on the findings of the report. Because the report should address the needs of the intended readership, and because intended readerships can be so varied, it is not possible for us here to provide detailed guidance for each type of readership and each type of report. Instead we provide general advice together with more specific guidelines and heuristics.

6.2 WHY REPORT AND DISSEMINATE

For researchers conducting a case study, there are intrinsic and extrinsic motivations to report and disseminate the case study. For a doctoral student, reporting the case study and the findings as a thesis for examination is a necessary part of the process toward conferment of the doctorate. For a professional researcher, the quality and quantity of publications from the case study may strongly influence his or her reputation among peers, subsequent access to grants, and career progression [162]. For a Principal Investigator of a case study funded by a grant, there is often a requirement to provide a final report to the grant funder. The grant funder is frequently a public body (e.g., the Engineering and Physical Sciences Research Council in the United Kingdom), but may be a charity (e.g., the Wellcome Trust) or a commercial sponsor (e.g., IBM Hursley Park for the third author's case studies).

Besides the intrinsic and extrinsic motivators to reporting and dissemination for the researchers, there are a range of benefits to the research community and to society in general. For example, reporting the case study can help others:

- To better understand what constituted the case study, for example, what was planned and replanned, what was not planned, what was done, what was found, what conclusions were drawn.
- To judge whether, and how, to include the findings from the study in a meta-analysis or systematic review. With case studies, it is very unlikely that the findings could be included in a statistical meta-analysis but as Pickard et al. [140] recognize, for software engineering research, such findings may be included in simpler meta-analyses such as vote counting. With the increasing use of Systematic Literature Reviews by the software engineering research community (e.g., [97] and [110]) there is increasing importance placed on the ability to judge the degree of admissibility of a case study to a systematic review.
- To better understand the scope of applicability of the findings of the study, for example, when the findings would and would not apply in another situation.

- To make better-informed decisions about when, where, and how to conduct new case studies, and what specifically those studies should investigate.
- To make better-informed decisions about policy and practice.

Reporting the results of a case study, and disseminating artifacts of that study, is inevitably a balance between a researcher's duty and goal to publish their results, and the participating company's and individuals' integrity [8]. We have discussed legal, professional, and ethical issues in Chapter 3.

6.3 THE AUDIENCE FOR THE REPORT

Each report written of the case study must consider the intended readership, or audience, of the report and this means that the composition of the report (e.g., its length, structure, and content) should be appropriate to the audience.

The types of audience interested in reports of the case study or dissemination of case study artifacts include the following:

- *The sponsor(s) of the case study.* For example, the sponsor(s) will want to know whether the case study has produced desirable and feasible findings.
- *Stakeholders and participants in the case study.* For example, the case study could be used to improve some aspect of software engineering within a particular organization.
- *Practitioner communities.* For example, the case study could be used to improve some aspect of software engineering across the industry.
- *Government and policy making bodies.* For example, the case study could be used to influence policy making or evaluate a previously implemented policy.
- *Research communities.* For example, the case study could open up a new avenue for research.
- *Educational communities.* For example, the case study could be used as a detailed example for teaching students about particular issues, or the artifacts from the case study could be used to help students learn how to organize and analyze data and report on that analyses.

A natural audience for reports on the findings of a case study will be the participants, stakeholders, and sponsors of that study. But there is a much wider community of researchers and practitioners who would also benefit from the results of the study. And, as already recognized, researchers may want to examine detailed aspects of the study design and conduct, or may want to replicate the study.

One significant difficulty arises where there are many different types of reader. A sensible strategy may be to write different reports for each identifiable type of reader. Of course a particular reader may be categorized in more than one type. For example, with a case study of a software project the project leader for that project constitutes one type of reader. But that project leader is also a software practitioner and a line manager in the company in which that project took place. Therefore, there may be one detailed report prepared for the project leader about his or her particular project, and that project leader may be the only intended reader of that report. A second more general report may be prepared for project leaders at the company, which would still be relevant to the project leader involved in the case study.

Example 6.1:   For the PM case studies, some of the audiences at IBM Hursley Park were: the senior manager at IBM who was sponsoring the research, the mentor at IBM who supported the PhD student, the Project Leaders of the *candidate* projects for case study, the Project Leaders of the projects actually studied, a variety of stakeholders in each project, and other stakeholders at IBM Hursley Park. Some of the audiences in the research community were the Principal Supervisor of the PhD and the other supervisors, the Examiners of the final PhD thesis and progression reports toward that thesis, other PhD students and researchers, other academic staff in the department, and others researchers met at, for example, academic conferences. Other audiences included software professionals encountered at other kinds of conferences.

Example 6.2:   Study XP was presented in different formats to different audiences, for example, to the involved companies in seminar format, to the research community in journal format [86], to practitioners in a magazine format [86], and in the form of a doctoral thesis [83]. The journal format paper is structured similar to Table 6.1, although the outline hierarchy differs slightly. For more details, see Chapter 10.

6.4   ASPECTS OF THE CASE STUDY TO REPORT AND DISSEMINATE

We have stated that a case study cannot be completed successfully without reporting at least the findings of the study. Besides the findings of the study we make a distinction between the following:

- The case study protocol and related research instruments, for example, question-naire templates and letters of introduction. Making these documents available to others helps them to judge the credibility and value of the case study, and also supports replication of the study. Page limitations on journal articles and conference papers often prevent researchers from reporting the full details of the case study and so this detail may need to be reported separately, perhaps as a technical report. As a contrasting example, software engineering research has begun to employ *lab packages* [183], which are detailed reports, together with perhaps other resources such as source code, that provide important information on how an experiment was designed and conducted.
- The case study artifacts, for example, the raw and refined data that was collected and generated during the case study. Raw data is almost always refined in some

way, as the researchers organize and analyze the data. For ethical and logistical reasons it may not be feasible or desirable to make some of these artifacts, particularly the raw data, available for others. But making artifacts available to others allows them to independently replicate the analysis, or alternatively to conduct new analyses. Also, artifacts can be used to test a new analysis technique as a trial, or to teach various case study techniques to students. As one contrasting example, the PROMISE group (visit http://promisedata.org) provides data sets for researchers to build and test prediction models. For PROMISE, it is the *data*, ideally with explanations of that data that is disseminated to researchers. Making artifacts available to other researchers allows those researchers to assess the quality and quantity of that data and, therefore, its appropriateness to other research problems. For example, Rainer and Gale [150] assessed the quality and quantity of open source software at SourceForge, and Deng and MacDonell [40] assessed the quality of the International Software Benchmarking Standards Group (ISBSG) data set.

- Experiences and lessons learned *by the researcher(s)* about the design, conduct and reporting of their case studies. For example, we report on some of our experiences in Part II of this book.

6.5   WHEN TO REPORT AND DISSEMINATE

When to report and disseminate information on the case study will partly depend on the readership, partly depend on the status of the case study, and partly depend on professional and ethical requirements. For example, once a sufficiently substantial and stable case study protocol has been prepared, it would be appropriate to seek peer review on that protocol, ideally before the data collection has begun. As another example, the researcher may have completed an ethical approval process, requiring the preparation of a report on the proposed case study, before the fieldwork can begin.

Given the above, it is evident that reporting does not only take place once the case study analysis has concluded, but often takes place in one form or another during the design and conduct of the case study, for example, as reports of interim findings. Conversely, it may be that information on a case study is disseminated for the first time many years *after* the case study completed, for example when the results are reinterpreted in the context of subsequent research; or perhaps when there is a need to respond to an enquiry from other researchers who would like further information on the details of the study (for example, when there is some scientific dispute); or perhaps after the lifting of an embargo for competitive or confidentiality reasons.

When a report should be made available to the readership is of course not the same as when one should start preparing the report. There are often several reports that the researcher knows will need to be prepared, such as a final report to the grant funder, the thesis, the case study protocol and research instruments, interim progress reports to supervisors or sponsors, and interim reports to participants. One rule-of-thumb is to start preparing for these reports as early as feasible.

6.6   GUIDELINES ON REPORTING

6.6.1   The Generic Content of an Academic Report

Robson defines a set of characteristics for a case study report [162]:

- To describe what the case study was about.
- To communicate a clear sense of the studied case.
- To provide a "history of the inquiry" so the reader can see what was done, by whom and how.
- To provide basic data in a focused form, so the reader can have confidence that the conclusions are reasonable.
- To articulate the researcher's conclusions and set them into a context they affect.

Reporting the case study objectives and research questions is quite straightforward. If these are changed substantially over the course of the study, the changes should be reported to help the reader better understand the case and the case study.

Describing the case might be more sensitive, since this might enable identification of the case or its subjects. For example, "a large telecommunications company in Sweden" is most probably a branch of the Ericsson Corporation. However, the case may be better characterized by other means than application domain and country. Internal characteristics, like size of the studied unit, average age of the personnel, and so on, may be more interesting than external characteristics like domain and turnover. Either the case constitutes a small subunit of a large corporation, and then it can hardly be identified among the many subunits (and one must be clear that the subunit does not necessarily represent the entire corporation), or it is a small company and hence it is hard to identify it among many candidates. Still, care must be taken to find this balance.

Providing a "history of the inquiry" requires a more substantial level of detail than the pure reporting of used methodologies, for example, "we conducted a case study using semistructured interviews." As the validity of the study is highly related to what is done, by whom and how, the sequence of actions and roles taken in the case study must be reported. On the other hand, there is no room for every single detail of the case study conduct and a balance must be found.

Data is collected in abundance in a qualitative study, and the main focus of the analysis is to reduce and organize the data in order to provide a chain of evidence toward the conclusions. To establish trust in the study, the reader needs relevant snapshots of how the raw and refined data support the conclusions. These snapshots may be in the form of for example citations (typical or special statements), pictures, or narratives with anonymized subjects. Further, categories used in the data classification, leading to certain conclusions, may help the reader follow the chain of evidence.

Finally, the conclusions must be reported and set into a context of implications, for example, by forming theories. A case study can not be generalized in the sense of being representative of a statistical population, but this is not the only way of achieving and transferring knowledge. Using analytic generalization as an alternative approach, conclusions can be drawn without statistics, and these conclusions may be interpreted and related to other cases. Communicating research results in terms of theories, and generalizing based on theory, are both underdeveloped practices in software engineering research, as identified by Hannay et al. [68].

Example 6.3: Martin et al. [124] conducted an ethnographic case study in a small software company of their testing practices. In their report, several sequences of dialogues within the company brings "live" to the description. For example:

G *"We've never figured out a way we can test it other than get someone with 500 users."*

D *"No, I can spike test but that's not a proper test..."*

P *"No, ...you could actually write a program that makes several PCs make loads of connections."*

Guidelines for reporting experiments have been proposed by Jedlitschka et al. [77] and evaluated by Kitchenham et al. [95]. Their work aims to define a standardized structure for reporting experiments that enables cross-study comparisons, for example through systematic reviews. For case studies, the same high-level structure may be used, but because case studies have a more flexible design, and are often based primarily on qualitative data, it is not appropriate to seek to standardize the low-level structure for reporting case studies.

We have modified the Jedlitschka et al.'s [77] guidelines to make them more applicable to case studies. In making these modifications, we have drawn on our own experiences, as well as taken account of Kitchenham et al.'s [95] evaluation of the Jedlitschka et al.'s guidelines. The resulting structure is presented in Table 6.1.

In a case study, the theory may constitute a framework for the analysis; hence, there are two kinds of related work: (a) earlier studies on the topic and (b) theories on which the current study is based.

The design section corresponds to the case study protocol, that is, it reports the planning of the case study including the measures taken to ensure the validity of the study.

As the case study is of flexible design, and the data collection and analysis may be more closely intertwined, the data collection and analysis sections may be combined into one section however some adjustments are needed. For example, the coding scheme often constitutes a natural subsection, and for a comparative case study, the data collection and analysis section may be structured according to the compared cases. For a longitudinal study, the timescale may constitute the structure of the data collection and analysis section. The results section also includes an evaluation of the validity of the final results.

**TABLE 6.1   Proposed Reporting Structure for Case Study Reports Using the
Linear-Analytic Structure (Based on Jedlitschka et al. [77] and Kitchenham et al. [95]).**

Section headings	Subsections
Title	
Authorship	
Structured abstract	
Introduction	Problem statement
	Research objectives
	Context
Related work	Earlier studies
	Theory
Case study design	Research questions
	Case and subject selection
	Data collection procedure(s)
	Analysis procedure(s)
	Validity procedure(s)
Results	Case and subject descriptions, covering execution, analysis, and interpretation issues
	Subsections, which may be structured, for example, according to coding scheme, each linking observations to conclusions
	Evaluation of validity
Conclusions and future work	Summary of findings
	Relation to existing evidence
	Impact/implications
	Limitations
	Future work
Acknowledgments	
References	
Appendices	

6.6.2 Reporting Recommendations from Evaluative Case Studies

A characteristic that often distinguishes an evaluative case study from other kinds of case study is the preparation and reporting of recommendations. When preparing recommendations, the researchers should think carefully about making recommendations that are credible, beneficial, and feasible. The credibility of the recommendations should be demonstrable through a well-designed and conducted case study, however the researcher will also need to ensure that the design and conduct of the case study is not just intellectually rigorous, but also relevant to the stakeholders who will be interested in the recommendations. This is clearly a case study *design* issue, as well as a reporting issue.

The benefits and feasibility of the recommendations are dependent on the researcher having a good knowledge of the situation to which those recommendations will apply. This includes a good knowledge of the constraints on changes that can be made to that situation, and a good knowledge of the constraints on the decisions and actions that the stakeholders can take. Stakeholders will likely have different goals, which are based on the respective roles of the stakeholders, and these differences can potentially lead to disagreements among the stakeholders over what are the beneficial and feasible decisions and actions to take. Robson [162] suggests that the researcher could present recommendations in terms of options, where each option is supported by different explanations and judgments. Naturally, each option should be supported by appropriate findings from the case study. For example, within the context of evaluating software methods, Kitchenham and Pickard [109] suggest that the researcher compare the performance of the evaluated method in three possible ways:

- Compare against a "sister" project, where the trial project and comparison project have similar characteristics and where the two projects are typical projects in the organization.
- Compare against an appropriate company baseline. This approach relies on the organization collecting data on projects as a standard practice.
- Compare against a random sample of appropriate components or activities.

Robson [162] also advises that the researcher should seek "buy in" from the stakeholders. This may be practically and ethically difficult where there is a diversity of stakeholder goals and problems. In these situations, the researcher may need to focus on the priorities of the sponsor of the case study. Again, this is an issue that the researcher may need to consider during the design of the case study, for example, to consider those activities that need to be undertaken during the case study to prepare the stakeholders for receiving and considering draft and final recommendations. Rosemann and Vessey [164, 165] propose a systematic approach called *Applicability Checks* that is based on the focus group method and concentrates on three dimensions of relevance critical to practitioners: importance, accessibility, and suitability.

In the process of developing recommendations, the researcher will often need to change their mode of thinking from observation and analysis, to design and engineering; or phrased differently, the researcher will need to change their thinking from description and explanation, to the more subjective and value laden prescription and justification.

6.6.3 Reporting to Stakeholders, Including Sponsor(s)

We suggest that case study researchers consider the following actions when preparing reports for stakeholders:

1. Identify and prioritize the stakeholders.
2. Clarify the goals and problems and other issues of particular relevance to the respective stakeholders. This can be done by
   - Asking the stakeholders directly and explicitly.
   - Reviewing previous reports prepared for the stakeholders.
   - Learning, through engagement with the stakeholders over time, the goals, problems, and concerns of those stakeholders.
   - Reviewing published literature that seeks to identify and understand the goals, problems and concerns of particular stakeholders. For example, at the *11th International Conference on Agile Software Development* (XP2010), Freudenberg and Sharp [57] asked conference participants to identify and vote on the most pressing question or issue the practitioners would like to be researched. From the responses, Freudenberg and Sharp derived the 10 most pressing issues. These issues could then help researchers investigating Agile methods to better understand the goals, problems, and concerns of practitioners.
3. Find out the kinds of report (e.g., structure, typical content) preferred by the priority stakeholders. This can be done by
   - Asking the stakeholders directly and explicitly.
   - Reviewing previous reports prepared for the stakeholders.
4. Prepare reports that address the concerns of the priority stakeholders in a format preferred by those stakeholders.

An example structure for reporting to stakeholders is given in Table 6.2.

We noted in Chapter 3 that it can be difficult to agree a common set of objectives with industrial partners. Even if the case study has a clear set of objectives that are pursued effectively, there can still be a diversity of stakeholder goals and problems, together with organizational politics. These conflicts can be difficult to take account of when preparing reports of the case study.

Example 6.4:   Taipale et al. [200] conducted a study to better understand where research on software testing should be directed. A summary of the four main phases of

TABLE 6.2   An Example Reporting Structure for Case Study Reports to Stakeholders.

Section Headings and Subsections

Title
Authorship
Executive summary
Summary of recommendations
Body of report, to include introduction, detailed findings and recommendations
Bibliography and references
Appendices, to include detailed theory, methodology, data and results
Acknowledgments

TABLE 6.3 Identifying and Ranking Issues for Research in Software Testing (From Taipale et al. [200]).

Phase	Description of Phase
1	Conduct of a literature review and, concurrently, the conduct of interviews with experts. This phase resulted in a list of software testing issues.
2	Consolidate the list of software testing issues from Phase 1 in three steps: (1) Consolidation by researchers. (2) Review of revised list of issues by a 10 member steering group, comprising representatives from industry and research. The representatives from industry were drawn from automation, engineering and telecommunications companies. This review consolidated the list of issues but also added additional issues. (3) Revise the list based on feedback from the panel after the panel had formally met.
3	Ranking of issues by a 10 member expert panel. Again, the panel comprised representatives from industry and research, but this panel had a more balanced composition of membership between the different types of company and also included representation from a small testing company.
4	Final review and refinement of the ranked list of issues.

the study is presented in Table 6.3. The study resulted in a ranked list of testing issues, a realization of the need to clarify the relationship between software development and software resting, and a hypothesis to provide direction to their further research.

6.6.4 Reporting the Context of the Case Study

The software engineering research community has recognized, for some time, the potential effects of context on the findings of research studies. For example, Kitchenham et al. [105] in their preliminary guidelines on empirical research in software engineering have encouraged researchers to specify as much of the industrial context as possible. Also, the very definition of a case study that we use in this book recognizes that context cannot easily be separated from the case being studied. The full specification of context, together with the separation of the case from that context, are particularly challenging aspects of case study research. Nevertheless, the researcher should still seek to describe and classify characteristics of the context as these characteristics will likely affect the generalizability of the findings of the study, as well as help the reader better appreciate the contribution of the study.

In the absence of any well-developed framework for characterizing the context of software engineering phenomena, we briefly consider here a bottom-up approach advocated by Basili and Shull [13], together with a top-down approach proposed by Petersen and Wohlin [138].

Basili and Shull [13] recognize two difficulties with being able to make statements about the effectiveness of processes in different contexts:

- There are many sources of variation between one development context and another.

- It is not clear *a priori* what specific factors influence the effectiveness of a process in a given context.

Basili and Shull [13] expect it to be an almost impossible task to predict *ahead of time* what factors are likely to affect the results of applying a process in one environment or another. On the other hand, Basili and Shull "know" that these variables do exist, and that the research community is able to reason about their influence when the researchers worked "bottom up" from their particular studies. This leads Basili and Shull to argue for families of studies where the studies look at a similar phenomenon of interest in similar and varied contexts. Families of studies provide a framework to support the opportunistic identification of context variables.

Petersen and Wohlin [138] have proposed a preliminary framework for describing the context of industrial research. The framework is organized into several facets and then, within each facet, into several elements. Petersen and Wohlin recognize that the facets and elements are incomplete and will need to be refined and extended in further research. They also recognize that for any given study it is unlikely that the researcher will be able to specify all facets and all elements for that study. The researcher will therefore need to make a judgment on what contextual information to report. The framework is summarized in Table 6.4.

TABLE 6.4   Preliminary Framework for Describing Context [138].

Facet	Element
Product	Maturity
	Quality
	Size
	System type
	Customization
	Programming language
Processes	Activities
	Workflow
	Artifacts
Practices, tools, technique	CASE tools
	Practices and techniques
People	Roles
	Experience
Organization	Model of overall organization
	Organizational unit
	Certification
	Distribution
Market	Number of customers
	Market segments
	Strategy
	Constraints

Example 6.5: In the PM case studies at IBM, several factors were reported as the sociotechnical characteristics of the two projects studied as case studies. The factors are summarized in Table 6.5.

TABLE 6.5   The Socio-technical Context of Project at IBM Hursley Park.

Size of support team
Size of planned development team
Size of planned management team
Assignment of work between support team and development team
Role(s) of project leader
Strategic value of product
Purpose of project
Type of product
Release sizes
Number of features/design changes
Platform
Project status meetings
Project duration (in weeks)
Product delivery week
Determination of project duration
Business process
Organization
Composition of management team
Project success

6.6.5 Reporting to Students

Students often have little professional experience of industry, or enterprise-level technical knowledge. Consequently, students can sometimes find it difficult to appreciate the significance of practitioners' goals, problems, and concerns; or the significance of researchers' concerns with validity and reliability. Understandably, students' goals and problems tend to relate to assessments (e.g., passing an exam), to progression on their program of study, and of course to learning the subject. Students therefore often have a different perspective to researchers and to practitioners.

Reporting case studies to students can therefore be very valuable for two different reasons: first, case studies can help teach students about industrial scale software engineering; second, case studies can help teach students about how to study industrial scale software engineering.

Whereas reports to practitioners and other researchers often take the form of "self-standing" reports, it may be necessary to provide much more explanation to students of relevant theory and knowledge, both of industrial scale software engineering and of research methodology. On the other hand, a teaching environment can often support a more flexible and interactive approach. Such an approach that can take place over

TABLE 6.6   An Example Reporting Structure for a
Teaching Case Study to University Students.

Section Headings

Title
Authorship
Introduction to the case study
Overview to the software project
Definitions
The context of the project
The project's schedule, workload, and capability
Software features and the project plan
Project urgency and other project behavior
Teams and functional areas of the project
Dependencies between functional areas
The reasons for the dependencies
The impact of the dependencies
Managing the impact of changes on the project
References
Appendices

an extended period of time and involve a variety of different types of reporting and dissemination, for example, lectures, tutorials, practicals, and reading material. This gives the lecturer potentially greater flexibility in what he or she chooses to report of the case study, as well as how those reports are made. An example structure for a teaching case study focused on project management is given in Table 6.6

Example 6.6:   For the PM case studies, the two *research* case studies have been converted into shorter case studies for teaching and assessment on an advanced project management module, part of the MEng Computer Science degree programme at the University of Hertfordshire in the United Kingdom. The Project C teaching case study comprises 15 pages of text and figures describing and analyzing the project. This is accompanied by an appendix on the research methodology, together with a second appendix describing how the findings are visualized in the figures. The Project C teaching case study is used as a detailed example for discussion of the project management concepts that are raised each week during the teaching program. The Project B case study, similar in size and format to the Project C case study, will then be used as the basis for the formal assessment on the module. A simplified structure for the case studies is presented in Table 6.6.

6.6.6   Ad Hoc and Impromptu Reporting

There may be situations where a participant in the study, such as a team leader in a project, asks for an update on the case study. The researcher needs to be very careful about what is, and is not, said in these often informal, ad hoc situations. The researcher should be particularly cautious about sharing any confidential or personal information in these situations. These issues are discussed later in this chapter and also in Chapter 3.

6.7 FORMATS AND STRUCTURES FOR A REPORT

In software engineering research, and unlike a number of disciplines in the social sciences, the accepted types of publication in the community are journal articles and conference papers. Because of page limitations however neither of these types is particularly suited to reporting in detail on large-scale case studies. This presents a problem for the software engineering case study researcher. For example, a number of compositional structures proposed by Yin and Robson (discussed later in this section) would not necessarily suit journal and conference publications. Benbasat et al. state that due to the extensive amount of data generated in case studies, "books or monographs might be better vehicles to publish case study research" [19]. One possible strategy is to design for a series of publications, each publication addressing particular aspects of the case study, with perhaps a summary paper providing an overview. This strategy is likely to be more feasible and effective for case studies with a strong theoretical foundation, or for replications of a previous study. For a case study that is exploratory, this strategy will be harder because the researcher will need to explore and then develop an understanding of the case before she or he can "design" for a series of publications.

Yin [217] suggests four main formats for reporting a case study:

- A narrative describing and analyzing a single case study. (These narratives could also include tables, figures, etc.) Yin recognizes that such reports are likely to appear as books (or theses) because journals cannot accommodate the space needed for such a report.
- The description and analysis of more than one case, with each case presented in one or more chapters as a narrative. As with the singlecase narrative, these reports are likely to appear as books or theses.
- The presentation of one or more cases in a question-and-answer format. Each case is reported in its own right, with that report structured according to the questions.
- A cross-case description and analysis of multiple case studies. In this format, cases are not presented individually, but the report is structured according to issues and, for each issue, each of the cases is described and analyzed with regards to that issue.

In addition to the four formats, Yin suggests several compositional structures for reporting case studies in general [217].

Linear-analytic. The standard research report structure, for example, problem, related work, methods, analysis, conclusions. A version of this structure is presented in Table 6.1.

Comparative. The same case is repeated twice or more to compare alternative descriptions, explanations, or points of view.

Chronological. A structure most suitable for longitudinal studies.

Theory-building. A structure that presents the case according to some theory-building logic in order to constitute a chain of evidence for a theory.

Suspense. A structure that reverts the linear-analytic structure and reports conclusions first, backing them up with evidence. Practitioner reports often take this "reverse structure," with the executive summary presented first.

Unsequenced. For example, a "structure" used when reporting general characteristics of a set of cases.

Robson [162] briefly discusses several alternative approaches to presenting a case study as a written report in contrast to, for example, an oral presentation or video. While the approaches discussed by Robson do not appear to have been explicitly used yet in software engineering research, some aspects of these approaches do appear to have been recognized and adopted in software engineering. Three of Robson's approaches most relevant to software engineering case studies are as follows:

Portrayal. "A broad and accurate reflection of a case's complex "transactions" is both more important than, and antithetical to, a focus on analysis" [162, p. 423]. Software engineering research recognizes the importance of describing software engineering phenomena, for example describing a software engineering process. Lonchamp [122] makes a distinction between a *descriptive* attitude and a *prescriptive* attitude. With the descriptive attitude, the researcher studies an existing process to answer the question *how software is (or has been) actually developed?* Within this "attitude", researchers may adopt an expressive approach, where the actual process is described more or less formally for understanding, communication, education, and so on. Alternatively, the researcher may adopt an analytic approach, where the description of the actual process is studied through more formal techniques, for a deeper understanding, for improvement, comparisons, forecasting, and so on. With the prescriptive attitude, the researcher defines a desired process, to answer the question *how should software be developed?* Again, this "attitude" is refined into two further approaches: guiding and enforcing. Robinson et al. [161], Curtis et al. [37], and Wolf and Rosenblum [216] are all examples of software engineering research that has taken a descriptive attitude toward investigating software engineering phenomena.

Adversarial statements. Two "positions" are adopted, one supporting some innovation, intervention, change or decision; the other opposing that innovation, and so on. No reconciliation is attempted between the two positions; instead reconciliation or compromise is left to the reader. Software engineering research recognizes the importance of competing theories and hypotheses, but to the best of our knowledge there is no software engineering case study that has been reported using this adversarial approach, although Orlikowski [131], for example, does present competing theories. The journal *IEEE Software* often includes a feature in journal issues that provides a point and counterpoint on some subject or topic, each written by a different person. These features are rarely adversarial in tone, however.

Dialogue. Different positions, of which there may be more than two, are presented as a form of discussion. Again, we are not aware of any software engineering case study that has been reported this way. But again, software engineering research recognizes that within a software engineering situation there can be many participants and stakeholders each with their own perspective. Baddoo et al. [11, 12], for example, investigated the motivations of programmers, project managers, and senior managers and presented those motivations using, among other things, multidimensional scalogram analysis. While this presentation was not a dialogue in the way intended by Robson, the reporting does make explicit the different positions of the three stakeholder groups.

A recently emerging approach used to report on findings in software engineering research is the concept of the *stereotype*. For example, Kasurinen et al. [87] used a survey and interviews to study test case selection and prioritization. They identified eight categories of observed effects on test case selection and then used these categories to distinguish between two stereotypical approaches to test case selection and prioritization: risk-based selection and design-based selection. These stereotypes were then used as a basis for reasoning about the choices and behaviors of different organizations for testing.

Example 6.7: Rainer's doctoral thesis [144] employed a combination of formats and compositional structures. For the formats, there was one chapter describing aspects of the two cases (software projects) studied which used some of the compositions summarized by Yin and also offered a portrayal of the progress of the two projects. After this chapter, there were then three chapters that each reported on an issue and compared the two cases according to that issue. A further chapter sought to synthesize the findings into one whole, including drawing on theoretical material presented earlier in the thesis. There was therefore a complex compositional structure to the thesis, which reflected the complex description and analysis undertaken during the case studies. See Chapter 11 for more details.

For the academic reporting of case studies, the linear-analytic structure is the most accepted structure, but it is possible to combine different structures. For example, Rainer (see example) has used a broad linear-analytic structure, but within that structure he has reported findings using chronological, comparative, and theory-related structures, as well as the unsequenced structure to report general characteristics and quotations from participants in the case.

6.8 WHERE TO REPORT

Where one should report is again dependent on the readership, on the status of the case study, on the timing of the report, and on professional requirements. There are of course a range of opportunities to report to the academic community, for example through peer-reviewed journals, international and national conferences, workshops, theses, and technical reports. There may also be opportunities to publish online, for example on the respective University's research blog. In each case, the researcher should carefully consider the degree to which the interim or final findings, or artifacts, of the case study map to the aims and scope of the respective opportunity to publish. There may also be a range of opportunities to report to industry, with examples being practitioner journals and magazines, and industry conferences. For companies who have participated in the research there are likely to be opportunities for presentations to the company. For grant funders, there is likely to be the obligation to make one or more reports on the project. Increasingly, software engineering researchers have their own professional home page on the internet, or a personal home page, and these of course provide opportunities to publish findings and to disseminate artifacts.

6.9 ETHICS AND CONFIDENTIALITY

Ethical, professional, and legal requirements can place restrictions on what can be reported, and there can sometimes be tensions between "academic freedom" and these requirements. The researchers must have the right to maintain their integrity and adhere to agreed procedures during the case study. Also, companies may not know academic practices for publication and dissemination and they may, as a consequence, need to be informed about these practices. The researcher should therefore take great care in deciding what to report, and may need to regularly consult with appropriate participants, stakeholders and other governance bodies such as ethics committees.

Information is not only sensitive when published outside of the company. Data collected from, and opinions stated by, individual employees may be sensitive to other participants and stakeholders within the company, such as line managers [192]. From a publication point of view, the relevant data to publish is rarely sensitive to the company since data may be made anonymous. However, it is important to remember that it is not always sufficient to remove names of companies or individuals. These companies and individuals may be identified by their characteristics, particularly if they have been selected from a small sample of people or companies.

Results may be sensitive to a company if, for example, the results reveal deficiencies in their software engineering practices, or if the company's product comes out last in a comparison [8]. Conversely, this risk may affect respondent's behavior, for example, overstating a project's performance. The chance that this may occur must be discussed upfront and made clear to the participants of the case study. In situations where violations of the law are identified during the case study, these must be reported, even though "whistle-blowers" rarely are rewarded.

Giving feedback to the participants of a study is critical for building and maintaining long-term trust, and for the validity of the research. First, transcripts of interviews and observations should be sent back to the participants to enable correction of raw data. Second, analyses should be presented to them in order to maintain their trust in the research. Participants must not necessarily agree on the outcome of the analysis, but feeding back the analysis results increases the validity of the study.

Example 6.8: In the XP, QA, and REVV, studies issues of confidentiality were handled through Nondisclosure Agreements and general project cooperation agreements between the companies and the university, lasting longer than one case study. These agreements state that the university researchers are obliged to have publications approved by representatives of the companies before they are published, and that raw data must not be spread to anyone but those signing the contract. The researchers are not obliged to report their sources of facts to management, unless it is found that a law is violated. In order to ensure that interviewees were not cited wrongly, it was agreed that the transcribed interviews were sent back to them for review in the XP and REVV studies. In the beginning of each interview, interviewees were informed about their rights in the study. In study QA, feedback meetings for analysis and interpretation were explicitly a part of the methodology (see Figure 12.1). When negotiating publication of data, we were explicitly told that raw numbers of defects could not be published, but percentages over phases could, which was acceptable for the research purposes.

The studies were conducted in Sweden, where only studies in medicine are explicitly regulated by law; hence there was no approval of the studies by a review board beforehand.

Example 6.9: For the PM case studies at IBM, confidentiality was handled through a Nondisclosure Agreement. This included the requirement that all publications intended for external dissemination were reviewed by IBM prior to their publication. In practice, this review was undertaken by the company mentor who very often gave constructive advice on how to communicate the issues while also maintaining sufficient confidentiality. There was a feedback session to the project manager and assistant for each of the two projects studied.

6.10 CONCLUSION

In this chapter, we have considered the reporting of the findings of the case study together with the dissemination of artifacts from the case study. Reporting of findings and dissemination of artifacts are surprisingly challenging activities within case study research. Because of the diversity in the types of audience for the reports and dissemination, and because of the range of types of findings and artifacts that could be reported and disseminated, this chapter has focused on more general guidelines, supported with examples.

CHAPTER 7

SCALING UP CASE STUDY RESEARCH TO REAL-WORLD SOFTWARE PRACTICE

7.1 INTRODUCTION

Empirical software engineering research is often conducted in real-world settings with complex and multifaceted characteristics. These characteristics will be difficult to capture and understand in depth if the case study is scoped too narrowly, for example, scoped to a single, small-scale unit of analysis.

Many real-world software engineering cases involve software artifacts, such as code repositories, design descriptions, test suites, and requirements documents, and each of these artifacts may be very large and complex. Investigating these artifacts can therefore produce immense amounts of data to analyze. If one also adds the potential complexity and size of industrial software processes, organizations, methods, tools, and so on, case study research may need to be scaled up from small single case investigations to a combination of multiple large-scale case studies, in order to achieve deeper empirical understanding of real-world software engineering. Thus, one of the greater aims that we, as a software engineering research community can embrace, is to make our research truly relevant by not limiting its investigations to small and convenient "toy" examples. Instead the community should extend our methodological tools to reach for a deeper understanding of the real complexity of real-world, large-scale software engineering.

Case Study Research in Software Engineering: Guidelines and Examples, First Edition.
Per Runeson, Martin Höst, Austen Rainer, and Björn Regnell.
© 2012 John Wiley & Sons, Inc. Published 2012 by John Wiley & Sons, Inc.

While embracing this important aim to large-scale studies, we must also recognize that research projects are conducted with limited resources and often with specific and focused goals that are specified in a contract with the research project sponsors. Thus scaling up to a complex, large-scale setting involves cost-benefit trade-offs between available research resources and the added value of an extended case study investigation that takes the committed research goals into account.

This chapter presents and discusses the aims of scaling up and the dimensions of scale in case study research. The chapter also discusses some of the challenges that may emerge when conducting large-scale case study research.

7.2 THE AIMS OF SCALING UP CASE STUDIES

There are at least two aims to scaling up case study research that are related and can be combined:

1. *Extending the scope* of the study to encompass a more comprehensive research agenda with extended research questions and thereby extended and more relevant results.
2. *Increasing the validity*, of the study so that the knowledge that is created from the cases that are studied becomes more trustworthy and useful. The purpose may for example be to increase the external validity and thereby provide case study results that are more generalizable and easier to assess if they are transferable to cases with common characteristics.

The first aim to scaling up involves a widening of the scope of the study, while the second aim seeks to improve the precision of the study within its current scope. Each of these aims may lead to increased benefits of the research results, as well as increased research costs and challenges with managing the added complexity of the research project.

Often these aims can be fulfilled using a series of case studies over time. For example, an investigation may first start with a small-scale case study and then be followed by a scaled up study as the first study reveals the need for a wider scoped study of the research question. The larger scope may, for example, better cover a phenomenon that turns out to be more complex than first anticipated. Another reason for following up the first investigation with a subsequent, larger scale case study may be to extend the data collection to address external validity issues and thus better support a generalization of the achieved knowledge to a wider context.

Extending the scope and increasing the precision may help to achieve the ambition to cope with real-world complexity by including large-scale objects of study with high complexity and many details. This may result in the benefits of both deeper and more comprehensive knowledge, but may also require huge efforts in data collection and analysis. For example, if we want to investigate how to improve the verifiability of software requirements in a case study, the results may call for an extended investigation of how to improve the general coordination and alignment of the requirements engineering, verification, and validation activities.

Example 7.1: Regnell et al. conducted a large-scale case study as described in detail in Chapter 14, denoted the REVV study. This case study includes 6 geographically distributed companies and 11 researchers at 2 universities producing transcriptions of 30 interviews comprising a total of approximately 217,030 words (319 pages of text). The total effort spent so far is approximated to 1700 h of researcher effort. The REVV study scaled up from a single to a multicase case study over time [172], with the purpose of increased scope in terms of more comprehensive research questions and more extensive data collection. There was also a purpose of increased validity behind the scaling up, as the partner companies wanted to know more about how others are dealing with the software engineering challenges under study. The study thus both widened and deepened over time.

7.3 DIMENSIONS OF SCALE

As a consequence of the two aims to scaling up case study research, case studies may scale up along (at least) four dimensions that each introduce additional benefits but also additional costs:

1. *Time* is one dimension along which researchers can increase the scale of the study. The temporal scope of a case study can be enlarged in terms of duration, so that research questions can be studied over time and valid results can be drawn while reducing the risk that the knowledge gained is only a transient phenomenon or do not cover aspects of evolution over time. Studies that follow a phenomenon over a long duration of time are often called *longitudinal* (a detailed example is provided in Chapter 11). Another approach is to increase the temporal resolution of a case in terms of increased precision in unit of time, so that research questions can be studied based on a richer data set that more accurately represents phenomena changing quickly over time [146].

2. The *number of cases* is another scaling dimension to consider. If budget and sponsor interest permit, researchers may make the effort to include more cases in order to further extend context and increase validity of the knowledge gained. The research questions and generalization objectives is a basis for selecting further cases, and the sampling strategy can be either to increase the variability in the data set and see if theory maturity is approaching, or to get "more of the same" to increase the certainty that our conclusions are general and transferable. As the number of cases are increased, iteration back all the way to the conception of the case study purposes may be needed, as new evidence may turn previous beliefs up-side down.

3. The *number of research questions, propositions, concepts, and measures* can be scaled to address the purpose of an increased case study context. For example,

a large-scale case study of a software project over time could investigate a very wide range of concepts, in contrast to a small-scale case study of a specific software inspection instance. However, even the study of software inspection could be scaled up to a large scope with many instances and variables of interest that are both directly and indirectly related to the evolving human activity of scrutinizing existing software artifacts.

4. The *number of involved researchers* can be increased when there is a sponsor that is willing to support an enlarged research budget on an interesting phenomenon that benefit from being investigated by many researchers in parallel. This is analogous to software engineering projects that seek to shorten lead-time while increasing the level of parallelization in order to utilize more resources efficiently and effectively. However, this may be easier said than done. Similarly, a complex activity such as research may also exhibit limitations in terms of how easy it is to gain a desirable yield from a resource increase. Nevertheless, it is our strong belief that we need to take on the challenges of synchronization among multiple researchers (or even multiple research teams), as well as the challenge of aligning disparate goals of individual researchers, in order to form a productive community effort to tackle the really important issues in contemporary and future software engineering. Also the number of researchers need to scale up, as our study object of large-scale software engineering does!

Scaling along any of these dimensions is certain to render increased size and complexity of the research endeavor. A longitudinal case study will over time accumulate a large base of data as the studied software engineering context evolve, with potentially contradictory evidence that are inter-related in complex manners. Likewise, as the number of cases increases the amount of data rapidly gets more and more complex to analyze, as the size and intricateness of the data are increased, and more variation among cases is introduced. Also, increases in the number of research questions and the number of researchers pose specific challenges in both effort in data collection and in inter-researcher communication.

The remainder of this chapter is devoted to further discussion some important aspects of scale; longitudinal case studies, multiple case studies, and multiresearcher case studies, respectively.

7.4   LONGITUDINAL CASE STUDIES

Publications in software engineering research refer to "longitudinal studies" or "longitudinal case studies" [120, 190, 197]. These two terms tend to refer to the duration of the case or cases being studied, as opposed to the period of time over which the study of the case has occurred. For example, studies of open source software are typically retrospective, longitudinal case studies because the researcher is exploiting a respository of source code that has accumulated over a lengthy period of time. Godfrey and Tu [62], for example, retrospectively examined the full Linux kernel as it evolved over the period 1994 to late-1999. In addition to the period of study, there is also the frequency of data collection activities during that period. For example, Storey et al. [197] created a tool to support source code documentation and then designed a longitudinal study to observe the use of the tool by developers, taking snapshots of the code at monthly intervals over a 2-year period.

Taken together, as the period of study increases and the frequency of data collection activities increase in that period so the longitudinal case study becomes increasingly demanding of the researcher's resources, in particular the effort required for the study. As the quantity of data increases there are increasing demands on quality assurance (e.g., an increasing number of interviews to transcribe and send to interviewees for review) and also on the resources required to organize and analyze the data that has been collected. In addition, there are likely to be more changes in the case being studied with a need to change the case study design and maintain the case study protocol. Also, with the increase in resources there is likely to be an increase in the effort required to coordinate those resources, for example, as more researchers are involved in the project, and as more participants in the case are interviewed. Further resources will be required as the number of cases increases, for example, through the need for cross-case analysis and reporting, and again the need to coordinate resources.

Longitudinal case study research is particularly appropriate for the larger scale, complex phenomena where there is a need to collect both quantitative and qualitative data. Two good examples of such phenomena are software projects and software product lines. Longitudinal case study research would also appear to be particular appropriate where one is interested in the success of some activity, for example, the impact of software quality assurance activities on the performance of software as used by customers "in the field," or the success of a software project. Shenhar et al. [181] provide a model of software project success, comprising four dimensions: project efficiency, customer satisfaction, business performance, and preparation for the future. Of these four dimensions, only the first dimension can be adequately assessed in the short period after completion of a software project. The other dimensions may require from months up to many years to properly assess. This means that a contemporaneous, longitudinal case study—a study undertaken at the time the case occurs—is more suited to studying immediate outcomes such as project efficiency, while a retrospective, longitudinal case study—a study undertaken after the case has completed—may be more suited to studying the longer term outcomes such as business performance and preparation for the future.

The tendency in software engineering research to focus on either small-scale cases (an exemplar being software inspections) or on relatively low-effort research methods (e.g., surveys, a series of one-off interviews) or on the analysis of already collected data sets (e.g., estimation models, open source software) is an indication that the software engineering research community both recognizes the demands of longitudinal case study research but also that the community can only rarely allocate sufficient resources toward such studies. As an unfortunate consequence of this situation, there is little information or empirical evidence available in the software engineering research community on the resource demands of such longitudinal case studies. Kitchenham et al.'s work on the DESMET evaluation methodology [104] provides some heuristics. McLeod et al. [126] reports detailed and insightful information on the conduct of a longitudinal case studies, summarized here in Example 7.3. We further discuss resource issues in Section 8.4.

Example 7.2: The PM study comprised two longitudinal case studies of software projects at IBM Hursley Park, between mid-1995 and mid-1998. Each case commenced with about 6 months of preparation (e.g., identifying appropriate cases), followed by approximately 12 months of data collection (the two projects each lasted 12 months and occurred concurrently), with a further 12–18 months of analysis and reporting, giving a total of approximately 3 years to design, conduct and report the two case studies. The field researcher was onsite full-time for the first year of the project, and then visited the site weekly for several months, subsequently reducing the frequency of visits. These two cases are discussed in Chapter 11.

Example 7.3: McLeod et al. [126] conducted a single holistic explanatory case study of an information systems project at AlphaCo (a pseudonym), a large manufacturing company. The case study was conducted between mid-2005 and mid-2007, and involved an initial 8-month period that coincided with the main project activity. During that period, the field researcher visited the site for two or three days per week, averaging about 12 h per week in visits. For one 7-week period, the researcher visited the site every day. After that 8-month period, there were a number of follow-up visits to the site, together with regular phone and email contact. The researcher participated in 36 meetings, for example: interviews with an external project manager, vendor meetings, project team meeting, weekly meetings with a contractor, and training sessions. These 36 meetings totaled almost 47 h. The researcher also conducted 33 interviews with a variety of stakeholders. These interviews totaled almost 24 h. In total, 558 h was spent on site with AlphaCo.

7.5 MULTIPLE CASE STUDIES

The second approach to scaling up case studies is to broaden the study to more than one case. Studying more cases naturally leads to more information about the studied phenomenon. This is not only due the increased amount of data collected from the informants but also based on the characteristics of the selected cases themselves. If cases with different characteristics provide similar information about a certain topic, it indicates a robust finding. On the other hand, if different information is provided from similar cases, the cause of the difference must be searched in other aspects. Hence, the characteristics of the case itself is important.

7.5.1 Multiple Cases and Replications

Conducting multiple case studies has some similarities to the notion of replication of experiments. The main purpose is to get another set of data points that brings light

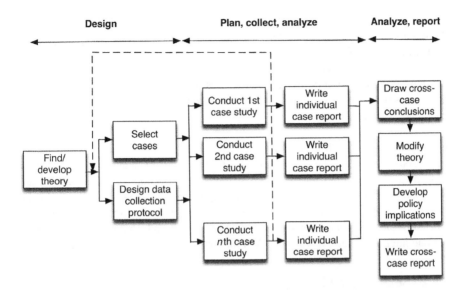

FIGURE 7.1 Example process for multiple case study. Adapted from Yin [217].

to the phenomenon under study. However, multiple case studies should not be mixed up with the notion of statistical replication and statistical sampling. For case studies, analytical replication and case selection apply. Statistical methods rely on sampling and representativeness, while case studies rely on the cases and their characteristics, whether it be typical or special in some sense.

There exist many different types of replication and different terms for replication. Gomez et al. surveyed replication type classifications, and found 18 different classification schemes in the fields of social science, philosophy, and business [63]. Shull et al. propose for experimental replications in software engineering to distinguish between *exact* and *conceptual* replications [183]; the first category trying to replicate the original experiment as close as possible, and conceptual replications trying to investigate the same underlying concept, but with different experimental procedures. Juristo and Vegas note that the exact replications are rare in empirical software engineering, and therefore they argue for conceptual replications and that we learn from differences between experiments, rather than similarities [79].

As defined in Section 3.2.10, case studies may be *literally* replicated, that is selected to predict similar results, or *theoretically* replicated to achieve contrasting results for predictable reasons. Instead of thinking in terms of samples, as for the statistical replications, the notion of theory is central to bring forward the conclusions from one case to being verified or rejected in another. Figure 7.1 illustrates how a multiple case study may be conducted, including theory development and modification. Verner et al. [208] published guidelines specifically for the conduct of multiple case studies in software engineering.

Example 7.4: Karlström and Runeson [85, 86] conducted the XP case study with three units of analysis, see Chapter 10. First, two companies were studied, analyzing the use of eXtreme Programming in a stage–gate management process. The companies were working in different domains, defense and automation, respectively, but since the conditions with requirements on processes and documentation are similar, they are seen as two units in a similar context. The third unit is a different type of company, and hence seen as a different case.

Example 7.5: Regnell et al. conducted the REVV case study with six embedded cases, see Chapter 14. The study started at one company [172], at which the interview instruments were piloted, and then a set of interviews were conducted, in total 11, later extended to 15. Five other companies were approached and new cases were added to the study, each of them comprising 3–4 interviews, giving a total of 30 interviews. One additional company was intended to be part of the study, but since we only could get one interview there, it was not taken into the study.

7.5.2 Selecting the Cases

In a multiple case study, the same principles apply as to selecting the first case (see Section 3.2.10). However, selecting the second case should be conducted to match the first case. In addition to the general principles of being "typical", "critical", "revelatory", or "unique" in some respect [19], certain characteristics of the software engineering context under study may be considered to find variation points. For example

- Size and age of company.
- Application domain—for example, telecom, banking, automation.
- Application type—for example, embedded, database, mobile.
- Business model—market or contract driven.
- Customer—private, public, internal.
- Process—plan driven or agile.
- Key quality characteristic—for example, performance, reliability.

Aspects of case study context are discussed in more depth in Section 6.6.4.

Sometimes, the researcher has little or no control over the choice of case or cases. For example, cases may be made available through a collaboration contract, or via a contact network. However, the characteristics of the cases may still be used to choose among candidate cases, and also for analyzing and reporting the case study. Selection from candidate cases is discussed in Chapter 11.

When approaching the second and subsequent cases, the research instruments may be adjusted based on the findings from the first case. In particular, the first case may be used as a pilot case to explore the phenomenon under study, and the following cases may be used for more in-depth investigations. Being a flexible research design, the case study may change during the course of the study. However, the objective of the research must remain the same, especially when investigating contrasting cases in the same study, where the same concepts are studied in different cases and contexts. Also, we advise that the researcher takes care not to communicate information about previous cases, both for confidentiality reasons, and to avoid biasing the interviewees with a preconceived view of the phenomenon under study.

A natural question for a researcher to ask is "How many cases do I need in a multiple case study?" There is no single and simple answer to that question. The notion of sample size is not relevant, because case studies are not concerned with statistical sampling. Only one case is needed to reject a hypothesis while it is not possible to prove any universal theories, independently of how many cases you study.

In statistical tests, the significance level (e.g., $p < 0.05$ or $p < 0.01$) is arbitrarily chosen and established by convention within a research community. A similar logic holds for the number of cases needed in a multiple case study. The needed number depends on the certainty you want to achieve (comparable to statistical significance). Further, it also depends on how different are the rival theories being studied which the research. Yin advices that "you may want to settle for two or three literal replications when the rival theories are grossly different and the issue at hand does not demand an excessive degree of certainty" [217, p. 51].

When adding cases, as well as when adding new interviewees to report in a case, the *saturation* criterion may apply [34, p. 143]. Saturation occurs when each new interviewee or new case does not make any substantive, additional contribution to the issue under study. The researcher recognizes that the responses of interviewees, for example, or the general patterns in the data are unchanged with each new interviewee or new case. Saturation is not a quantitatively measurable entity, but is still a feasible criterion when judging the validity of a case study.

For theoretical replications, when different results are predicted, the number of cases needed to achieve certainty also depends on the complexity of the studied phenomenon.

Example 7.6: Hall et al. [67] conducted an extensive multiple case study with 13 companies on process improvement programs. They arranged in total 44 focus group meetings involving approximately 200 software professionals. The focus group of participants discussed topics related to process improvement and the discussions were analyzed using quasi-statistical approaches. The focus group findings were followed up in a survey in 85 companies, thus combining qualitative and quantitative data collections, as well as flexible and fixed designs.

7.6 MULTIRESEARCHER CASE STUDIES

Scaling up case study research by involving more researchers, and perhaps also multiple research groups at several universities, may be required in order to tackle comprehensive research objectives and large cases and contexts. Further, if we, for example, seek to fulfill the purpose of increasing the external validity of our results within a limited time frame, we may choose to incorporate more researchers to cut the lead-time of studying multiple cases by undertaking them in parallel.

Although there are many benefits from a knowledge creation perspective by scaling up to multiresearcher case studies, there are two obvious drawbacks: increased cost and increased complexity of the research process. It is often up to the research sponsor to decide if the cost increase is worthwhile, while the process complexity hopefully can be tackled by an increased capability of the research methodology.

Example 7.7:   Regnell et al. (see Chapter 14) conducted a multiresearcher case study, involving 10 researchers, from two different universities, interviewing representatives from six different companies. The research questions cover the comprehensive area of Requirements Engineering and Verification and Validation alignment based on a data collection from 30 interviews with practitioners. Challenges specific to the context of multiresearcher case studies were encountered, for example, regarding alignment among researchers and the research artifacts produced.

There are several challenges from a research method perspective that arise with increased size and complexity of research artifacts, as well as from the increased complexity of the research process itself:

Alignment of research objectives. Increasing the number of researchers brings an increasing number of research interests to the project. Setting the scope in research projects is always critical, and more so as more resources are put at stake. It is a challenge to make the best use of the benefit of the plurality and width of experiences that many researchers bring, while minimizing the risks of spreading resources over unfocused research questions. Working hard on the formulation of research questions helped in the REVV study. The result of an extensive viewpoint-alignment process on establishing research questions is shown in Table 14.1 in Chapter 14.

Alignment of data collection. When distributing the data collection among several researchers or even research groups, there is a risk that unintended variability in the method of data collection arises that in turn may introduce a confounding factor to the analysis. When scaling up to multiresearcher case studies, it is important to invest effort in aligning data collection procedures and practices across researchers and research groups. In Chapter 14, we describe how explicit and elaborate coding guides (Appendix D) and case study protocols have been put in place to help overcome this challenge.

Alignment of data analysis. The analysis and its subsequent interpretation need to be synchronized across the researchers to ensure that the analysis (e.g., the coding) is performed consistently. In part, the coding can be carried out for selected pilot data sets, where the coding scheme is established in an iterative manner. This may enable a shared understanding at an early stage of how to apply the coding principles.

A great opportunity with multiresearcher case studies is the availability of many perspectives, expert areas, and experiences. This opportunity, if properly fostered, may turn the analysis and interpretation into new knowledge that would not have been possible with a more narrow set of competences.

The alignment of data analysis among researchers can be improved by using concrete examples to encourage feedback and discussions of specific data items. Discussions at the "instance level" (e.g., particular fragments of data) can be more productive compared to abstract discussion where no illustrative or particular exemplars are given. In general, we recommend to use physical meetings and face-to-face workshops at regular intervals combined with frequent video conferencing and phone calls to keep the analysis aligned for the duration of the research project. If multiple, collaborating research groups are physically distributed and frequent colocated meetings are not be feasible, then communication tools such as on-line video discussions may be acceptable alternatives.

Alignment of reporting. When many researchers are involved, it is even more important to have a publication strategy that is agreed upon within the project. A rich set of conclusions from comprehensive data analysis of large data sets may be difficult to include in the format of a single journal paper. The division of results into coherent and interesting research reports and artifacts, and the allocation of these to among the involved research groups, is vital. Also, as the number of companies providing case sites increases, there is an increasing need to plan for the process of gaining consent to publish from the stakeholders in these companies. It may be possible to agree on some strategy or policy upfront with these companies or, alternatively, agreement may need to be sorted out on a publication-by-publication basis.

7.7 CONCLUSION

In this chapter we reviewed the reasons for scaling up case study research, and considered some of the main dimensions along which scaling occurs, that is, the duration and temporal resolution of the study; the number of cases; the number of research questions, propositions, hypotheses, and concepts; and the number of researchers and research groups. Each of these dimensions increases the size and complexity of the case study, introduces additional challenges, and has implications for effort, time, and resources to undertake such studies. Increasing the number of researchers and research groups is one way of attempting to accommodate the increases in size and complexity that arise from the other dimensions. For example, with more researchers there is more opportunity to study more cases or study cases over a longer period of time. Increasing the number of researchers introduces a range of challenges around alignment of research objectives, data collection, data analysis, and reporting. Examples of large-scale case studies can be found in Part II, including a longitudinal case study in Chapter 11 and a multiresearcher, multiunit case study in Chapter 14.

CHAPTER 8

USING CASE STUDY RESEARCH

8.1 INTRODUCTION

Case studies have started to gain attraction and acceptance within software engineering. Even purely qualitative studies are accepted, and the community is learning to distinguish between "toy" cases and real-life case studies. Case studies are starting to get used for different purposes.

In this chapter, we address different areas of use for case study research and also touch upon future development of case study research. Section 8.2 addresses how to read and review case study research reports, and which quality criteria should apply for the conduct and reporting of case studies to allow their publication. In Section 8.3, the needs for, and methods for synthesizing evidence from several case studies are elaborated. The economics of case studies, that is, the return on investment in case study research, is discussed in Section 8.4. The issue of specialization of case study research for software engineering is elaborated in Section 8.5. Finally, the use of case studies as drivers in software process improvement is discussed in Section 8.6.

8.2 READING AND REVIEWING CASE STUDIES

Case study reports may be read for at least three purposes: (i) to review a manuscript and judge whether a case study report should be published or not, (ii) to learn from

Case Study Research in Software Engineering: Guidelines and Examples, First Edition.
Per Runeson, Martin Höst, Austen Rainer, and Björn Regnell.
© 2012 John Wiley & Sons, Inc. Published 2012 by John Wiley & Sons, Inc.

a published case study report for use in further research, or (iii) to learn from a case study for use in practice.

Reviewing empirical research in general must be done with certain care [202]. Reading case study reports requires judging the quality of the report, without having the power of strict criteria that govern experimental studies to a larger extent, for example, statistical confidence levels. This does however not say that any report can do as a case study report. The reader must have a decent chance of finding the information of relevance, both to judge the quality of the case study and to get the findings from the study and set them into practice or build further research on.

8.2.1 Development of Checklists

In order to guide the reading and reviewing, we developed checklists to guide the reader. These checklists were originally published in 2007 [73]. In the development of the checklists, a literature survey was first conducted. This resulted in a set of nine sources from the literature where checklists or material resembling checklists were found, as summarized in Table 8.1. This included journal articles, textbooks, and "handbooks" in different domains, such as education, social science, and software engineering.

The checklists from the identified sources were merged into one long checklist with several items overlapping. This list needed to be condensed in order to be useful. This was done by taking both the user role and the case study phase into account [73]. It resulted in 46 items grouped per case study phase, design, data collection, data analysis, and reporting.

This checklist was validated in a series of courses and workshops, including a PhD course on case study research. The validation was done by letting participants use the checklist in the review of published case study articles, and during this process reflect over the usefulness of checklist items. During the first evaluation, it was found that there was a need to define a more condensed checklist for reading case study reports, as described in Section 8.2.3.

TABLE 8.1   Sources for the Checklist Items

Author	Type	Domain
Corcoran [35]	Journal	Education
Esterhuizen [52]	Handbook	International policy
Kitchenham et al. [109]	Journal	Software engineering
Kyburz-Graber [113]	Journal	Education
Perry et al. [134]	Tutorial	Software engineering
Robson [162]	Textbook	Social science
Stake [196]	Textbook	Social science
Wohlin et al. [215]	Textbook	Software engineering
Yin [217]	Textbook	Social science

8.2.2 Checklists for Conducting Case Study Research

In Appendix A.1–A.4, the checklists for different phases of a case study are presented. These are intended to be used by researchers *conducting* case study research. After each phase, the corresponding checklist may be used to check the completeness of the conduct. Preferably, one researcher takes a quality assurance role in using the checklists to monitor the conduct of the case study.

8.2.3 Checklists for Reading and Reviewing Case Studies

The criteria and guidance for performing and reporting case studies are relevant for the reader as well. However, in our work with derivation of checklists for case study research [73], evaluation feedback found them being too extensive for practical use, and asked for a more condensed checklist for readers and reviewers, for example, when reviewing a manuscript for publication or assessing the quality of research in a systematic review.

The reader's and reviewer's checklist is presented in Appendix A.5. The numbers on the checklist items refer to the items of the checklists for each phase, if more in depth criteria are needed to in the review.

8.2.4 Development of Practice

How should the research community relate to the growing acceptance of case study research? Which quality criteria should be set up for inclusion in proceedings and journals?

A research community is always under development. New technologies and methodologies are developed, or used, both in the field of study as such, and for the conduct of research, that is, the research methodologies. The quality criteria for conferences and journals must follow this development, and sometimes this development leads to new conferences and journals.

However, this does *not* imply that the requirements on what is reported, is always growing. It is apparent from research fields where case study methodology is an accepted practice for long, that the methodological parts of their papers are quite condensed. When the joint understanding in the research community is established, and converged toward a well-defined practice, the need for detailed descriptions of each methodological step is reduced.

Important means for the methodological development are journal editors' and program chairs' work to enforce practices and guidelines. By setting up and adhering to criteria for methodological standards, in addition to writing and referencing standards, the implementation of good methodological practices may be boosted.

8.3 IDENTIFYING AND SYNTHESIZING USE CASE RESEARCH

Research implies "standing on others' shoulders," that is, starting off based on other researchers' findings. This is an established policy and practice in most fields of research. However, there exist different methods to review the state of research. With the continuous growth of available research papers and fora to publish research in, the needs are stressed for more systematic methods to ensure that all relevant literature is covered in a review.

8.3.1 Identifying Primary Studies

In order to review the current state of research, *systemic mapping studies* (SMS) and *systematic literature reviews* (SLR) are conducted. The original studies searched for are referred to as *primary studies*, while the synthesis studies as such are referred to as *secondary studies*. Mapping studies aim at providing a thorough overview of all kinds of research within a defined scope. Typical results of an SMS include a map of conducted research, characterized, for example, with respect to research type, and domain-specific classes. An example map for a mapping study on software product line testing is presented in Figure 8.1. Systematic literature reviews aim at synthesizing

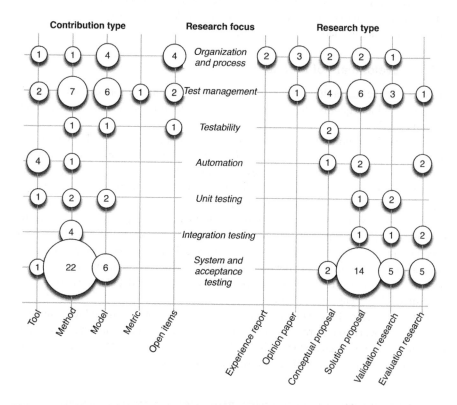

FIGURE 8.1 Example outcome from a mapping study [50]. The mapping of product line testing research is done along three dimensions: type of contribution, research focus, and research type. The size of the circles, and the numbers in the circles, represent the number of studies.

the empirical evidence related to a specific research question. Typical results of an SLR include aggregated findings from the primary studies. The main characteristics of SLRs and SMSs are summarized in Table 8.2.

Example 8.1: Runeson et al. [168] reviewed empirical studies on defect detection techniques, that is, software inspections and testing. They identified 10 experiments and 2 case studies, comparing inspection and testing. Based on a qualitative analysis of the outcomes, they conclude

- "For *requirements defects*, no empirical evidence exists at all, but the fact that costs for requirements inspections are low compared to implementing incorrect requirements indicates that reviewers should look for requirements defects through inspection.
- For *design specification defects*, the case studies and one experiment indicate that inspections are both more efficient and more effective than functional testing.
- For *code*, functional or structural testing is ranked more effective or efficient than inspection in most studies. Some studies conclude that testing and inspection find different kinds of defects, so they're complementary."

The search procedures to identify primary studies are similar for both types of reviews. Mostly, databases are searched with a defined set of search strings. Identified papers are then manually classified with respect to the actual research question, and possibly evaluated against some quality criteria. Searches may be complemented by tracing new papers via references in the studies already found, so called "snowball sampling." Since the database searches give huge share of false positives, alternative approaches are evaluated, starting with the "snowball sampling" and using the database searches for validation [50, 171] as well as identifying which fields of the database entries give best results [41].

The use of systematic reviews in the software engineering domain has been subject to a growing interest in the last years. Kitchenham et al. recently published a review of 53 systematic reviews in software engineering during 2004–2008 [110]. In 2004, Kitchenham proposed a guideline adapted to the specific characteristics of software engineering research, based on adaptations primarily from the field of medicine. This guideline has been followed and evaluated [29] and updated accordingly in 2007 [97].

8.3.2 Synthesis of Evidence from Multiple Case Studies

For systematic literature reviews, the evidence from the primary studies have to be synthesized to make the review meaningful. For studies with quantitative data, there are meta-analysis methods available that help synthesizing evidence from several studies. An example partial outcome from a systematic literature review is shown in Figure 8.2.

Meta-analytical procedures include statistical analysis applied to the original data from the primary studies (i.e., the raw data) or the original analyses (i.e., the

TABLE 8.2 Difference Between Mappings Studies and Systematic Literature Reviews, According to Kitchenham et al. [96]

SLR Elements	Systemic Mapping Study	Systematic Literature Review
Goals	Classification and thematic analysis of literature on a software engineering topic.	Identifying best practice with respect to specific procedures, technologies, methods or tools by aggregating information from comparative studies.
Research question	Generic—related to research trends. Of the form: which researchers, how much activity, what type of studies, and so on.	Specific—related to outcomes of empirical studies. Of the form: Is technology/method A better or not than B?
Search process	Defined by topic area.	Defined by research question that identifies the specific technologies being investigated.
Scope	Broad—all papers related to a topic area are included but only classification data about these are collected.	Focused—only empirical papers related to a specific research question are included and detailed information about individual research outcomes is extracted from each paper.
Search strategy requirements	Often less stringent if only research trends are of interest, for example, authors may search only a targeted set of publications, restrict themselves to journal papers, or restrict themselves to one or two digital libraries.	Extremely stringent—all relevant studies should be found. Usually SLR teams need to use techniques other than simply searching data sources, such as looking at the references in identified primary studies and/or approaching researchers in the field to find out whether they are undertaking new research in the area.
Quality evaluation	Not essential. Also complicated by the inclusive nature of the search that can include theoretical studies as well as empirical studies of all types making the quality evaluation of primary studies complicated.	Important to ensure that results are based on best quality evidence.
Results	A set of papers related to a topic area categorized in a variety of dimensions and counts of the number of papers in various categories.	The outcomes of the primary studies are aggregated to answer the specific research question(s), possibly with qualifiers (e.g., results apply to novices only).

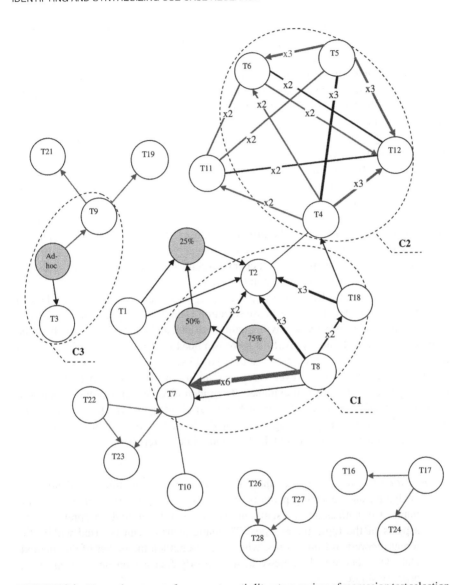

FIGURE 8.2 Example outcome from a systematic literature review of regression test selection techniques [51], showing empirical results for cost reduction variable in the study. Nodes represent different techniques, where shaded ones are reference techniques. Arcs between nodes indicate empirical comparisons. Gray arrows represent "lightweight" empirical result while black arrows indicate "medium weight" result. A line means that the studies have similar effect; an arrow points to a better technique. Thicker lines represent more studies. Dashed circles surround clusters of techniques that are compared in two or more empirical studies.

synthesized data). In the first case, data from primary studies are pooled and statistical analyses are applied to the pooled data. Different methods exist, depending on whether the effect sizes of the studies are homogeneous, that is, giving similar results, or heterogeneous, that is, giving different results due to some unknown factor [69, 127, 140]. In the second case, analyses may be applied to the effect size of the primary studies. One basic method is "vote counting," which is not recommended for use in software engineering [140].

Even though the statistical theory is well established for meta-analyses, their application to software engineering is debated, especially when it comes to similarity and differences between the primary experimental studies. Miller [127] states about reusing experimental material, "although from a simple replication point of view, this seems attractive, from a meta-analysis point of view this is undesirable, as it creates strong correlations between the two studies." Pickard et al. comments on the other hand on the outcome of the primary studies [140] "the greater the degree of similarity between the studies the more confidence you can have in the results of a meta-analysis." Hence there is a conflict or between what is desirable from a statistical point of view, and from a learning point of view.

Case studies are not driven by sampling logic, but by replication logic, as defined in Section 2.3.4, hence the issue of case selection is not bound by the sampling logic. Further, case studies mostly deal with qualitative data, and hence the issues about the statistical methods do not apply. Still there is a need to synthesize knowledge from qualitative case studies, and there exist methods to support the synthesis.

Cruzes and Dybå [36] surveyed secondary studies in software engineering, which include synthesis of empirical evidence. They identified several synthesis methods, many from medicine (see, e.g., Dixon-Woods et al. [45]) of which seven methods were used in software engineering. These methods are briefly introduced below. For more detail, consult Cruzes and Dybå [36] and related references.

Thematic analysis. Thematic analysis is a method that aims at identifying, analyzing and reporting patterns or themes in the primary studies. At minimum, it organizes and presents the data in rich detail, and interprets various aspects of the topic under study. Thematic analysis can be used within different theoretical frameworks, which can strengthen the power of the method. Outside a theoretical framework, it is mostly focused on description of the primary studies.

Narrative synthesis. Narrative synthesis adopts a narrative approach to summarizing the findings of primary studies. It tells a "story" that originates from the primary evidence. Raw evidence and interpretations are structured, using, for example, tabulation of data, groupings and clustering, or vote-counting as a descriptive tool [163]. Narrative synthesis may be applied to studies with qualitative or quantitative data, or combinations thereof.

Comparative analysis. The comparative analysis method is aimed at analyzing complex causal connections. It uses Boolean logic to explain relations between cause and effect in the primary studies. The analysis lists necessary and sufficient conditions in each of the primary studies and draws conclusions from presence/absence of independent variables in each of the studies. Causal relations are more frequently studied using experimental methods, but may also be found using qualitative data.

Case survey. The case survey method aggregates existing case study research by applying a set of structured and tightly defined questions and answers, to each primary study [123]. The survey instrument must be tailored to fit the research questions in the primary studies. The data from the surveys are quantitative, and hence the aggregation is performed using statistical methods [114]. However, since the literature is a nonrandom sample of the phenomenon under study, conclusions should be drawn with care.

Metaethnography. Metaethnography resembles the qualitative methods of the primary studies. It aims to synthesize by induction and interpretation of the primary studies, to understand and transfer ideas, concepts and metaphors across the different studies. The metaethnography translates studies into one another, and synthesize the translations into concepts that go beyond individual studies. Interpretations and explanations in the primary studies are treated as data in the metaethnography study.

Meta-analysis. Meta-analysis are, as mentioned above, based on statistical methods to integrate quantitative data from several cases. Since most case studies are based on qualitative data, meta-analyses are rarely applicable to synthesizing case study research. Even for studies with quantitative data, the lack of probabilistic sample is major threat in applying meta-analytical procedures to case studies.

Scoping. Scoping analysis aims at giving an overview of the research in a field, rather than synthesizing the findings from the research. Scoping are also referred to as mapping studies. Kitchenham et al. define the difference:

> In contrast [to systematic literature reviews], a mapping study reviews a broader software engineering topic and classifies the primary research papers in that specific domain. The research questions for such a study are quite high level and include issues such as which subtopics have been addressed, what empirical methods have been used, and what subtopics have sufficient empirical studies to support a more detailed systematic review. [96].

Hence, scoping is focused on the metalevel question of which research is conducted, rather than which synthesized evidence has come out from the research.

8.3.3 Current State of Synthesis

In their systematic review of systematic reviews in software engineering (referred to as a tertiary study, i.e., a review of secondary studies), Cruzes and Dybå [36] identified 49 secondary studies in software engineering between 2005 and middle of 2010. Two of the studies were based only on quantitative studies, while the majority

TABLE 8.3   Number of Secondary Studies in the Tertiary Study by Cruzes and Dybå [36], Using Different Synthesis Methods

Goal/Method	Scoping	Decision Support	Knowledge Support
Thematic analysis	4		4
Narrative synthesis	3	1	5
Comparative analysis		2	2
Case survey			1
Metaethnography		1	
Meta-analysis			2
Scoping	16	1	7

The secondary studies are grouped with respect to their goal.

were composed of qualitative or mixed-method studies. The synthesis methods used in the secondary studies include all the seven methods, presented above. The distribution over the methods is shown in Table 8.3, where the secondary studies also are grouped with respect to the goal of the synthesis: scoping, decision support, or knowledge support.

The large number of scoping studies can be noted, even though they were entitled systematic reviews or synthesis studies. Out of the 49 secondary studies, 23 studies have scoping as a goal, and 24 studies use scoping methods to synthesize research. The software engineering community has a lot to learn from other fields of research, such as medicine. In a similar study on qualitative research on health and healthcare, Dixon-Woods et al. conclude that 19 out of 42 papers used metaethnography to synthesize findings [45], which is a much more powerful approach than those used in software engineering. Here is hence a lot to gain in future synthesis of empirical evidence in software engineering.

8.4   THE ECONOMICS OF CASE STUDY RESEARCH

One of the opportunities for further work in software engineering research is to better understand the practical requirements and constraints on different kinds of case study design, particularly where investigators study the development of large, complex software systems over an extended period of time. This would allow researchers to make an economic argument to practitioners about when the benefits of a case study, or case studies, will outweigh the potential costs of such studies.

Although, unfortunately, the software engineering research community has not directed any sustained attention toward the economic arguments for conducting different kinds of research study, there is some relevant work that has already been published in the field. This work has focused on the costs and benefits of conducting technology evaluations using different research strategies and methods. Three sets of work are briefly considered here: Zelkowitz et al.'s [218] empirical study of evaluation techniques, the evaluation of methods within the DESMET methodology, and Wohlin et al. [213] and Herceg's [70] frameworks for organizing costs and benefits of evaluation methods.

8.4.1 Costs and Benefits of Evaluation Techniques

Zelkowitz et al. [218] report one of the few studies that has collected empirical evidence on the costs and benefits of different evaluation techniques. Using a questionnaire survey, Zelkowitz et al. asked researchers, industrialists, and students to rank over a dozen evaluation techniques on a number of criteria. A careful study of the findings of the study suggests that

- Researchers and industrialists appear to have a clearer opinion on the practicality of an evaluation technique compared to the validity of the techniques.
- Researchers and industrialists appear to have different opinions over which techniques are practical or impractical, with some agreement that replications are impractical. Interestingly, researchers and industrialists also have different opinions over the techniques that are more or less likely to produce valid results.
- There appears to be little association between the practicality of a technique and its validity. Of particular relevance to our discussions, industrialists consider case studies to be easy to conduct but are neutral on the validity of case studies (neither reporting them as more or less likely to produce valid results).

8.4.2 Evaluation of the DESMET Methodology

DESMET [104] was developed in the late 1980s through a UK government-funded collaborative project between industry and academia. It was developed in response to the recognition that software methods and tools continued to proliferate without supporting evidence on the benefits of these new methods and tools over existing approaches. The DESMET methodology aims to establish the measurable effects of using a technology; but also to establish the appropriateness of a technology, that is, how well the method or tool fits the needs and culture of a particular organization. The methodology provides guidance on nine broad research methods together with advice on the appropriateness of each method, given such factors as the evaluation goals, constraints and capabilities of the organization planning to undertake an evaluation. A full exposition of DESMET can be found in series of papers, most of which are published in the journal of the *ACM Special Interest Group on Software Engineering (ACM SIGSOFT)* [89–93, 101–103, 106–108, 173]. The project to develop the DESMET methodology also undertook evaluations of the DESMET methodology itself.

A summary of the cost, time, and risks of the various DESMET evaluation methods is summarized in Table 8.4 (restructured from the original tables in the DESMET methodology [89]).

8.4.3 Frameworks for Organizing Methods of Evaluation

Wohlin et al. [213] present a framework for organizing methods of evaluation that recognizes the escalation in costs that would be incurred by an organization when conducting different kinds of evaluation. A modified version of their framework is

TABLE 8.4   Summary of Cost, Time, and Risks of the DESMET Evaluation Methods

Method	Time	Cost	Risk
Feature analysis experiment	Short	High	Low
Feature analysis case study	Long	Medium	High
Feature analysis screening	Short	Medium	Very high
Feature analysis survey	Medium	Medium	Medium
Quantitative effects analysis	Very short	Very low	Very high
Quantitative experiment	Short	High	Very low
Quantitative case study with within-project baseline	Long	Medium	Low
Quantitative case study with organization baseline	Long	Medium	Medium
Quantitative case study with cross-project baseline	Long	Medium	High
Quantitative survey	Very short	Low	Low
Benchmarking	Short	Medium	N/A

TABLE 8.5   Comparison of Two Classification of Evaluation Methods

Evaluation Environment	Research Method	Wohlin et al. Classification Method to Evaluate Software Process	Herceg Classification Industrial Evaluation Methods	Costs and Benefits
Desktop	Survey	Literature study	Expert discussion and opinion	Low
		Basic impact analysis	Feature/vendor literature study	
		Detailed impact analysis	Academic literature study	
			Internal field study	
			External field study	
			Historical data study	
			Theoretical analysis	
Laboratory	Experiment	Limited experiment	Feasibility test	Medium
		Full experiment	Experiment with nonrandom data	
			Formal experiment	
Production project	Case study	Pilot project	Pilot project	High
		Standard project	Project case study	
			Replicated project case study	

included in Table 8.5. The table indicates that as one proceeds from literature studies through to case studies of standard projects, the costs for performing the evaluation increases, the similarity of context increases and the confidence in the evaluation increases. Given industry's focus on costs, it is reasonable to suppose that an organization would undertake some kind of formal or informal literature review as a first step in evaluating a proposed technology. Indeed, Wohlin et al. state that "...a suitable first step [to evaluate new technology] is always to study the available literature to obtain a baseline concerning the state of the art in the area and also to get some information about best practices" [213, p. 11].

Aside from the costs of conducting an evaluation, Herceg [70] recognizes the costs incurred from the adoption of an inappropriate technology. These costs include the opportunity cost of not finding critical information of interest, the already incurred and unrecoverable costs ("sunk costs") of integrating the inappropriate technology, costs arising from reversing the integration of the inappropriate technology, and finally the additional costs of finding and inserting an appropriate technology. The first of these costs can potentially be directly addressed with a careful literature review, and such a review could provide a foundation for subsequent decisions over technology evaluation and adoption. Herceg combined the methods proposed by Wohlin et al. [213] and Zelkowitz et al. [218] to develop a revised classification, also presented in Table 8.5. As with Wohlin et al., Herceg recognizes the increase in both costs and benefits as one proceeds from the desk based to production targeted evaluations. Herceg also suggested three methods of evaluation to avoid: nonexpert opinion, vendor opinion, and demonstration. Demonstrations may however be useful for contributing information to an evaluation, rather than constituting an evaluation themselves.

8.5 SPECIALIZING CASE STUDY RESEARCH FOR SOFTWARE ENGINEERING

We recognized in Section 2.5 that the case study research strategy tends to be more suited to particular kinds of research question (i.e., *how* and *why* questions) and to particular kinds of phenomena (i.e., a phenomenon that cannot be easily separated from its context). Easterbrook et al. [47] suggest that a research program (which may be an individual research project, for example by a doctoral research student, or the broader program of a research community) progresses through stages of research questions and that different research strategies may be more suitable at these different stages. For example, where there is already a well-established theoretical framework, case studies seeking theoretical replication become more feasible and also more suitable, and it follows that the *design* of the case study can be much more firmly based on, or related to, that theoretical framework.

The software engineering research community would most likely benefit from the development and application of more specialized variants of the generic case study research strategy, with each of these variants being orientated toward particular research questions or particular phenomena. For illustration, we review two examples of specialised case study research strategies: the longitudinal chronological case study (LCCS), and the controlled case study.

8.5.1   The Longitudinal Chronological Case Study Research Strategy

The longitudinal chronological case study research strategy is being developed by Rainer [147] as he reflects on his past experiences of undertaking case studies of software projects at IBM Hursley Park. The case studies are described in Chapter 11. The software projects that Rainer studied were inherently complex, occurred and changed over time, contained multiple perspectives due to the presence of many different stakeholders, had a relatively small number of data points in relation to the number of attributes of interest, and contained a large volume of fine-grained, diverse data types some of which were naturally generated or collected close to the occurrence of the events to which that data referred. These characteristics of software projects appear to present specific challenges to case study research.

Rainer [147] distinguishes between a longitudinal case study that looks at phenomena over a *period of time*, and chronological studies that investigate phenomena using a relatively fine-grained *contiguous temporal structure*. A longitudinal chronological case study therefore investigates a phenomenon over a period time, but with a fine-grained contiguous temporal perspective. A quantitative time-series could be understood as a kind of narrowly focused longitudinal, chronological study although such time-series lack the diversity of types of data anticipated in the LCCS research strategy. Rainer has complemented the LCCS research strategy with the multidimensional timeline (MDT), a technique for visualizing multiple dimensions of behavior over time, using qualitative and quantitative data [146].

The LCCS strategy is more formally defined as follows:

> The longitudinal chronological case study research strategy is an empirical investigation, at a relatively fine-grained level of granularity, of a relatively large scale, complex phenomenon that occurs over time, where
>
> - The investigation exploits large volumes of naturally occurring data that is qualitative and quantitative in nature, and that has been generated, or collected, close to the time at which the events of interest occur; however the investigation is not restricted to the exploitation of naturally occurring data but also collects new, complementary data, for example, through interviews.
> - The analysis of data intentionally retains the temporal dimension, where feasible and appropriate.
> - The reporting of the results also seeks to retain the temporal dimension, again where feasible and appropriate.

A number of challenges remain to be addressed in the development of the LCCS research strategy. For example

- Large and complex phenomena are inherently hard to study, requiring considerable time and resource.

- While a large volume and diversity of naturally generated and researcher-generated data is desirable it is also hard to organize, analyze, and report concisely and effectively.
- Where there is a lack of appropriately established theoretical frameworks, a LCCS would inevitably be exploratory that can add additional demands to the research, not least the risk that the case study design will more frequently change.
- Where there is a lack of appropriate theoretical frameworks, it is even more difficult to use analytic generalization to generalize the findings of the case study to a broader class of projects.
- The formalization of the LCCS research strategy has begun to occur after the original case studies and there is a need to further develop and evaluate the research strategy.

The LCCS research strategy's explicit focus on behavior over time, and sequences of change, allows the researcher to investigate the chain of causal relationships because temporal sequence is a necessary condition for such investigations.

McLeod et al. have recently published a paper [126] on longitudinal case study research in software engineering. The paper is based on McLeod et al.'s experiences of applying a longitudinal qualitative approach to the empirical case study of a software development project in a large multinational organization.

8.5.2 Controlled Case Studies

Salo and Abrahamsson [174] report on the development and application of the controlled case study to the investigation of an Agile software development project. The controlled case study approach combines design principles from experiments, case studies and action research. This integrated approach seeks to support investigations that take place within a close-to-industry setting and that strive for replication, in-depth data collection, and the ability to change the process being investigated. The approach accommodates both quantitative data (e.g., time, size, and defect) and qualitative data (e.g., diaries, postmortem sessions, and final interviews) together with the respective data collection and analysis techniques. The approach is organized into three main phases: design, implementation, and learning; and then within those phases, the approach is further organized into a series steps with associated outcomes. The approach has been used predominantly with student subjects, however future studies have been designed to include representatives of industry developing their own software in a specified research setting. As with all research strategies that focus intensely on a small number of cases there is the problem of generalizing the results of studies that use that research strategy.

8.6 CASE STUDIES AND SOFTWARE PROCESS IMPROVEMENT

Case study research lends itself naturally to software process improvement (SPI) because of the focus of case studies on individual sites within their natural context.

TABLE 8.6   Matrix of the Suggested Credibility of Knowledge for Software Practitioners (based on Rainer et al. [143])

Source of Knowledge	Type of Knowledge	
	Opinion	Empirical
Local	1 (most credible)	2
Remote	3	4 (least credible)

Rainer and Hall [151] reviewed 39 publications describing SPI activity for 14 organizational sites in 11 large organization, including Boeing, Hughes, Motorola, NASA, Siemens, and Telcordia. The 11 organizations include all five of the organizations that had, at the time, been awarded the *IEEE Computer Society Award for Process Achievement*. Twelve of the 14 sites have been assessed at CMM Level 3 or higher. While not all of the 39 publications were explicitly case studies, the publications did focus on SPI within specific sites in the content of specific organizations.

In related work, Rainer et al. [143] used content analysis to analyze discussions of the motivation to undertake SPI. The discussions were taken from four published papers and from qualitative data collected through a focus group as part of the *Practitioners, Processes, and Products* (PPP) project [153].

The analysis suggested that developers want evidence of the benefits of SPI and that they probably want local empirical evidence. But the analysis also suggested that practitioners seem to discount empirical evidence in favor of local opinion, and also that practitioners prefer local expertise. This presents an apparent contradiction: developers value empirical evidence, but also seem to discount empirical evidence. Rainer et al. [143] sought to resolve this contradiction through suggesting a matrix of the credibility of knowledge for the software practitioner, distinguishing between types of knowledge and sources of knowledge (Table 8.6).

In this matrix, local opinion may be the most credible type of knowledge *to practitioners* and remote empirical evidence the least credible. This ranking of knowledge, if correct, is a stark contrast to the ranking of knowledge by academics, that is, to value independent empirical knowledge over local opinion. Rainer et al. [143] suggested three reasons to explain software practitioners apparent preference for local opinion:

1. A local expert possesses application domain knowledge of the application being developed, as well as technical knowledge of the methods being used to develop that application.

2. A local expert has the opportunity to *demonstrate* his or her expertise over time in that situation to colleagues. Related to this, the time taken for a local expert to state their opinion is almost always going to take a much shorter amount of time than it would take to conduct and report an empirical investigation. Therefore an "answer" through local opinion is available much quicker than through empirical evidence.

3. A local expert may also have authority, and hence power, in the local situation by virtue of his or her expertise. That expert may therefore be able to more strongly influence decision making, in contrast to the 'passive' influence of independent empirical knowledge.

Riemenschneider et al. [160] conducted a field study of 128 developers in a large organization that implemented an adaptable lifecycle methodology that had been developed for the company under the leadership of an external consultant. Riemenschneider et al. used five established theoretical models of individual technology acceptance to seek to explain the acceptance behavior of the developers. They found that, like previous research on technology adoption, developers must regard the methodology as useful. But they also found that developers intentions to use the new methodology were driven by the presence of an organizational mandate to use the methodology; the compatibility of the methodology with how developers perform their work; and the *opinions* of developers' coworkers and supervisors toward using the methodology.

Dingsøyr and Moe [42] conducted a longitudinal case study of employee participation in the development of an electronic process guide for a medium sized company. Dingsøyr and Moe studied developer and project manager usage with respect to three factors: frequency of use, used functionality, and the reported advantages and disadvantages of the process guide. They found that employees who had participated in the workshops to develop the guide accessed the guide, on average, 65% more than the nonparticipants. Dingsøyr and Moe concluded that employee participation has a long-term positive effect on electronic process guide usage, with the implication that users of an electronic process guide should be involved in developing that guide. The implication here for the credibility of knowledge is that participation creates a situation where employees can create and share context-specific opinions and local expertise on the relevant technology.

More generally, there is a significant implication to contrast between the knowledge valued by practitioners and the knowledge valued by researchers: even if researchers could demonstrate a reliable and beneficial relationship between SPI and organizational performance, there would still be the problem of convincing practitioners that the evidence applies to their particular situation. This is where case studies can be highly valuable, particularly when the case study is conducted in the site and context to which the findings are intended to apply. For example, Pino et al. [141] report a systematic review of published case studies of SPI in small-to-medium enterprises (SMEs).

8.7 CONCLUSION

The use of case studies in software engineering research have emerged over two decades and has been gradually accepted by the research community. There are different kinds of use of case studies; for the academic search for knowledge in separate case studies and in synthesis from multiple studies; for practical use as decision support, and as means for process improvement.

We foresee further development of the case study practice in software engineering, especially when it comes to research synthesis and case studies as a driver for evidence-based practices in industry. We hope that this book will contribute to strengthening the validity of case study research, and help the research community move forward on understanding and improving software engineering practices.

PART II

EXAMPLES OF CASE STUDIES

CHAPTER 9

INTRODUCTION TO CASE STUDY EXAMPLES

9.1 INTRODUCTION

Chapters 10–14 report the experiences of the authors in the design, conduct, and reporting of a range of case studies. The experiences are presented as narratives, structured according to the main stages of a case study presented in Section 2.6, linking these experiences to the guidelines and advice reported in Part I of this book. The narratives provide detailed real examples of the design, conduct, and reporting of case studies. These examples are intended to complement the abstracted guidelines reported in previous chapters. As such these experiences represent a state-of-practice and are not intended as a benchmark for best practice.

There are mistakes and weaknesses in the design, conduct, and reporting of these case studies and the motivation for reporting these limitations is to encourage others to improve their case studies rather than to reinforce a repetition of these limitations. Also, these experiences are obviously described from a particular perspective and it is likely that other participants in the case studies, researchers or practitioners, would have alternative experiences that would complement and perhaps on occasions contradict the experiences reported here.

The case study examples are selected to illustrate some varying types of studies. The study characteristics are summarized in Table 9.1. The *Scale* characteristic is relative so that, for example, the XP and RMT cases are smaller in scale but not small in the sense of being "toy" or trivial cases.

Case Study Research in Software Engineering: Guidelines and Examples, First Edition.
Per Runeson, Martin Höst, Austen Rainer, and Björn Regnell.
© 2012 John Wiley & Sons, Inc. Published 2012 by John Wiley & Sons, Inc.

TABLE 9.1 Characteristics of the Case Study Examples of Part II

Study	Design	Data	Collection	Analysis	Scale
XP	Two cases, three units	Qualitative	Interviews	Coding and comparative	Smaller
PM	Two cases, several units	Qualitative and quantitative	Interviews, observations, and documents	Coding, and statistical and simple quantitative	Longitudinal
QA	One case, three units	Quantitative	Archival data and metrics	Statistical	Iterative
RMT	One case, several units	Qualitative and quantitative	Interviews and direct observation	Thematic and simple quantitative	Smaller
REVV	One case, six units	Qualitative	Interviews	Multilevel coding	Larger

The case example in Chapter 10 is a study aimed at investigating how agile practices, especially eXtreme Programming (XP), function in a traditional stage–gate project management context. Two researchers interviewed people at three companies, two of which were in a similar context and the third in a different context. The first two companies had launched pilot projects, using XP within their traditional stage–gate project management models, and the study aimed at capturing experience from them. Interviewees were selected to represent both management and engineering perspectives at the two companies. The interviews were recorded and transcribed. The analysis first identified codes in the data and then summarized statements in brief "slogan" format. The analysis then gathered statements grouped by categories, originating from the codes. Then, a comparative analysis was conducted across companies: managers versus engineers and agile versus non-agile teams. The limited size of the study enabled two researchers conduct both the interviews in a few days and the analysis using standard spreadsheet tools. The study was reported to different audiences, ranging from a PhD committee to the practitioners.

Chapter 11 presents two longitudinal studies, each lasting for over a year. One researcher was present full time in the company, gathering archival data and interviewing participants on project management practices (PM). The studies had a particular focus on project schedules and time to market. The analysis used a combination of qualitative and quantitative data analysis techniques. For example, qualitative data were coded and once coded could then be analyzed using simple nonparametric statistics. Visualizations were also used to communicate the complexity of behavior over time. One challenge for longitudinal studies is that because the study takes place over an extended period of time, there is an increased likelihood that the phenomenon being studied will change over time and, as a result, the case study design and conduct will need to change. This raises a significant threat to the validity of such studies and emphasizes the importance of maintaining a formal case study protocol. Unfortunately, no formal case study protocol was maintained, although electronic and hardcopy logbooks and other interim reports were maintained and many still exist for reference.

In Chapter 12, an iterative case study is presented, with focus on management of quality assurance activities (QA). The study ranged over more than a year and was conducted in seven distinct cycles, which evolved over time. The initial cycles were exploratory, while the later cycles were confirmatory and explanatory. The study has a flavor of action research, since it aims to improve the QA and its iterative nature. However, the researchers only derived data, analyzed them, and proposed solutions, while the company personnel were responsible for implementing the improvement proposals, thus giving distinct roles to researchers and practitioners. Three different projects (units of analysis) were studied within one company: one post hoc and two while the projects were running. The collected data were mainly quantitative statistics on defect reports in the company; analyses were consequently mostly done using statistical methods. The quantitative data put some constraints on the flexibility of the case study, since data have to be collected in the same way to allow comparisons; and statistical generalization is not possible as the cases are not sampled from a well-defined population.

The case study in Chapter 13 reports experiences of evaluating and selecting a requirements management tool (RMT) for a software development company. The study investigated the state-of-practice in the target organization to identify and prioritize needs, and the study identified the need to improve the management of requirements. This need motivated the subsequent work, that is, to use the DESMET methodology to identify and evaluate RMTs, to recommend a particular RMT to the company, to support the deployment of that RMT, and to evaluate the subsequent adoption of the RMT. Three particular challenges were settling on appropriate units of analyses, because the study examined a range of very different activities (e.g., selection of candidate RMTs compared to postdeployment evaluation); choosing an appropriate RMT for the company while not being able to demonstrate the cause–effect relationships of the RMT (because of the complexity of both RMT and the software development process); and generalizing the results of the evaluation to other situations (because the chosen RMT may not be appropriate to the needs of a different company). Again, no formal case study protocol was maintained, partly because the primary focus of the research was on evaluating the RMTs and so on rather than investigating the evaluation process itself.

Finally, a multiresearcher, multiunit case study on the alignment between requirements engineering and validation and verification (REVV) is presented in Chapter 14. The study is an example of a large-scale case study involving 11 researchers at 2 universities conducting 30 interviews at 6 different companies distributed over 5 sites. The planning, data collection, analysis, and interpretation of qualitative data were conducted as a multiresearcher endeavor, comprehending almost 1700 h of effort. The study rendered many lessons learned related to a large-scale case study research on issues such as the scoping of research questions, iteration in the research process, and effort trade-offs among the different tasks needed in a large-scale case study. One specific benefit of scaling up the scope of a case study to several companies is the opportunity of cross-company learning, as the involved companies can benchmark their current practices with respect to the studied phenomena. Furthermore, when enlarging the set of researchers to involve more areas of expertise, the analysis and interpretation can benefit from a multiperspective view on the collected data. In general, we believe that in order to tackle some of the greater software engineering research quests, we need to develop our capabilities in conducting a large-scale case study research in a collaborative manner reaching across our global research community.

CHAPTER 10

CASE STUDY OF EXTREME PROGRAMMING IN A STAGE–GATE CONTEXT

10.1 INTRODUCTION

This chapter reports the experience of the first author conducting a case study on the introduction of eXtreme Programming (XP) [17] practices in a context that is governed by plan-driven practices and a stage–gate approach to project management [33]. The cases in the study come from three different application domains—automation, defense, and telecom—and are denoted ABB, Ericsson, and Vodafone for the corporation names, respectively.

10.1.1 Methodological Status

At the time of the study (2003–2004), qualitative research was not fully accepted in the software engineering domain, and the overall share of empirical studies was low [61]. Seaman's seminal paper [176] inspired the use of qualitative methods, but guidelines from the social science were mostly used [162].

Case Study Research in Software Engineering: Guidelines and Examples, First Edition.
Per Runeson, Martin Höst, Austen Rainer, and Björn Regnell.
© 2012 John Wiley & Sons, Inc. Published 2012 by John Wiley & Sons, Inc.

10.2 CASE STUDY DESIGN

10.2.1 Rationale

We undertook the study in response to questions raised at an industrial seminar on eXtreme Programming [17] and Agile development methods held in 2003. The Software Engineering Research Group at Lund University sponsored the seminar, which included representatives from more than 20 different software companies. The representatives were very much interested in agile development, but they were not sure whether or how it might coexist with their existing project management models. Their interest prompted us to study the feasibility of applying agile methods in the context of large software development projects using stage–gate project management models. A stage–gate model has a waterfall [166] characteristic for the project management (Figure 10.1), but this does *not* imply the development process be waterfall. Still it was not clear how an extremely agile development process could coexist with the waterfall project management process.

10.2.2 Objectives

A PhD student (Karlström) studied the introduction of XP in a small-scale software development project [84], and wanted to expand his knowledge into the use of XP in a large-scale software development. Through the research group's contact network, we identified two teams at two different companies—branches of ABB and Ericsson—that were piloting XP practices in a stage–gate project management models. Later, we added a third company to the study—a branch of Vodafone—that was interested in launching agile practices. The first two companies were operating in domains that require quite high degree of formalism and documentation in the development process, namely, automation and defense. The third company was acting in the telecom

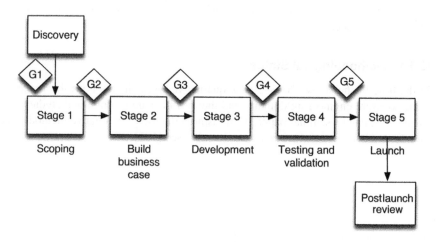

FIGURE 10.1 Stage–Gate™ model from Cooper [33].

services domain, which is less formal, although still quite plan driven. The first two cases focused on the practitioner and lower level management, while the third case studied mid- and top-level management only.

To narrow the scope of the investigation, we decided to focus on the decision point gate 3 (or G3 as shown in Figure 10.1), that is, deciding on whether to start full-scale development, as this is considered a crucial point in projects. At this point, it is decided whether the project should proceed into full-scale development and a large increase in resources is to be allocated. The subprojects that were investigated, however, were far beyond G3 and as such could only describe what happened at G3 in retrospect as the participants remember it. Hence, we had to focus on the projects as a whole instead.

10.2.3 Cases and Units of Analysis

When the case studies started, ABB and Ericsson companies had applied the XP practices for about a year in two subprojects. The intention was to interview project members about their experience of using XP in the stage–gate context. The Vodafone case was added afterward, and was more in the transition toward using agile practices. The ABB and Ericsson cases are considered two units of analysis in a general context, with similar characteristics, while the Vodafone case is considered a separate, holistic case study, as depicted in Figure 10.2. ABB and Ericsson, however, also have different characteristics. In the ABB case, products are developed for a general market; while in the Ericsson case, the product was developed for a specific customer, with the intention to go to a broader market at a later stage. This difference was not considered a hinder to treat the two companies as different units of analysis in the same context since the customer interface in the Ericsson case was organizationally distant from the project; they had no direct interaction with the customer.

At the time of the investigation, the Ericsson team had completed their implementation, had subsequently been split up, and had its members reassigned to various assignments. The ABB team was late in the implementation stage of the product. Furthermore, specific focus was set in the study on the interfacing between the XP team and the surrounding environment as this is where contrasts between the two

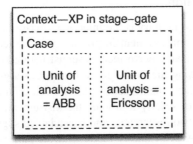
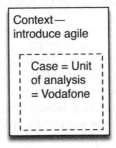

FIGURE 10.2 Overview of the contexts, cases, and units of analysis.

were thought to appear most clearly; hence, we decided the units of analysis be the XP projects, with a specific focus on their interaction with the environment. This implied that the focus moved away from the original G3 decision toward the interface between the project management process and the agile projects in general.

10.2.4 Theoretical Frame of Reference

The theoretical framework for the study was constituted by quite a large amount of experience reports on the use of XP. Reviewing the literature, we found that there was a mismatch between the information available and the interests of the companies. The companies work with stage–gate models [33] to produce their products, which are aimed at a broad market rather than at a specific customer. First, much of the agile literature focuses on a contract situation, developing bespoke products or components for specific customers, rather than a market situation, developing products or components for a general market. Second, there was at the time almost no research on integrating agile into stage–gate models, except for preliminary research performed by Wallin et al. [211] and a study by Lindvall et al. [121].

10.2.5 Research Questions

The intentions of the research were not phrased in terms of research question, but as an aim: "The study aims to investigate the effects of introducing an agile software development process within a traditional stage gate model style project management system. The study specifically aims to identify the main problems with this combined approach as well as key success factors" [86].

For the Vodafone case, attitudes toward future introduction and agile practices were studied, rather than experience from already introduced practices [83, Chapter 7]. Hence, we consider the Vodafone case being a separate context.

10.3 PLANNING

10.3.1 Methods of Data Collection

The main source of information in this enquiry is the interviews performed with the development team members and the management in proximity to the teams in the studied organizations. The interviews were performed as semistructured interviews, more in the form of a discussion, using the interview instrument as a guide of areas available to discuss. Interesting facts mentioned were followed up immediately with each interview subject instead of strictly following the instrument. The interview instrument was constructed by two researchers and was adapted slightly as the interviews progressed. Adaptations were primarily made with the purpose of gaining further information about statements made by previous subjects. The interview instrument is presented in Appendix B.

10.3.2 Selection of Data

Multiplicity was achieved mainly through the selection of interviewees in different roles in each company. In the ABB case, one department manager, one subproject manager, and three developers were interviewed. In addition, quantitative data were collected on defect reports in the ABB case. In the Ericsson case, one department manager and three developers were interviewed. In the Vodafone case, 11 interviews were conducted, but they had a slightly different focus, since there was no distinct project applying XP practices, rather some agile principles were applied to the company as a whole, as defined by the different contexts in Figure 10.2.

10.3.3 Case Selection Strategy

The companies were selected from the contact network of the researchers, and at the same time attempts were made to achieve as large variation as possible among the cases. The cases are characterized in Table 10.1. At the time of the study, an industrial PhD student from the defense branch of Ericsson belonged to the research group who paved the way to the XP team at Ericsson Microwave.[1] The branch of automation within ABB has a long tradition of cooperation with the research group and, in addition, the PhD student did a summer internship at the company some years ago. The Vodafone case was selected based on personal contacts by the PhD student.

10.3.4 Case Study Protocol

No formal case study protocol was developed for the case studies. However, since the duration of the study was so short—9 interviews in 3 days with 2 researchers for the first case and 11 interviews for the second case over a short time frame— the consequences were not so serious. For case studies with longer duration of the data collection period, the protocol becomes more critical to maintain consistent study procedures, although it is important for any case study as a record of the research project. Furthermore, to enable replications of the study, the protocol is a critical resource.

10.3.5 Ethical considerations

The interviews at Ericsson and ABB were protected by an already existing nondisclosure agreement between the companies and Lund University. For the Vodafone case, a new agreement was signed. One complication related to Swedish law is that the individual researcher and student owns the intellectual property rights and, second, that nondisclosure aspects are regulated by law for university–company collaborations. Hence, the University cannot sign a contract on behalf of the researcher, and any nondisclosure agreement is meaningless, since it is superseded by the law. Corporate

---

[1] Ericsson Microwave is now a part of the SAAB Group.

TABLE 10.1 Overview of Cases in the XP Study

Company	Product Type	Customer Type	Business Model	SE Methodology	Management Model	Goal
ABB	Real-time industrial control and automation system	Industrial customers	Market	Normally traditional, pilot team using XP	Stage–gate	Agile SW team integration into gate model
Ericsson	Embedded radar control and target tracking	Military	Product line with contracts	Normally traditional with some iteration, pilot team using XP	Stage–gate, iterative	Agile SW team integration into gate model
Vodafone	Complex HW/SW system of systems	Consumer mass market	Market	Traditional	Stage–gate	Agile influences in gate model

lawyers, however, have several examples of lawyers not familiar of this part of the law and insist on signing nondisclosure agreements with the researchers.

10.4 DATA COLLECTION

The main method for data collection was semistructured interviews, which were considered feasible for this descriptive and explanatory type of study. The interview sessions followed a "timeglass" structure (see Section 4.3) with an open introduction, more specific questions in the middle, and ending with very open questions. The interview instrument consisted of the following main sections (see Appendix B for more details):

- Introduction.
- Personal, group, and company background.
- General experiences of introducing XP.
- Experiences of combining XP and gate models.
- Ending.

The interviews were approximately 1 h in length with two researchers interviewing one subject. Some notes were taken during the interview, but the main form of documentation was the sound recording intended for transcription as a part of the analysis. In the first interview, technical problems arose with the recording equipment, due to the duration of the interview. After some time it stopped recording. The equipment was tested for shorter periods of time, but not for the full-time period of the interview. This indicates that the technical equipment to be used for data collection must be tested thoroughly.

10.5 DATA ANALYSIS

The interviews were transcribed, almost literally, although pauses, sighs, and passages that were obviously out of scope of the interview were not transcribed. The PhD student transcribed most of the interviews, but for some of the Vodafone interviews, other students were hired for transcription. The expansion rate was in the magnitude of 1:8, that is, 1 h of interview took 8 h to transcribe.

During the course of the analysis, information takes on several forms at different levels of abstraction. The subjects act in and observe the reality within their organization. Their reflections and observations on the area of research are discussed in the semistructured interviews and recorded as an audio file. These recordings are then fully transcribed and interesting quotes are identified. Next, quotes are coded and grouped to support each other and finally individual results are identified from these groups. The grouping was conducted using plain tables in a word processing program.

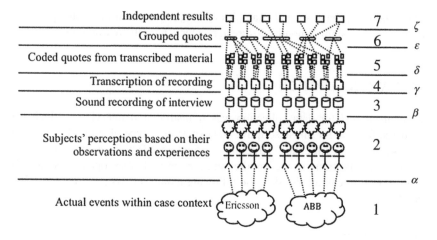

FIGURE 10.3 Overview of information and transformation in the analysis process [86].

The grouping was conducted individually by both researchers, and then discussed to find a common view.

The different forms that the information takes in this enquiry are numbered 1–7 in Figure 10.3. The first form is the actual event in the study context. The second form is the subject's perception of the event, and so on, as labeled in Figure 10.3. Each change in form is due to some kind of treatment, and we refer to this change in form as a transition. The transitions are denoted α through ζ in Figure 10.3 and later analyzed from a threat to validity perspective.

The main categories of analysis identified in the study were as follows:

- Communication—horizontal, vertical, and internal.
- Planning and estimating within the project.
- Continuous feedback.
- Quality aspects.
- Technical aspects.
- Attitudes.
- Gate model and its adaptations.

The coded data were stored in tables together with references to the individual interview statement that the data were based on in order to ensure full traceability. These tables were then used to identify results across interview subjects and companies and to draw the final conclusions. The analysis was possible to handle for two researchers, analyzing nine interviews, without any specialized tools. The excerpts from the transcripts were possible to print on a big sheet of paper, which helped giving an overview.

TABLE 10.2 Example Table part, Corresponding to One Interview with an Engineer

Category	Summary of Interview Statements
Communication (V: vertical, H: horisontal, I: internal)	V: Reporting path (106, 258); no insight into work (120–121); no good customer role (134); CRC cards (141) I: Competence spreading on pair programming (168–176); H,V: own terminology hinder (226, 278–282) H: Problem in technical interfaces (237–242); communication problems not only related to XP (265); combination of different methods (337–338) I: Awareness about progress (383).
Planning	Two week iterations (136); good time estimates in second project (298–299); priorities on requirements changes (342); good sense for time consumption [378, 390–391].
Follow-up	Reporting of time and resources (274); ideal time hard to communicate (278–282); product versus paper as status reports (349–352); follow-up meeting biweekly (195–196, 379); under control (198).
Quality	Better quality (174, 460); no big bang (177); ensured by unit tests (207–209).
Technical issues	Planning game (132, 278–282); small releases (136, 189–191); metaphor; simple design; testing (136, 158, 161, 421); refactoring (162); pair programming (136, 168); collective ownership (166–168); continuous integration (370); 40 h week; on-site customer (134); coding standard; test first has spread (425).
Attitudes	Bad support from the process (115); started study circle (117); the team very much satisfied with XP (223, 477); resistance from management (229–231, 245, 478); continued working the same way despite directives (253); requirements engineers positive (341); halfway product versus predictability (392–395).
Tollgates	No gate decisions (78); bad support from the process (115); independent of the technical process (416); and business process (96); documents must be prepared, cannot be skipped (319, 323–329).

Numbers in parentheses refer to lines in the transcribed interviews.

The results of the case study comprised one descriptive part, primarily related to the main categories, and one cross-case analysis, comparing three contrasting perspectives on the observations: agile versus nonagile teams, management versus engineers, and Ericsson versus ABB. These results are derived from summaries of interviews that were documented in one Excel sheet: one row for each interviewee, one column for each category. An example from the sheet is shown in Table 10.2, which corresponds to an interview with an engineer (although transposed for readability reasons).

The contrasting perspectives are also derived using the summaries data table. For the contrasting views, columns are sorted so that the interviewees representing each perspective are seen together (Figure 10.4). When analyzing one category, the category column is studied across interviews. For contrasting analyses, interview rows are

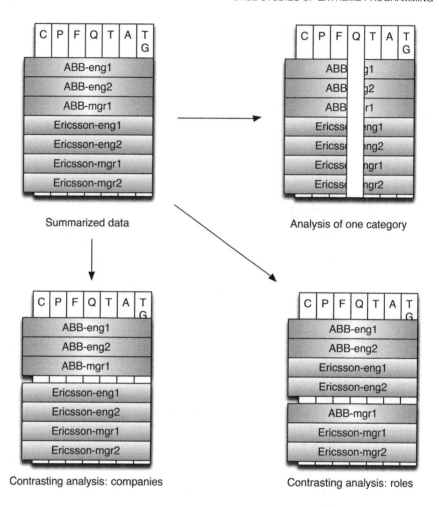

FIGURE 10.4 Examples of sorting the summarized data for analysis.

grouped by companies or roles, and compared across groups. The outcome of one of the contrasting views is presented in Table 10.3. During the in-depth analysis, the underlying interview transcripts are consulted in order to utilize the richness of the interview data.

As an example of the analysis procedure, the observation that "Engineers find agile project work 'under control?,' while managers feel they are loosing control" in Table 10.3 can be traced to "Under control" in the Follow Up category of Table 10.2, referring to a statement at line 198 of the interview transcript:

> One of the major advantages were our biweekly meetings with the whole group. We could then study our progress, see what we had missed and where we were beyond target. I felt that it gave us control over how far we have come, and how much time was left.

TABLE 10.3 Summary of Observations on the Contrasts Between Management and Engineers [86]

Finding	Management versus Engineers
Level of abstraction	Management dislike handling the detailed level issues.
Iteration frequency	Engineers adjusted better to the higher frequency than the management.
Good microplanning	Management find sometimes, paradoxically, good microplanning as a problem, since they are concerned with macroplanning.
"Under control"	Engineers find agile project work "under control," while managers feel they are loosing control.
Attitude	Engineers are positive toward agile methods, while managers are skeptical.

Similar statement exist in interviews with four other engineers. Here is one quote from the other company:

> Researcher: Can you give an example of something specific which you think works very well? Interviewee: Yes, specifically that you have everybody's work under control. We have so short cycles. The short cycle time is the biggest advantage and that we always – and now I exaggerate slightly – but we have always something executable.

The management skepticism is reflected in the following quote:

> They worked in a manner that was not described in any process description. This implied that our line managers, SQA and others had no reference to measure the against, and ask "have you done this and that?"

In the journal publication [86], the conclusion on these issues were reported as follows:

> 6.5.2. Under Control
> All people involved in the projects have a strong feeling of being in control, with the exception of management, which of course is a major threat to success. This is in contrast to the feeling of uncertainty that both teams experienced, hampering progress in previous projects...

In the practitioner-oriented publication [85], it was briefly summarized as follows:

> Teams experienced less confusion and expressed a sense of having their work "under control."

This case study, which actually appeared to be two different studies, comprising three study objects in total, is quite small in terms of data collection. Nine interviews are conducted for the Ericsson and ABB part (and 11 for the Vodafone part). Still, thanks to the two cases across which we were able to do cross-case analysis, quite some conclusions could be drawn about the studied issue. The access to company cases through our existing network was critical for the success, which probably also implied mutual trust in the relationships.

10.5.1 Threats to Validity

Each transition in Figure 10.3 introduces additional validity threats to the results, depending on the treatment performed in the transition. Treatments, the validity threats introduced, and countermeasures taken are summarized in Table 10.4. These countermeasures can also be seen in part throughout the study design, as one of the goals of a good study design is to minimize the effects of threats. Some of the transitions in the analysis were performed redundantly by two researchers independent of each other. The results of the individual analyses in these transitions were compared with and aggregated into a common analysis result.

The analysis performed in the study is of the inductive type, implying that patterns, themes, and categories of analysis come from the data itself in contrast to being imposed prior to the data collection, as is the case in deductive analysis.

10.6 REPORTING

The case studies were reported in several different ways to different audiences. Examples of case study reports are shown in Figure 10.5.

10.6.1 Academics

Being a part of a PhD project, the PhD thesis was one way of reporting the case. However, since the thesis was conducted in a tradition where theses may be compiled from several papers, the case study reports constitute two chapters in the thesis [83]— one of those is an earlier version of a paper in Empirical Software Engineering [86]. This paper follows the traditional linear analytic report structure.

10.6.2 Practitioners

The three cases together are reported in a practitioner-oriented publication in IEEE Software [85]. Here, the methodological parts of the study are played down, and a more practitioner-oriented style is used. The introduction of the paper is written as a fictitious dialogue between a project manager and a developer about agile planning, which captures some of the findings from the study. Short sections on theory and research methodology are presented in sidebars.

In addition, the case study results were reported orally at industry seminars, and in a poster format at industry seminars.

TABLE 10.4 Overview of Threats and Countermeasures Taken in the XP study

Transition	Treatment Description	Threats	Countermeasures
α	Original observations	Misconceptions, misunderstanding, lack of objectivity.	Use several sources with similar perspectives; identify inconsistencies between interviews.
β	Interview	Misunderstandings, omissions.	Feedback to subjects before final results; multiple researchers during interview.
γ	Transcription	Audibility of source.	Use high-quality microphone and recording equipment.
δ	Identifying quotes and coding	Misunderstanding, misinterpretation of intent.	Feedback to subjects before final results; multiple researchers in quoting and coding.
ϵ	Grouping	Incorrect grouping due to effects of previous threats.	Previous countermeasures; multiple researchers in grouping.
ζ	Identifying specific results	Incorrect results due to effects of previous threats.	Previous countermeasures; multiple researchers in grouping.

Letters refer to transformation steps in Figure 10.3.

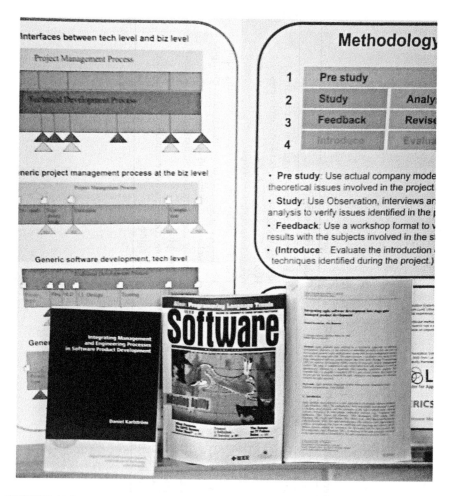

FIGURE 10.5   Different reporting formats for the case study: poster (behind), PhD thesis (left), practitioner article (middle), and academic article (right).

10.7 LESSONS LEARNED

During the case study, we learned several lessons:

Method selection. The type of research question for this research fits nicely to the case study methodology. The focus was a contemporary phenomenon, where the borderlines between the studied phenomenon and its context are not clear. The flexible research type was also feasible since our original aim was to study a specific event, and when this was not possible to study in the cases, the flexibility allowed a shift of focus in the study.

Case selection. The cases were selected based on the researcher's existing contact network. Due to the timing of the research, we could only study pioneers, adopting agile practices. This is a common situation for studies on new phenomena, and is not possible to avoid. If you want to study a new phenomenon, early adopters are the only ones to study. However, it is important to follow up early adopter studies with studies of cases with slower adopters of technology or methodology.

Case study protocol. Being conducted by only two researchers, the communication and decisions within the research project were kept informal. The study would have gained from a more formal case study protocol, not the least for archival reasons. The material is still available in electronic and physical archives, but a case study protocol would help providing a summary of events and decisions, which must be derived from raw data in the absence of protocol.

Equipment and tools. The technical sound recording equipment failed at the first interview session. Lessons learnt are that the equipment used for data collection should be robust and well tested. Regarding the analysis, standard word processing tools were considered sufficient to handle the data in the study. More critical was the ability to get overview of the data in sheets and graphs. Such features are improved in analysis tools of today, and might have helped in this study as well.

Transcripts. Transcriptions take time and some of them were done by others. This is always a trade-off. If the number of interviews is large, some transcriptions may be done by others, but at least some should be done by the researchers. Nuances and context factors are easily lost in the transcription process, and the fact that the transcription forces the researchers to spend much time with the material is a benefit in itself for the analysis.

Reporting. The attempts to publish a case study with qualitative data in recognized software engineering journals were not met with enthusiasm. An editor of *IEEE Transactions of Software Engineering* rejected the manuscript with the following motivation:

> The paper is based mostly on interviews with little quantitative project data
> to back any observation or conclusion. Such papers are not suitable for a
> journal like TSE.

Luckily, other journals were more open to qualitative studies, resulting in publications both in *Springer's Empirical Software Engineering* journal [86] and *IEEE Software* [85]. Review comments then summarized:

> The study was very well designed. The design approach is backed up by
> literature and a description of subjects, research strategy, research methods,
> how the analysis was done, the threats to validity and how they were
> addressed are all presented.

CHAPTER 11

TWO LONGITUDINAL CASE STUDIES OF SOFTWARE PROJECT MANAGEMENT

11.1 INTRODUCTION

This chapter reports the experiences of the third author as he undertook two longitudinal case studies of software projects at IBM Hursley Park, as part of his PhD research. The two projects are referred to respectively as Project B and Project C to retain consistent identifiers with previous publications [144–147, 152, 154, 155] on these case studies.

11.2 BACKGROUND TO THE RESEARCH PROJECT

In the mid-1990s, IBM Hursley Park and Bournemouth University, both in the United Kingdom, had already agreed to undertake a research project. A PhD student would be the primary researcher for the project. The aim of the research project was very broadly defined: essentially the PhD student would identify one or more problematic situations at the company and would work toward understanding these situations and seeking solutions or resolutions to these situations. The project was initiated prior to the recruitment and selection of the student. Also, the objectives imply an opportunity for action research.

Case Study Research in Software Engineering: Guidelines and Examples, First Edition.
Per Runeson, Martin Höst, Austen Rainer, and Björn Regnell.
© 2012 John Wiley & Sons, Inc. Published 2012 by John Wiley & Sons, Inc.

IBM Hursley Park and the University advertised the student post and jointly participated in the selection and recruitment process. It had been agreed that the student would relocate close to the company and would, at least for the first few months, work full time at the company, traveling to the University when it was appropriate to do so. This arrangement would ensure that the researcher had direct and immediate access to the personnel working on projects. The researcher shared an office with a long-serving employee of the company, who was one of the people responsible for process improvement. This person took on a formal role of company mentor, distinct from the formal line manager (who was also the sponsor of the research project). Formally, the student was a nonsalaried contractor and also a Research Assistant at the University. There were professional, legal, and ethical responsibilities that came with holding both of these posts. The student worked onsite full time at the company for about 9 months and then relocated to the University, subsequently traveling regularly back to the company, initially twice a week and then less frequently. The student commenced the project in June 1995.

11.3 CASE STUDY DESIGN AND PLANNING

At the time of the study, there were few formal guidelines and checklists available specific to software engineering research on case studies, so advice was sought from other disciplines, such as management science, information systems research, organizational science, social science, and psychology. Yin's textbook [217] and Benbasat et al.'s article [19] were two reference texts for the design and conduct of the case studies.

11.3.1 Rationale

Once the researcher was in-post, the initial objective was to conduct a series of interviews with stakeholders about the problems and challenges confronted during software development and software project management, and whether these problems and challenges should be the focus of the research. Advice was also sought from the company mentor. At the same time, work commenced on a review of the research literature.

11.3.2 Objective

A high-level objective to focus on project schedules and time-to-market was developed over an extended period of time (from June 1995–December 1995). In January 1996, a major decision on the plan, to focus on project schedules and time-to-market, was taken by the company line manager, the principal PhD supervisor for the project, and the student. The plan would evolve considerably over the course of the case study.

11.3.3 Definition of the Case

The case was defined as a software project that has successfully completed its plan phase and had been planned to complete in approximately 12 months. This was considered a suitable timescale for a student, for example, to allow some time for schedule slippage in the software projects to be studied, as well as to provide sufficient time for analysis and reporting (e.g., the doctoral thesis and defence).

11.3.4 Units of Analyses

Units of analyses emerged during and after the data collection and during the analysis. Initially, the unit of analysis was the same as the case, but over time a number of units of analysis emerged: behaviors that the project participants or the researcher conjectured related to software project schedules; reports of waiting in the software project; reports of progress (e.g., no progress, poor progress, and good progress) on the project; reports of overdue work on the project; and sociotechnical characteristics of the project. Other units of analysis were considered but not pursued. For example, within a project there are features being developed and each of these features had its own development plan. Therefore, one could define a feature development plan as a unit of analysis embedded within the project plan units of analysis that was, in turn, within the case being studied. Overall, a multiple, embedded case study design was adopted.

11.3.5 Theoretical Frame of Reference and Research Questions

There was an ongoing tension between a desire to take a grounded theory-like approach to the study, in which a theoretical framework emerged from the phenomenon, advice in the empirical software engineering research community at the time to commit upfront to a set of theoretical propositions, and a desire from IBM that the study should produce practical results. A further complication was the limited empirical work and related theoretical frameworks published in the field at the time on these topics, for example, there was little empirical work on the study of software project behaviour over time, with research tending to focus on individual activities or team activities. Given these tensions, two contrasting research questions emerged. These questions persisted for the duration of the research (and have continued since the research). The two questions are as follows: *What happens on software projects? How does one reduce time-to-market?*

11.3.6 Case Selection

Given the nature of the research questions and the decision to undertake case studies, all projects being undertaken at the time at the company were potential candidates for case study. Criteria for short-listing projects and then selecting projects were therefore based more on pragmatic criteria. The company mentor and the student identified a candidate list of 18 projects that were due to commence shortly and would finish in about 12 months. The student interviewed managers of many of these projects. Most projects were retained as candidates, with a small number of projects being eliminated, for example, because the project manager was not comfortable with the proposed research. Initially five case studies were selected for longitudinal case study, however, as the research progressed, it became clear that it was not practical for one researcher to collect and analyze data for five projects and the number of active case studies was reduced to two. Data have been collected, however, for other projects.

Cases were short-listed and selected on the basis of availability (e.g., that the projects were occurring at the time and within the required time period) and accessibility (e.g., the degree to which the student and the company mentor considered the project participants would be more willing to participate and cooperate in the research).

Overall,

- Two case studies were completed (cases B and C).
- Two further cases were started, but not completed (cases A and G) due to practical constraints.
- Three cases had some data collected (cases H, K, and M), but these data have not been analyzed.
- Four cases had no data collected, but data were available (cases I, L, and N1 and N2).
- Four cases were deferred (cases D, E, F, and J).
- One case did not respond to the approach from the investigator (case O).
- Two cases were considered, but were not approached (cases P and Q) as there were already a sufficient number of cases.

11.3.7 Replication Strategy

With five cases initially, the intention was to seek theoretical replication between the cases on the basis of a theoretical framework that would be developed as part of the research. Some consistent theoretical propositions were developed and subsequently tested statistically. Without an *a priori* theoretical framework, it is difficult to select cases on the basis of literal replication, particularly as each project is expected to be unique in some ways.

11.3.8 Case Study Protocol

No formal case study protocol was developed for the case studies. A monthly log book/journal was maintained for the entire duration and numerous other documents were also generated, for example, interim analyses.

11.3.9 Quality Assurance, Validity, and Reliability

Because the documentation was generated for the purpose of the project and not for the purpose of the case study, there are threats to the validity and completeness of the documentation. For example, issues may not be discussed at meetings and even if they are discussed they may not be documented in the meeting minutes. Information can be accidentally missed of the minutes, and other information (e.g., acronyms, colloquialisms) may not be clearly defined in the documents because such information is standard terminology in the organization. Also, the researcher may not have identified relevant information in the documentation or may have misinterpreted that information. Two feedback workshops, one for each project, were organized to provide the opportunity for the project's manager and assistant to comment on the interim and draft final results. In addition, the company mentor was actively involved in the design, conduct, analysis, and reporting of the case studies. Together, the feedback workshops and the mentor provided two mechanisms for ensuring the quality of the case studies.

11.3.10 Legal, Ethical, and Professional Considerations

An appropriate nondisclosure agreement was signed with the company to ensure that confidential information was not disseminated outside the company. This agreement was binding beyond the duration of the research. Explicit ethical policy in software engineering research has advanced considerably since the conduct of the research project. In research publications relating to the IBM case studies that have been prepared since the completion of the project, the rule-of-thumb used by the student is not to publish any evidence beyond that explicitly reported in the doctoral thesis.

In addition to ethical responsibilities to the company, there were also ethical issues relating to individuals and to projects. With regards to projects, project managers may not want information on their respective projects divulged to other project managers, to project participants or other employees, or to senior managers. Also, individuals may not want remarks attributed to them. One project was not selected as a case due to the confidentiality concerns of the project manager. There were other instances where tape recorders were switched off or where interviewees waited until the tape recorder was switched off before the interviewee initiated conversation on a topic. In some of these situations, the interviewees did not explicitly state their concerns, and the student needed to be sensitive to what was implied by the interviewee's comments.

Besides the ethical responsibility to not divulge information, there can be the converse responsibility to divulge information. For example, the decision to disseminate the results of the research to the wider company was the responsibility of the line manager and not the student. Ethically, academics may have a responsibility to society to report the truth. In practice, the company mentor became a central source of advice for resolving confidentiality issues.

There was no known appropriate ethics board at the time at the respective University for ethics approval. Approval was sought from the academic supervisor, the company supervisor, and the company mentor, and of course there was informed consent for each participant interviewed. The collaboration between IBM and University had been explicitly set up for this research, so there was formal consent from the corporation.

The motivation for the senior line manager at the company to be involved in the research (e.g., he had the authority to initiate and resource the research project) was different from that of the mentor (e.g., the mentor has been assigned to the role) and different again for each project manager, and for the other project participants. It was for the project manager of each candidate case to decide whether his or her project was involved in the study, and then for participants in the projects to decide whether to be involved in interviews. The project manager also decided on whether to release project documentation to the researcher.

11.4 DATA COLLECTION

The majority of the data collection for the two case studies commenced in December 1995 and concluded by December 1996. Further case study activities (e.g., analysis and feedback workshops) continued well into 1997.

11.4.1 Sources of Data

Data were collected through a variety of sources, as summarized in Table 11.1.

The primary source of data used in the two case studies was the minutes of project status meetings. The status meetings were the highest-level meetings within the respective projects, occurred weekly or fortnightly, were typically attended by project stakeholders from across the respective projects, and were a naturally occurring phenomenon so that the researcher was not intruding on the projects. Overall, the status minutes provided a broad view of the project over the duration of the project. Naturally, minutes did not record all that was discussed at a meeting, or even necessarily the most important issues, and such meetings were unlikely to have discussed *all* the issues occurring within the respective project at the time of the meeting. Consequently,

TABLE 11.1 Sources of Data Used in the Two Case Studies at IBM Hursley Park

Source of Data	Project B	Project C
Interviews	8	9
Meeting minutes	51	76
Project status meetings	49	N/A
Design/Code/Test status meetings	0	37
Feature commit and approval meetings	N/A	34
Senior management meetings	1	5
Project review/postmortem	1	N/A
Researchers records of status meetings	2	N/A
Project schedules	1	2
Projector overheads (from presentations)	1	2
Project documents	6	7
Plans	3	1
Other documents	3	0
Risk assessments	2	2
Project "contract"	1	1
(including amendments for Project C)		
Feedback workshop questionnaires	1	2
Total number of "documents"	73	101

there are at least two levels of simplification with meeting minutes. First, in reporting the progress of a functional area within the project, the representative of that area will have likely simplified the progress of that area. Second, the minutes simplified the discussions that occurred at the meeting. Despite these simplifications, the minutes provided a large volume of "rich" information about the project over the duration of the project, and these data were rich enough to provide a substantive, longitudinal view of the software development process. Furthermore, the minutes provided a breadth of information and often contained a mixture of qualitative and quantitative data, and structured and unstructured data.

The meeting minutes were complemented by the other sources of data, principally interviews with project participants. Different roles were interviewed on the project, but these roles tended to relate to project management activities rather than software development and testing activities. This is a potential weakness of the case studies because it limits the evidence collected on different perspectives of the project. With over 50 participants in Project B and 19 participants in Project C, it would not have been feasible to interview all of them, even if each was only interviewed once.

The design of interviews varied. The intention was to prepare an interview schedule before each interview and those plans that were prepared comprised open and closed questions and were semistructured. But sometimes, for example, with an ad hoc meeting, an interview schedule was not possible. At other times, the interview presented an opportunity to explore current issues emerging on the project. An interview schedule, therefore, could not always be prepared. A standard template for interviews may be more feasible when the theoretical framework, research questions, and other technical aspects of the study have fully stabilized. For example, sometimes the interview was planned on the basis of the latest literature that was read, so the interviews were not necessarily consistent across subjects and projects.

Some interviews were recorded. Other interviews were not recorded for a number of reasons: the interview was unexpected (e.g., the researcher met the participant in the corridor or at coffee), there were technical issues with the recorder, or the interviewee did not want to be recorded. A final reason was that it became clear that there would not be the time and resources on the project to undertake a transcription of every interview recording, so the researcher relied on notes taken at the interview or written up soon after the meeting. Note taking is of course incomplete. For confidential reasons, all recordings have been destroyed since completion of the project.

For those interviews that were recorded, the recordings were not transcribed but were sometimes listened to again to clarify issues. With one project at the company (not Project B or C), an attempt was made to organize interviews with the project manager in pairs close to each other, for example, interview with subject A followed within a week by another interview with subject A. This arrangement initially occurred opportunistically, but later the project manager and the researcher recognized the value of such an arrangement because it provides an opportunity for both parties to reflect on what had been said recently.

Figure 11.1 indicates when data were collected over time for Project B. Figure 11.2 summarizes when research activity occurred across *all* the cases considered in the research project.

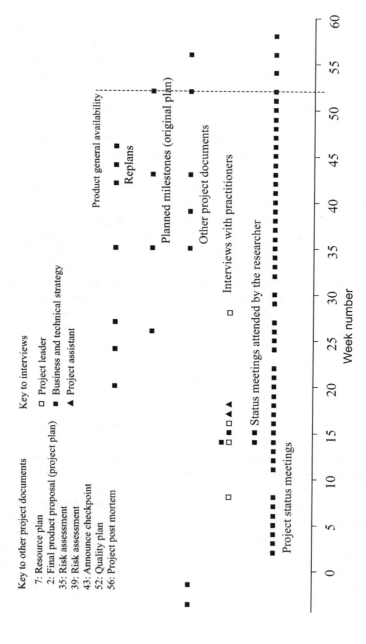

FIGURE 11.1 Plot of evidence collected and generated for Project B.

Case	Activity	Nov-96	Dec-96	Jan-97	Feb-97	Mar-97	Apr-97	May-97	Jun-97	Jul-97	Aug-97	Sep-97	Oct-97	Nov-97	Dec-97	Jan-99
A	Interview	1		3	3				1	1						
	Meeting			1												
	Minutes															
	Other															
B	Interview		1	2	4				1							
	Meeting			1	1											
	Minutes															
	Feedback															1
	Other															
								General availability (GA) of product to customers: Oct 97								
C	Interview		2	3	1		1		1	1						
	Meeting															
	Minutes															
	Feedback															1
	Other															
													GA: 14 Oct 97			
G	Interview			2	1	1		3								
	Meeting							2								
	Minutes															
	Other															
D,E,F	Interview			3												
H,I	Interview									2						
K,L,M	Interview										3					
Z			1													

FIGURE 11.2 Interviews conducted for all cases.

11.5 DATA ANALYSIS

The volume and variety of types of data collected during the case studies meant that several approaches were used to organize the data and to then analyze it. A number of concurrent activities of analysis emerged and, over time, it was possible not only to move toward a more fixed design for some parts of the analysis but also to start to organize and relate the different activities of analysis that were taking place. The main activities of analyses were as follows:

1. Identification and organization of information relating to planned and actual schedules, phases, milestones, decisions, and replans for each project. This analysis produced a framework around which the results of other analyses could be related. Data for schedules, phases, milestones, decisions, and replans were identified from project plans, meeting minutes, interviews, and other project documentation. This required careful reading of a significant quantity of documentation from the projects. The summarized data were recorded in spreadsheets and word processing documents.
2. Identification and coding of reports of waiting, progress of work, and overdue work for the functional areas in each project. This analysis was focused on

the three units of analyses: reports of waiting, progress of work, and overdue work on the projects. One objective of the study was to use these reports to test hypotheses about the prevalence of waiting in the projects; hypotheses that had been derived from the research literature, in particular from Bradac et al. [25, 26] and van Genuchten [204]. Another objective of the study was to use these reports as empirical data to explore a simple theoretical model developed as part of the research, that is, that work does not progress according to plan, that poor progress results in overdue work, and that this overdue work leads to waiting in other parts of the project (due to within-project dependencies) that consequently affects the progress of other items of work.

To identify reports of waiting, progress, and overdue work, the researcher not only browsed hardcopies of the meeting minutes but also searched using a text editor the electronic versions of the minutes, in order to identify and classify all relevant reports throughout the duration of the project. The reports were coded in various ways, for example, when the report was made; what type of work was progressing poorly, or overdue, or causing waiting; and what functional areas of the project were affected in some way by the poor progress, overdue work, or waiting. These codes were then counted in various ways to give, for example, the frequency of reports of waiting for each week of the project. These counts then allowed hypotheses testing using simple nonparametric statistics. The summarized data were first stored in spreadsheets and subsequently imported into statistical software for statistical analysis.

3. Identification and classification of other significant events on the project, such as reports in meeting minutes about significant design problems, or other difficulties emerging on the project. From this activity, a more specific set of data, subsequently referred to as "indicators of project urgency" was identified and then analyzed separately. Again, this required careful reading of a range of project documentation, and the summarized data were recorded in spreadsheets and word processing documents.

4. Identification and classification of decisions and actions made by the project management team to try to address the various problems emerging in the project. Again, this required careful reading of a range of project documentation, particularly the meeting minutes and interview notes, and the summarized data were recorded in spreadsheets and word processing documents.

5. Identification and classification of the sociotechnical context of the projects to support cross-case analysis and generalization. These data were identified primarily from interviews.

Clearly, much of the analysis concerned identifying and classifying data from the projects. The refined data then provided a basis for investigating a simple theoretical model and also for inferring how the two projects progressed and what management could do to address problems on the projects. In Robson's [162] terminology, the two case studies progressed from exploring, to then describing, to then attempting to explain the situation of interest.

11.6 REPORTING

A variety of reports were produced during and after the case studies. These included:

- A range of interim reports for review by the company mentor, the company sponsor, research colleagues, and the PhD supervisory team.
- Feedback reports on the draft final results for the respective projects. These provided opportunity not only for quality assurance for the case studies but also for the respective projects to reflect on their projects and perhaps learn from the feedback reports and that reflection.
- Several technical reports during the PhD and since its completion.
- Academic conference papers published during the case studies [154].
- The doctoral thesis [144], a copy of which was also given to the company sponsor. The thesis adopted elements of three of Yin's [217] reporting structures: the linear analytic structure; the comparative structure, where characteristics of the two projects studied were compared; and the chronological structure, where the behavior of each project was represented over time. Part of the structure of the thesis is summarized in Table 11.2.
- Academic conference papers published several years after the completion of the case studies [152].
- Journal articles that use the material from the two case studies to propose extensions to the reporting of case studies [146] and to propose the *longitudinal, chronological, case study* research strategy [147].

TABLE 11.2 Structure of Rainer's Doctoral Thesis

Chapter	Description
4	Discussion of theoretical models.
5	Project-level behavior. Description and analyses of the behavior of two software projects using the following structure: Unsequenced narrative reporting general information on Project B. Unsequenced narrative reporting general information on Project C. Description of the sociotechnical characteristics of Projects B and C using a comparative structure. A detailed narrative of Project B, complemented by chronological information presented graphically. A detailed narrative of Project C, complemented by chronological information presented graphically.
6	Comparative analysis of reports of waiting for Projects B and C, analyzing various aspects of waiting, for example, prevalence, source, and dependent points of waiting.
7	Analysis of reports of the progress of work, using a structure similar to Chapter 6.
8	Analysis of reports of overdue work, using a structure similar to Chapter 6.
9	Integration of the analyses from Chapters 5–8.

- Case studies for Projects B and C have been prepared to support teaching and assessment on the MEng Computer Science degree program.

11.6.1 Internal Reporting of Results

Some participants asked for an awayday to review the results of this research. Arranging an awayday was beyond the remit of the student. Some participants wanted to know how they compared to other projects, and this led to some careful responses from the student, for example, either explaining that it was not appropriate to provide comparisons or alternatively to provide general comparisons that need not reveal the identity of individual projects. Given the other communication channels in the organization, it may be that projects knew other projects were in the study.

11.6.2 Dissemination of Artifacts

Because of the nature of the qualitative data collected during the case studies, it is extremely difficult to "sanitise" the raw data. Similarly, the logbook that was maintained throughout the duration of the case studies also contains sensitive information that cannot be easily sanitized. For these reasons, artifacts from the case studies have not been disseminated to others.

11.7 LESSONS LEARNED

A range of lessons continue to be learned from the case studies. These include the following:

Flexible case study design. Conducting longitudinal case studies is a very challenging type of research for which careful planning is required. The longer the duration of the study, the more likely the case(s) being studied will change and, therefore, the more likely the case study *design* will need to change.

Theoretical framework. For exploratory studies where there is an absence of background theory, the researcher should think carefully about how he or she will organize the data collection and analysis.

Quantity of qualitative and quantitative data. In software projects and other software engineering activities, large volumes of qualitative and quantitative data are often naturally generated and collected by the participants in these activities (e.g., public and personal records of meetings). As these kinds of data are naturally generated and collected, it is a low-cost activity for the researcher to acquire copies of these data. The researcher should then think carefully about how these data should be analyzed and also about the problems of quality and validity that can arise with these kinds of data.

Resourcing the research project. During the design stage of the research, the intention was to conduct five case studies, but as explained earlier in this chapter, this proved to be too demanding for the resources available. Time and effort were expended on collecting data that were subsequently not used. In retrospect, this time could have been directed toward the collection of more data from the two case studies that were eventually studied (e.g., conducting more interviews) or toward the quality assurance of these data (e.g., writing up notes of interviews and asking the interviewee to comment on them).

Support from the participating company. It helps considerably to have an individual within the respective organization who can support the case study research on a day-to-day basis, in addition to having more senior line management support for the case study. For example, the company mentor may provide assistance with the following:

- The identification, short-listing, and selection of cases for study.
- Introduction to stakeholders and advice over how to approach these stakeholders.
- Reviewing reports and other documents prior to internal or external dissemination.
- Assistance with the interpretation of data.
- Clarification of company processes, procedures, and terminology.

CHAPTER 12

AN ITERATIVE CASE STUDY OF QUALITY MONITORING

12.1 INTRODUCTION

This chapter reports the experience of the first author conducting a case study on quality management in an iterative development environment. The study has a flexible design and primarily uses quantitative data, while qualitative data are taken in for explanatory purposes. The case comprises three projects within one company, developing consumer products with an extensive list of features, as requested by the market. Quantitative data are collected from defect management databases, project reports, and product plans.

A PhD student (Andersson) was given access to the premises and databases under a nondisclosure agreement. She worked part time at the company for about half a year. At regular intervals, every third or fourth week, a feedback meeting was held with the main contact person from the company, the PhD student, and the supervisor. At these meetings, the progress was followed up, and the next step in the study was decided.

A highly iterative software development organization is a very complex, contemporary phenomenon, without clear boundaries between technical and organizational issues. Hence, it is clearly feasible for a case study.

Existing case study methodology handbooks at the time [217] did not sufficiently define how to conduct such a study. Thus, a new case study process was needed to address the issues adherent to the situation, which has clear characteristics of the cyclicality of action research studies (see Section 2.2).

Case Study Research in Software Engineering: Guidelines and Examples, First Edition.
Per Runeson, Martin Höst, Austen Rainer, and Björn Regnell.
© 2012 John Wiley & Sons, Inc. Published 2012 by John Wiley & Sons, Inc.

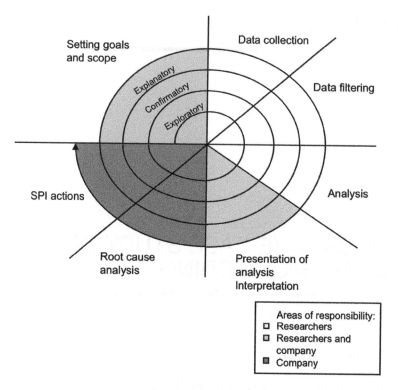

FIGURE 12.1   Process model for iterative case studies [7].

As we wanted to avoid the inherent bias of action researcher involvement, we split the roles of observation and action. The researchers in this context derived and synthesized the information from the case, while the company staff was responsible for the change part. In a pure action research study, researchers may be part of both.

We defined a spiral case study process (Figure 12.1) that has an iterative characteristic, similar to Boehm's spiral model [22], in order to enable stepwise adjustment of the goal and scope to the iterative findings. In addition, the case study process is defined to manage the interface between researchers and project staff, and explicitly show who has responsibility for the specific parts.

12.2 CASE STUDY DESIGN

12.2.1 Objectives

The overall goal of the case study was to understand the current test process with the intention of improving it. Improvement goals include reduced cost, increased quality, and improved planning and predictability. More specifically, the company aimed for a prediction model for defects to use as a basis for management decisions on internal and external releases. Second, we also wanted to replicate two earlier studies on defect distributions by Fenton and Ohlsson [53] and software reliability growth models by Stringfellow and Andrews [198].

The original intention was to develop a software process simulation model [88]. The purpose of the simulation model was to analyze the test process, similar to a study by Berling et al. [20]. The objective was then adapted during iterative cycles of the case study, first exploring the case, and then searching for explanations.

12.2.2 Cases and Units of Analysis

The company organized their work in projects, and hence it was natural to choose the management of the project as the unit of analysis. From the beginning, two projects were selected, and later a third project was added to broaden the basis for the study.

12.2.3 Theoretical Frame of Reference

There was no explicitly defined frame of reference at the time of conduct. However, there were two fields of theory that were implicitly behind the case study:

1. Fenton and Ohlsson's hypotheses on defect distributions [53].
2. Stringfellow and Andrews' work on software reliability growth models [198].

The initial research cycle were inductive, starting with observations, while later cycles were deductive, starting from theory or hypotheses.

12.2.4 Research Questions

The research set out two goals, one practical and one theoretical. The practical research goal was to provide the company with means for quantitative quality management of the test process, to support decisions, for example, on when to stop testing or release a product. The theoretical goal was to replicate the studies by Fenton and Ohlsson [53] and Stringfellow and Andrews [198], respectively, in new contexts.

12.3 PLANNING

12.3.1 Methods of Data Collection

The case study was conducted within a framework collaboration program between the university and the company under study. Issues of confidentiality and publications were regulated in a contract. The PhD student got access to the company premises and databases, at the same level as employees of the company.

When starting the case study, it was not decided how many iterations should be conducted, only that the study should be conducted in an iterative fashion with continuous feedback. The summary of iterations in Table 12.1 is hence defined cycle by cycle, rather than as complete plan.

TABLE 12.1 Overview of the Seven Case Study Cycles of the Case Study [7]

	Goals and Scope	Data Collection and Filtering	Analysis and Presentation	Interpretation and Improvement
1	Simulation model	Process models: Time reports and defect reports.	Build simulation model.	Very complex approach.
2	Exploratory	Defect reports project 1, 2.	Distribution of detection activities over time.	Response on specific events in each project.
3	Exploratory	Defect reports per feature group.	Distribution of detection activities per feature group.	Motivation for distribution.
4	Confirmatory	Defect reports project 3.	Same as in cycle 2 and 3.	Sufficient fit for practical use.
5	Explanatory	Qualitative data on feature groups.	Characteristics of feature groups.	Root cause analysis on causes and suggestions for each group; subset of defect reports.
6	Explanatory (prediction)	All defect reports.	Prediction of defect content with simple model.	Use of prediction model to improve planning.
7	Explanatory (prediction)	All defect reports; time data.	Software reliability growth models.	Use of prediction model.

TABLE 12.2   Characteristics of the Selected Cases

Project	Type	Duration (Scaled)	Size (Scaled)	No. of Defects (Scaled)	No. of Feature Groups	Collection
1	Application	10	10	10	10	Post hoc
2	Platform	13	15	25	12	Online
3	Application	9	20	15	12	Online

In the first research cycle, informal interviews were held to provide a general understanding of the development process and practices. The data were collected as meeting notes. The findings from the interviews were compiled into a qualitative process model.

In the later iterations, data from company databases and documents constitued the main source. Database queries were not only defined to the defect management system but also to the administrative systems to triangulate some data. For example, the defect reports had an entry telling the testing phase (function test, system test), and the company organizational information was used to cross-check that the issuer of a defect report in function test was actually working as a function tester. Project reports were studied to get information about dates for certain events, such as project start and delivery dates.

12.3.2   Case Selection Strategy

We analyzed data from three separate software development projects, which main characteristics of which are reported in Table 12.2. Two of the projects are application projects developing consumer products. One project is an internal platform project where the resulting product is used as a platform in other consumer products. Projects 1 and 3 are the application-type projects, whereas project 2 is the platform project. A project runs for approximately 1 year. The data for project 1 were collected retrospectively (post hoc) from the problem-reporting database, whereas the data for projects 2 and 3 were collected while the projects were running (online). The online approach made it easier to get help with interpretation and clarifications, since the people worked in the projects at the moment. However, the post hoc project was finished just a few months ago, so most people remained in the company, although they worked in new projects.

12.3.3   Case Study Protocol

No formal case study protocol was developed for the case study. However, the researchers kept a log of the data collected, analyses conducted, and issues raised and resolved in the feedback meetings.

12.3.4   Ethical Considerations

The research was partly concerned with finding similarities and differences in defect patterns between features. Some of the feature teams then wanted to benchmark themselves against the others. However, since the technical characteristics of the features were different, it was not possible to compare them side by side. We published the data and analysis at a feature level, but stated very clearly that the conditions for what are good and bad patterns may be different for different features.

12.3.5 Data Collection

Initially, when launching the case study, the scope was very broad. The goal was to develop a software process simulation model in order to analyze the test process, similar to the study by Berling et al. [20]. Unfortunately, the goal to build a model based on mostly quantitative information was not achieved. The scope turned out to be too large, since the available information at that time was not adequate for building the model on the required level of abstraction, and the goal had to shift toward a more general analysis of the process, based on what could be collected from the company's defect management database and other archival sources.

12.3.6 Exploratory Study

A second cycle of the case study was then launched, with an exploratory goal. Quantitative information, specifically in the shape of defect reports, was collected from two projects to gain knowledge about the studied object. The obtained defect distributions were analyzed over time and the behavior was analyzed with respect to specific events and test activities.

In the third cycle, the same defect reports as in the second cycle were further analyzed. A new attribute, the feature in which the defects were located, was used as the unit of analysis. The approach was still exploratory, and the analyses were descriptive in the form of bar charts. The findings were fed back to the organization during the presentation step of the case study process and discussed and expanded with qualitative information on the obtained defect distributions.

12.3.7 Confirmatory Study

The fourth case cycle used a confirmatory approach. Quantitative information from a third project was collected. The defect distributions obtained in cycles 2 and 3 were compared with the defect reports from the third project to investigate whether the observed trends from the previous cycles were found here as well. The analysis and interpretation were mainly based on statistical analyses and hypothesis tests.

12.3.8 Explanatory Study

The fifth case study cycle took an explanatory approach. This cycle can, in reality, be separated into several subcycles. Qualitative information was collected to characterize the subproject groups and to explain their behavior. The qualitative data were complementary to the data obtained from the defect reports database and used for explanatory purposes, for example, to properly interpret data fluctuation and to clarify differences between the projects.

The last two case study cycles were also explanatory, with the purpose of finding prediction models that could explain and predict future behavior. To start with, a simple prediction model of the number of defects to expect in a project was defined, based on the defect distributions observed in previous cycles. Afterward, software reliability growth models were applied to the defect distributions, and these models' ability to give appropriate predictions were evaluated and compared with the more simple approach from case study cycle 6.

12.4 DATA ANALYSIS

The data analysis was conducted in each cycle and included mostly descriptive statistics. The qualitative data were mostly connected with certain quantitative observations, and hence no separate analysis of the qualitative data was performed. After the last cycle, a separate analysis was conducted of the quantitative data to replicate the previous studies on defect distributions and software reliability growth models.

12.5 REPORTING

The findings of the case study were continuously reported in the feedback meetings. Mostly, only the main contact person was attending the meeting, while at other occasions, representatives from different feature teams were present.

The case study as such was reported in a journal publication, together with the proposed spiral case study model [7]. The replication studies were then published as separate journal papers [5, 6].

The company was concerned about publishing a number of defects, defect densities, and so on. However, from the research point of view, percentages and scaled data were sufficient, together with reporting the approximate magnitude of size of the systems under study (Table 12.2).

12.6 LESSONS LEARNED

Lessons learned from the case study are addressed below:

Quantitative data in case studies. Case study research mostly connected with qualitative data collection. Sometimes, it is even referred to as a *qualitative research design*, although we prefer to call it a *flexible research design* (Section 2.3). However, there is no conflict between collecting quantitative data and conducting a case study. There are however two concerns regarding quantitative data from flexible design studies:

1. The data collection may evolve over time, or some quantitative data may not be available for some projects. Hence, comparison cannot be done fully between the projects.

2. The cases are *not* sampled from a population, and hence the sampling logic cannot be used to generalize from case studies, be they based on quantitative or qualitative data.

Iterative case study. The iterative process for the case study was very effective in building up an industry – academia relation. In the feedback meetings, the company got incremental delivery of analyses, which they could use in the operational business. At the same time, the research could aim for a more long-term goal and general understanding of phenomena in software engineering. Using the post hoc project to start data collection from was also a useful practice to establish a baseline for further iterations.

Case study versus action research. Whether to label the enquiry a case study or action research is to some extent a matter of taste. However, we found it particularly useful to distinguish between the roles for *observation* and *action*. Being a researcher coming from the outside helps studying phenomena without the risk of being home blind. On the other hand, deciding and implementing improvement actions require commitment from the organization, which an outsider cannot encourage to the same extent as an insider.

CHAPTER 13

A CASE STUDY OF THE EVALUATION OF REQUIREMENTS MANAGEMENT TOOLS

13.1 INTRODUCTION

In this chapter, we report the case study of the evaluation of requirements management tools (RMTs) and the subsequent selection, deployment, and postdeployment
evaluation of a particular RMT at a software development company in the
United Kingdom.

The RMT evaluation reported here was undertaken as part of a collaborative project
between the University of Hertfordshire and 1Spatial Ltd., a software development
company based reasonably close to the University. At the time of the evaluation, the
company was a small- to medium-sized enterprise (SME), had been in business for
almost 40 years, employed about 100 staff full time, and provided software products and services to clients internationally in the field of spatial data analysis. The
company was ISO 9001:2000 compliant (previously ISO 9001:1994 compliant) and
in 2004 the company implemented the Rational Unified Process® (RUP®) subsequently integrating RUP into its ISO procedures and documents. Until 2004, partly
due to the lack of disciplined requirements management, the company was able to
complete only two major software builds per year. The company had already decided
to adopt an RMT to help improve software development, and the University and the
company worked together to identify, evaluate, and decide on the appropriate RMT

Case Study Research in Software Engineering: Guidelines and Examples, First Edition.
Per Runeson, Martin Höst, Austen Rainer, and Björn Regnell.
© 2012 John Wiley & Sons, Inc. Published 2012 by John Wiley & Sons, Inc.

for the company to adopt, and then to deploy the tool and subsequently review its deployment. The overall project lasted about 12 months.

RMT evaluation was formally undertaken as part of a Knowledge Transfer Partnership (KTP),[1] funded by the company and the UK's Technology Strategy Board.[2] KTPs employ one or more KTP Associates full time to work on the KTP project. A recent graduate was recruited as the Associate to work onsite as a practitioner at the company and to undertake the in-company RMT evaluation, deployment, and postdeployment review. At the time of the project, the Associate was employed by the University. Upon completion of the project, the Associate was then employed full time as an analyst with the company, although he has now moved to another company. To undertake the evaluation, the Associate received academic support from the University and commercial support from the company.

The preselection evaluation was performed primarily using a set of feature analysis methods, which are part of the DESMET [93, 103] methodology. The preselection evaluation and postdeployment evaluation used interviews and questionnaire surveys as additional methods of collecting data. Detailed information on the evaluation is reported by Sanderson [175]. For simplicity, we refer to the KTP Associate as the evaluator for the remainder of this chapter.

13.2 DESIGN OF THE CASE STUDY

13.2.1 Rationale

The case study of the evaluation was undertaken as part of the evaluator's MSc by Research project. The project was investigating the conduct of software technology evaluations in real-life settings, in particular the use of DESMET within a commercial environment. One particular focus of the research was on the economics of such evaluations, for example, the costs and benefits to companies of conducting software technology evaluations. There is limited published research on the economics of actual evaluations of software technologies in field settings, and the case study sought to contribute to the body of research in this area.

13.2.2 Objective

The case study took place in industry; however, the primary audience for the case study was academia and the objectives for the case study reflected that audience. The overall objectives were as follows:

- To undertake a tool evaluation in an industrial setting using a formal evaluation methodology.

[1] Visit www.ktponline.org.uk for more information.
[2] The Technology Strategy Board is an executive nondepartmental public body (NDPB), established by the UK Government in 2007 and sponsored by the Department for Business, Innovation and Skills (BIS).

- To deploy a requirements management tool in a commercial setting.
- To learn from that evaluation about the following:
  - Impact of commercial factors.
  - Impact of formal methods.
  - Cost and benefit of using a formal method.
  - Criteria appropriate to such evaluations.
  - Relationship between an evaluation and the technology adoption decision-making process.
- To learn from the deployment about adoption and assimilation of tools.
- To apply DESMET to a requirements management tool evaluation.

These objectives are decidedly broad and ambitious. For conciseness, this chapter focuses on the objectives of learning from the evaluation about the costs and benefits of using a formal evaluation method in a commercial setting.

13.2.3 The Case and Its Context

The case concerns the range of activities relating to the identification, selection, and evaluation of RMTs, the subsequent recommendation of an RMT to the company, and the deployment and postdeployment review of the adopted RMT. The nature of case studies is such that the case under study cannot be easily separated from its real-life context. There are however four demarcation lines that help to bound the case and distinguish the case from its context. First, the decision to adopt an RMT was made by the company prior to the start of the research project. Second, the decision on which particular RMT to adopt was made by the company and lies outside the scope of the research. In other words, the *recommendation* of a particular RMT represents one boundary of the case. Third, the postdeployment review of the adopted RMT was conducted as part of the research project. Finally, while identifying candidate RMTs, the evaluator sought suggestions and recommendations on RMTs to consider from partner companies and clients. Also, while gathering information on the short-listed RMTs, the evaluator made contact with the vendors of the RMTs. The majority of the evaluation activity therefore took place within one company, but the boundary of the case does not map cleanly to the boundary of that company.

The preselection evaluation process is summarized in Table 13.1. The evaluator identified 32 features required of the RMT and ranked these features using two scales: importance of feature and conformance. The importance ranking determined whether a feature was mandatory, highly desirable, desirable, or nice to have. Of the 32 features, 16 features were mandatory or highly desirable and 16 were desirable or nice to have (it is a coincidence that the split is 50:50). The conformance ranking is an indicator of the aggregation of factors like functionality, documentation, usability, and so on. In other words, the importance ranking signifies how important the feature is to the company, while the conformance ranking signifies how well "implemented" that feature needs to be in the respective RMT. For example, a mandatory feature could

TABLE 13.1   Activities for the Evaluation

No.	Activity Description
1.	Investigation of state-of-practice at company and identification of need for RMT.
2.	Selection of DESMET methodology as formal methodology for evaluation; within DESMET, selection of feature analysis method as primary method of evaluation.
3.	Initial evaluation of RMTs.
	3.1 Identify candidate RMTs through semistructured literature search and visits to vendor websites.
	3.2 Select candidate RMTs through application of heuristics.
	3.3 Identify user groups in company and select representatives of user groups.
	3.4 Identify features required by user groups of RMT.
	3.5 Prioritize features.
	3.6 For each RMT:
	3.6.1 Use standard "legacy project" as case study for evaluation.
	3.6.2 Evaluate RMT against mandatory and highly desirable features.
	3.6.3 Discontinue evaluation of RMT, if RMT fails on mandatory and highly desirable features.
	3.6.4 Evaluate RMT against other features.
	3.6.5 Undertake Webex tutorial of RMT.
	3.7 Analyze results of evaluations from activity 3.6, make preliminary recommendation to senior management in company, and review evaluation process in response to senior management feedback.
	3.8 Reevaluate short-listed RMTs on the basis of additional criteria from senior management, and present final recommendation.
	3.9 Company senior management make decision on which RMT to acquire and deploy.
4.	Deployment of acquired RMT.
5.	Postdeployment review of RMT.
6.	Evaluation of steps 3–5 to learn lessons for future evaluations.

have a low conformance (a minimum level of capability); conversely, a nice-to-have feature may need to have a high level of conformance.

13.2.4   The Units of Analyses

About 30 RMTs were identified for evaluation and, of that number, 8 were short-listed for initial evaluation. One unit of analysis therefore concerns the activities by which RMTs were identified and selected. A second unit of analysis was the evaluation of a particular RMT so that, in principle, there were eight instances of this unit of analysis (the eight RMTs). The analysis of this unit is complicated however because six of the eight RMTs were dropped at different points during the evaluation (as each RMT failed to achieve a standard set during the evaluation) leaving the final two RMTs recommended to the company and from which the company should choose. In Table 13.1, the main activities relating to this unit of analysis occur in stage 3. A third potential unit of analysis was the implementation of the DESMET feature analysis method, as this method underpinned the main activities of evaluation. A final unit of analysis, and the one considered in this discussion, is the overall case itself. For each of these units, one can consider how the findings relating to that unit could generalize. The issue of generalization is considered in more detail at the end of this chapter.

13.2.5 Theoretical Framework

There is limited theory (e.g., causal explanations) available in the academic literature on software evaluations, although there are a range of arguments for why such evaluations are important. On the basis of the arguments for the importance of evaluations, there is also a wide range of methods and methodologies for conducting evaluations. For example, Jadhav and Sonar ([76]; published after the case study reported here was conducted) provide a structured review of 52 of these resources, organized into four categories: methodologies for software selection, software evaluation techniques, software evaluation criteria, and systems/tools to support decision makers in software selection.

There is however very little empirical evidence on the costs and benefits of conducting software technology evaluations, although these issues are discussed in the literature [70, 213, 219]. Similarly, there are arguments for the value of RMTs (e.g., as an electronic repository to manage the large, complex, and changing requirements of projects), but little published empirical evidence on the efficacy of these RMTs or on how to select an RMT (however, one example by Matulevîcius exists [125]). There are a large number of RMTs available from which to choose. A review of the literature identified various gaps in the published literature and these gaps helped demonstrate the value of conducting the case study.

13.2.6 Research Questions

Given the rationale for the case study, and the focus in this chapter on the objective of learning from the evaluation about the costs and benefits of using a formal evaluation method in a commercial setting, the research question was:

RQ1. What are the costs and benefits to a company of undertaking software technology evaluations?

13.2.7 Propositions, Concepts, and Measures

An indicative summary of some of the concepts and measures used in the case study is given in Table 13.2.

13.2.8 Case Study Protocol

No formal case study protocol was developed or maintained for the case study; however, detailed information on the actual conduct of the study is presented by Sanderson [175].

TABLE 13.2   Definition of Concepts and Measures

Concept or Measure	Definition
DESMET	A methodology developed to evaluate software methods and tools.
Feature analyses methods	A set of evaluation methods within the DESMET methodology. The four methods that make up the set are feature analysis experiment, feature analysis case study, feature analysis screening, and feature analysis survey. Feature analysis screening and feature analysis case study were the two main methods used in the case study. The feature analyses methods rank products according to weighted criteria. The methods can therefore indicate the more appropriate product, but cannot provide insights into the effectiveness of the method.
Feature importance	Importance ranking determined whether a feature was mandatory, highly desirable, desirable, or nice to have.
Feature conformance	Conformance ranking is an indicator of the aggregation of factors like functionality, documentation, usability, and so on.

13.2.9 Methods of Data Collection

Several methods of data collection were used because of the different activities taking place in the case study. A semistructured literature review was conducted to identify candidate RMTs for the evaluation (see activity 3.1 in Table 13.1). A set of structured interviews were conducted to identify features and to subsequently prioritize these features. A subjective scoring of the RMTs by the evaluator was undertaken, together with the collection of qualitative notes on respective RMTs. The evaluator estimated the effort and other costs consumed (e.g., licenses, training costs, and support costs) during the evaluation, deployment, and postdeployment review. The evaluator also estimated the qualitative and quantitative benefits to the company of undertaking the evaluation, deployment, and postdeployment review. These methods are discussed in more detail in Section 13.3.

13.2.10 Methods of Data Analysis

For the investigation of the economic argument concerning the costs and benefits of the evaluation to the company, data were analyzed in several ways. The evaluator determined the nonquantifiable benefits of an RMT by gathering qualitative information from staff at the company and estimated the quantifiable benefits of the RMT, again by gathering estimates from staff at the company. The evaluator also calculated the costs of the evaluation itself (principally a daily cost of effort expended) and the costs of implementing and maintaining the software (e.g., license costs, training, and support costs), and then estimated the *cost-savings* incurred by comparing the costs estimated for the RMT that was adopted against the costs estimated for the "runner-up" RMT.

13.2.11   Case Selection Strategy

The case itself was selected on the basis of availability, that is, KTP project presented an opportunity to conduct an evaluation of RMTs and to study that evaluation process. The identification and selection of units of analyses were then determined by decisions made during the evaluation. For example, the choice of DESMET as the evaluation methodology and the choice of feature analyses methods as the main evaluation methods occurred because of several objectives and constraints. The choice of RMTs was based on several criteria developed to identify and select RMTs.

13.2.12   Data Selection Strategy

The strategy for selecting data was driven primarily by the activities listed in Table 13.1 and by the guidelines of DESMET feature analyses methods.

13.2.13   Replication Strategy

There was no strategy for replication on the basis that there was no comparable RMT evaluation previously conducted or even comparable evaluations of other technologies. Also, such evaluations are likely to quickly become out of date; so, while the design of the study might be reused, the outcomes from a study may be different. Future case studies of the evaluation of RMTs are, therefore, likely to adopt a strategy of theoretical replication, although currently there is limited theory in this area.

13.2.14   Quality Assurance, Validity, and Reliability

To help ensure that data collected were representative of a broad range of stakeholders at the company, a set of user groups were identified and people from these user groups were approached to complete questionnaires and also review interim results. A summary of the user groups and their roles is provided in Table 13.3.

TABLE 13.3   User Groups and Roles in the company

User Group	Roles
Analysts	Elicitation, analysis, specification, validation, and management of requirements. Direct interaction.
Product and Project Managers	Status reporting, traceability reporting, prioritization Some direct interaction.
Architects	Creating design and architecture artifacts. Indirect interaction.
Developers	Implementing the requirements into the system and possibly creating design artifacts. Indirect interaction.
Testers	Creating test script artifacts. Indirect interaction.
Customer Support	Supporting released products require knowledge of requirements. Indirect interaction.
Consultants and Sales	Interacting with customers. Indirect interaction.

DESMET recognizes that feature analysis is prone to subjective assessments and inconsistencies between evaluators. To help increase the rigor of the evaluator's subjective "scoring" of the features of each RMT, a set of requirements from a legacy project previously completed by 1Spatial were used as test data for the evaluation. In other words, the evaluator sought to simulate a situation were requirements analysts would be using the respective RMT to manage a set of requirements.

Due to the short evaluation period for each tool, assumptions had to be made concerning the stability of the RMT. With only one evaluator using the tool, there was no opportunity to rigorously test multiple users working on the same project at the same time. This was a significant and risky assumption to make, and had to be made due to the availability of resources. Evaluation copies of tools were mostly single fixed licenses, which did not give the opportunity for testing concurrency. Therefore, the evaluator had to make assumptions about stability of the RMT because of the constraints on resources.

With only one evaluator, there are the risks of bias and errors of omission. For example, it is possible that the evaluator either underassessed or overassessed some functionality, with the consequence that an RMT was underscored or overscored incorrectly. One implication here is that an RMT should have been retained for further assessment when in fact it had been removed and, conversely, that an RMT should have been removed when in fact it had been retained. Given the time and resource constraints of the commercial environment, assumptions concerning the subjectivity and rigorousness of the evaluation had to be made.

13.3 DATA COLLECTION

Data were collected in the following ways:

- A preliminary investigation of the state-of-practice of gathering, analyzing, and managing requirements was undertaken within the company. Fourteen employees with various roles in the company completed a questionnaire. A qualitative summary of problems, their impact, weak areas, and needs was constructed.
- Five structured interviews were conducted with employees of the company. These interviews were not recorded or transcribed. Instead, the evaluator made notes during the interviews.
- A representative from each identified user group was chosen to review the initial feature list and provide feedback for refinement. Upon completion of this review, the evaluation had settled on 32 features.
- Eight representatives from user groups were selected to rank the 32 features by importance and by conformance.
- A score sheet was completed by the evaluator for each evaluated RMT, comprising a subjective ranking of the product, together with qualitative information. Analysis of the score sheets and the qualitative comments subsequently provided the basis for the RMT recommendation to the company. The score sheet was

completed, together with the qualitative data, while the evaluator populated a trial version of the RMT with legacy data from previously completed project at the company.

- After the adopted RMT was deployed, the evaluator collected data through structured interviews with six employees in the company. Each interview lasted about 45 min. As with the predecision evaluation, the sample of candidates represented different departments in the company and included the different types of users of the RMT adopted. Three of the six interviewees were also interviewed during the predecision evaluation, providing the opportunity to investigate pre- and post-decision opinions. Again, none of the interviews were recorded or transcribed; instead, the evaluator took notes at the interviews.

- Using a revised version of the interview template for the six postdeployment interviews, the evaluator conducted interviews with representatives from three of the company's clients who used an alternative, market-leading RMT. Again, none of the interviews were recorded or transcribed; instead, the evaluator took notes at the interviews.

- A quantitative analysis of response times, from the RMT vendor, to support queries raised by the company during presales, postsales, and posttraining.

- The evaluator estimated the costs of the whole evaluation from predecision to postdeployment training and evaluation. This estimate covered effort and software costs. A nominal rate of £450 per day was used, as this was the amount the company charged a client for an analyst at the time.

13.4 DATA ANALYSIS

Different kinds of analyses occurred at different stages of the case study. To identify the features to be used in the feature analysis, the evaluator conducted a thematic analysis on the responses from the state-of-practice questionnaire that had previously been administered to 14 employees in the company. This analysis identified candidate features. A similar thematic analysis was conducted on the notes from the five structured interviews. The results of these two thematic analyses were merged. When collecting the *initial* information through questionnaire and interview, the objective was not to ask users to identify specific features for an RMT, but rather to gather information from users on the nature and problems of requirements and requirements management. The features were then extracted from this information.

A representative from each user group in the company (see Table 13.3) was selected to review the initial feature list and provide feedback for refinement. Representatives were chosen on the basis of their experience of working in the company, for example, their experience of the company's tailored RUP. The feature list was refined on the basis of the feedback from these representatives.

Eight representatives from the user groups were then asked to rank each of the 32 features on 2 simple numeric scales, one for *feature importance* and one for *feature conformance* (see Table 13.2). The evaluator then calculated the arithmetic mean and mode of the eight responses to determine the final rankings on the features on the two scales. The mode was used for the initial calculation. Where two modes occurred for the ranking of a feature, the mean was used to help decide which mode was more appropriate.

There were three phases of the actual evaluations of the RMTs, with an RMT being removed from the subsequent phases of the evaluation if that RMT failed to satisfy the respective evaluation threshold for a phase. The three phases were (1) screen the candidate RMTs based on the importance rankings, (2) assess the RMTs using the conformance rankings, (3) assess the RMTs using other information such as purchase and training costs and supplier viability. By the completion of the phases, the evaluator had the following analysis: quantitative information on importance rankings; quantitative information on conformance rankings; qualitative information on functional and nonfunctional features, including information on suppliers maturity, usability, efficiency, maintainability, compatibility, and security; and quantitative information on purchase, training, and operational costs. By the end of the three-phase evaluation, two RMTs remained and these were presented to the company for a decision over which to adopt.

When analyzing the data collected from the postdeployment interviews, the evaluator performed simple quantitative and qualitative analyses. For the quantitative analysis, the evaluator compared the rankings the interviewees provided for the features before the deployment with the rankings the interviewees gave after the deployment. For the qualitative analysis, the evaluator again performed some simple thematic analysis of the issues noted from the interviews.

Finally, the evaluator performed some simple quantitative analysis of the number of support requests raised with the vendor during the evaluation and after the deployment. The evaluator had collected data on the time it took for the vendor to provide satisfactory responses to the support requests.

13.5 REPORTING AND DISSEMINATION

The interim and final results of the evaluation were reported to practitioner and academic audiences. For the practitioners, there were ongoing formal and informal progress reports to 1Spatial, including a formal report recommending a particular RMT to adopt. There were also formal reports to the project management team of the KTP project. The project management team was made up of stakeholders from the company, the University, and the Technology Strategy Board. Also, a final report on the KTP project was prepared for the TSB, the main funder of the project. For the academic audiences, there have been two conference papers at academic conferences [148, 149], and a Master's thesis [175], together with a viva voce defense of the thesis.

In addition to qualitative and quantitative results relating to the research question, the case study also provided recommendations to researchers on how to better perform RMT evaluations in the future. These recommendations included heuristics for selecting a method or methodology for the evaluation of technology, together with heuristics for short-listing RMTs for evaluation. Examples of the heuristics for selecting an evaluation methodology include that the methodology has been recently developed, that the methodology has been successfully applied in industry, and that the methodology has been successfully applied by academia. Examples of the heuristics for short-listing include that the websites for the respective RMTs should provide sufficient quality and quantity of information on the RMT, and that the number of RMTs to short-list should be influenced by the resources and time available by the company to undertake an appropriate evaluation.

Given the variety of kinds of data available for the heuristics and the difficulty in assessing the credibility of all the data for each heuristic, it was not possible to define a procedure for consistently applying the heuristics, for example, a procedure for applying the eight heuristics to short-list RMTs. Also, it is very unlikely that any evaluation methodology or RMT would satisfy all the relevant heuristics; and moreover, the company did not have the time and resources to rigorously apply all the heuristics to every RMT on the market. Therefore, the evaluation methodology (i.e., DESMET) and the RMTs were selected on the basis of a judgment involving the respective heuristics. In case of the short-listing of RMTs, the first four heuristics listed above tended to be the most useful in the initial selection process.

13.6 LESSONS LEARNED

As a result of the case study, we learned several lessons:

Limitations of the study. The evaluation focused primarily on the *appropriateness* of the RMTs, for example, assessing the degree to which respective RMTs possessed features, such as traceability, that were appropriate to the company's needs. There has been no investigation of the cause–effect relationship between the RMT, or one or more features of the RMT, and improvements in requirements management or software development. Given the design of the evaluation, it is not possible to make any objective, empirically supported claim from our evaluation that any of the RMTs actually improve requirements management or software development.

More generally, cause–effect analyses are extremely difficult to study with software technologies because the effect of the technology is confounded by a range of other factors, such as the ability of the user(s) of the technology, the process for which the software technology is used as a resource, the need to integrate with other technologies, the quality of inputs to the process, and the controls placed on the process. Kitchenham et al. [98] briefly discuss these kinds of issues when considering the application of Evidence Based Medicine to software engineering. Fenton and Pfleeger [54] present a model of a repeatable process, using a simplified Structured Analysis and Design Technique diagram, that illustrates the presence of these factors.

The problems of generalizability. RMTs were evaluated in terms of 1Spatial's specific requirements and circumstances, and a particular RMT was recommended for adoption and deployment on that basis. The adopted RMT was not one of the market-leading RMTs, neither has it been frequently evaluated by other evaluators. In the case study, we do not claim that the adopted RMT is universally good or imply that other RMTs are universally bad. It is not appropriate therefore to attempt to generalize the *outcome* of the DESMET evaluation, that is, to generalize the recommendation to adopt the RMT adopted by 1Spatial. One alternative approach to generalization is to consider generalizing the claims about the cost-benefits of different methods of evaluation. On this point, the results from the evaluation appear to be broadly consistent with previous theoretical work [70, 213, 219]. A second alternative is to generalize through guidelines and heuristics for future evaluations, as we have indicated earlier in this chapter.

An alternative unit of analysis. Section 13.2.4 identified four units of analysis for the case study. As a counterexample, a very different kind of unit of analysis could have been the feature. With 32 features identified for the feature analysis, the evaluator could have chosen to examine each feature and compare the "outcomes" of each feature. Such a unit of analysis would be appropriate where an investigator was interested in the following kinds of questions (as examples): How are features identified by practitioners and by the evaluator(s) when undertaking a feature analysis of software technologies? How are a large number of features of different types, with different kinds of evidence, integrated to support the overall comparison of different software technologies being evaluated with those features? How does a particular feature contribute to the "causal" impact of a technology on the software engineering activity for which the technology is being used? For example, a traceabilty feature in RMTs can potentially help in the activity of monitoring, estimating, and managing the impact of requirements changes.

CHAPTER 14

A LARGE-SCALE CASE STUDY OF REQUIREMENTS AND VERIFICATION ALIGNMENT

14.1 INTRODUCTION

This chapter presents experiences from an ongoing large-scale, qualitative case study that will continue until at least the end of 2011. So far the study has involved 11 researchers at 2 universities (Lund University and Blekinge Institute of Technology, both in Sweden). The fourth author of this book is the project leader for the case study. The study currently includes six anonymous companies geographically distributed over five sites in Scandinavia. Thirty interviews have been transcribed and these transcriptions total approximately 217, 030 words (or 319 pages of text with an average of around 680 words per page). Spin-off studies of both a descriptive and prescriptive nature are anticipated to follow on from the large-scale study when it completes.

The focus of the study is the alignment and mutual coordination of two different subprocesses in software engineering, namely, requirements engineering (RE) and verification and validation (V&V, also called testing). Throughout this book, the study is referred to as REVV study.

REVV study turned out to be a much more complex endeavor than originally anticipated, and the sheer amount of data in the form of transcripts and quotes make the material difficult to handle. This chapter summarizes the experiences of this study from a methodological point of view. Preliminary results from the partial analysis of

Case Study Research in Software Engineering: Guidelines and Examples, First Edition.
Per Runeson, Martin Höst, Austen Rainer, and Björn Regnell.
© 2012 John Wiley & Sons, Inc. Published 2012 by John Wiley & Sons, Inc.

the data based on 11 interviews with a narrow focus have been published [172], while a more complete analysis remains to be published.

14.2 CASE STUDY DESIGN

REVV study is part of a larger, action research context, depicted in Figure 14.1. The study was intentionally designed with this larger context in mind. The results of the study, anticipated to be descriptive in nature, are intended to support further studies, with subsequent results that are intended to be prescriptive in nature. Thus, a detailed description and understanding of the problem of requirements and test alignment is intended to act as an empirical foundation on which to develop prescriptive solutions. This foundation will give the researchers and practitioners greater confidence in the relevance of the solutions to practice.

14.2.1 Rationale

REVV study was conceived at the start of a 10 year research program together with industrial partners in a research program that commenced in 2008. Several industrial partners pointed out the important challenge of managing the increasing amount of information in a large-scale software engineering, and in particular stressed the need for improving the current state-of-practice regarding the alignment and coordination between requirements and testing.

There were other candidate areas for the research, but a focus on the alignment and coordination between requirements and testing was considered by the partner companies to be among the most promising in terms of potential to make a major step in improving industrial practice. The primary rationale for the study from a practitioners' point of view was notably not to describe and create theory and provide deep problem understanding for its own sake; rather the main motivation came from its projected utility in the problem solving part of the research.

14.2.2 Objectives

The long-term expectation of the industrial partners from the research is to improve the competitiveness in software engineering, where a particular potential of productivity improvement in RE and V&V alignment was hypothesized. In joint workshops on research directions, practitioners' preconceived wishes on output from the research included tools, methods, processes, guidelines, and similar support to specifically address improved RE–V&V alignment. REVV study is thus part of a typical action research effort, where academic researchers together with industrial partner companies mutually exchange and develop knowledge, problem understanding, and solution designs, with the explicit aim to act in the real world and change the state-of-practice. This action research mode (as shown in Figure 14.1) includes a mutual exchange between practice and research, where problem understanding is informed by practice, while this understanding also changes the attitudes toward the problem in practice.

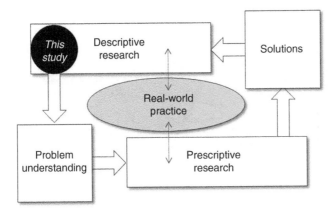

FIGURE 14.1 A general, comprehensive research cycle carried out in an action research mode. REVV study is part of a larger, long-term effort where real-world practice is aimed at being improved through a better problem understanding as a result of descriptive research as well as providing new, effective solutions as a result of prescriptive research in a collaborative design process together with practitioners.

Furthermore, the solutions should be empirically evaluated in the real world and, if successful, can potentially have a large impact on the evolution of practice.

14.2.3 Cases and Units of Analysis

The context of the REVV study is software engineering practice with respect to alignment and coordination of RE and V&V. The initial definition of the context was only tentative as the study aims to define the phenomena under study comprehensively. Figure 14.2 shows our preunderstanding of the context based on the discussion with industrial partner companies, while establishing our study objectives.

Each of the six investigated companies represents one unit of analysis. Although different in terms of, for example, size and application domain, they are similar in that they all put significant efforts on software development while having defined roles, processes, and artifacts for RE and V&V, respectively.

We could also view each company as one case if we would like to contrast the cases and report each case as its own case study, where transferability of results is investigated in cross-case analysis. If we view each company as one case, the units of analysis may be defined by the two different perspectives that we study in each case, namely, the requirements and the verification & validation perspectives, respectively.

In the analysis of the REVV study, we have, however, pooled all data from our 30 interviews together in order to enable analysis of a rich picture with large variations in the common context of RE and V&V alignment, and we thus call the REVV study a case study in singular, even if one could argue that it is a family of related case studies. Thus, the REVV study can be denoted as embedded (multiunit), single case study.

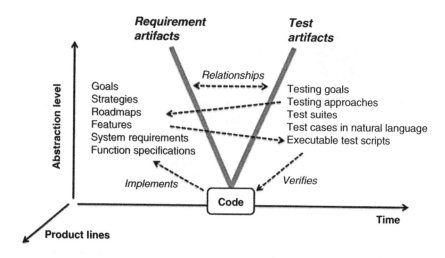

FIGURE 14.2 This conceptual model of the case study context [172] formed our preunder-standing of the phenomenon of RE and V&V alignment and acted as input to the formulation of research questions as well as design of the data collection instrument.

14.2.4 Theoretical Frame of Reference

In the literature review preceding the case study design, we encountered previous work on connecting requirements and testing, including Damian and Chisan [39], Post et al. [142], and Uusitalo et al. [203]. Uusitalo et al. [203] have conducted a series of interviews in order to investigate best practices in linking requirements and testing. The importance of linking requirements and verification is also stressed by Post et al. [142]. The challenges of scale in requirements engineering practice is discussed by Regnell et al. [157]. Communication gaps between subprocesses of software development are indicated as a driver for overscoping by Bjarnason et al. [21].

We decided in this study to build on existing work while designing our study and extend it to take into account a broader range of aspects of RE and V&V alignment, as indicated by the conceptual model of Figure 14.2. The existing work will also act as references to which we can relate the results. We also based some of our design decisions on our general methodological experience from some previous case studies by Regnell et al. [156, 158, 159], where we, for example, learned about the drawbacks of not having a formal case study protocol that is under version control as a solid reference on decisions taken.

While extending the scope of the study to include, for example, processes and communication among people in the organization, the theoretical frame of reference may also be considered very wide. Thus, we anticipate, in light of our future results, the need to extend the literature review with respect to general issues such as traceability, product line engineering, and evolution. The extended literature review should at least try to cover empirical studies in those research areas that to some degree relate to RE and V&V alignment. Indeed, during our journey of iterative data collection and analysis, we have found many relations between the phenomenon of RE and V&V alignment and other research areas of software engineering.

14.2.5 Research Questions

The research questions of the REVV study are summarized in Table 14.1, showing a subset of the many research questions that were conceived. Some research questions were abandoned and some were merged or otherwise rephrased in the process of defining a common view among all researchers about what to actually investigate. The process of arriving at a set of well-formed research questions is in general a creative and iterative activity, which was particularly emphasized in the REVV study where many researchers with various experiences and goals were working toward an agreement. The discussions involved many different aspects, including the rationale, objective, and theoretical frame of reference. The latter entails that the research questions should take into account what has previously been researched and then if a research question is similar to that of an existing study, replication or transferability aspects also need to be considered. In the REVV study, there was to the best of our knowledge no previous study with this comprehensive scope on the RE and V&V alignment phenomenon, but depending on which scope we chose in our discussion, the research questions became either very broad and general or very narrow and specific. We struggled to find a good balance with respect to abstraction level and arrived at a two-level question structure, as shown in Table 14.1.

In our discussions on which research questions to choose, softer issues also played a role, such as estimated available resources in terms of, for example, person hours, budget, and PhD thesis goals of the participating doctoral candidates. All these issues had to be balanced and this balance needed to be considered not only in the formulation of research questions but also in the planning and the iterative data collection. As it turned out, we also had to iterate back to our research questions as preliminary findings gave us a better understanding of the phenomena. This iterative nature of the study

---

TABLE 14.1 A Subset of the Research Questions Defined in the REVV Study

Main Research Questions—Subquestions

What is the current state-of-practice in RE–V&V alignment?
   What are the challenges in RE related to V&V?
   What are the challenges in V&V related to RE?
   What are the artifacts, processes, and roles related to RE–V&V alignment?
   How does RE–V&V alignment relate to the development modes of product line engineering, outsourcing, and open source?

What is the future wanted situation in RE–V&V alignment?
   How can the current alignment be improved?
   What are the expected benefits of an improved RE–V&V alignment?
   How can RE–V&V alignment be measured?

was vital as otherwise we would have risked investing all our research resources into a preplanned direction that we actually knew little about up front. We wanted to avoid being trapped in small iterations and frequent changes causing extra work without a general plan to stick to. At the same time, our general plan needed to be flexible as our scope was only vaguely understood and we did not know in advance where the data collection and analysis would take us.

The research questions need to be revisited and revised when we feel they have to. In a large study like this, we often iterate back to research questions even in the reporting stage, while, for example, writing scientific papers. In particular, during paper writing on a partial result of an analysis chunk, we need to consider how a crisp formulation of research questions can give the reader a good understanding of the (sub)objectives of the reported study. This was the case when we wrote the first paper from the study focusing on one company and on one (refined) research question [172]: What are the challenges of RE–V&V alignment in a large-scale industrial context? We then chose to include an overview of the interview instrument in the paper as a representation of the more detailed research questions.

14.3 PLANNING

The planning of the REVV case study was in practice intertwined with the design in an iterative manner as our goals and research questions were influencing, for example, the interview guide. In essence, we were dealing with planning and design at two levels simultaneously: (1) high-level design in close interaction with our industry partner and research program leader, and (2) detailed design and planning mainly carried out in discussions among the researchers.

The large-scale nature of the REVV study entailed that many stakeholder goals and perspectives were involved in the process, which was both an advantage due to the great pool of experience available and a disadvantage in terms of efficiency. The project leader several times had to make decisions that excluded some stakeholders' goals or perspectives to keep the planning process going. Furthermore, the geographical distribution over two main university sites as well as five industrial sites of the interviewed companies severely hindered the kind of corridor and coffee-break talk that can help effective consensus-building. (This obstacle is analogous to the software engineering challenge of global distributed development.)

Our initial plan was documented in the form of written documents and slide presentations. Figure 14.3 shows a representation of a late version of our plan and its deliverables. The figure also indicates how iteration took place. The activities presented in the figure should not be interpreted as steps in a waterfall-like process, but rather as parallel activities with mutual dependencies. The activities toward the left side of the figure have consumed a larger proportion of the effort distribution early on, compared to those activities toward the right side of the figure.

The plan represented by Figure 14.3 included work packages that can roughly be mapped to these five main activities:

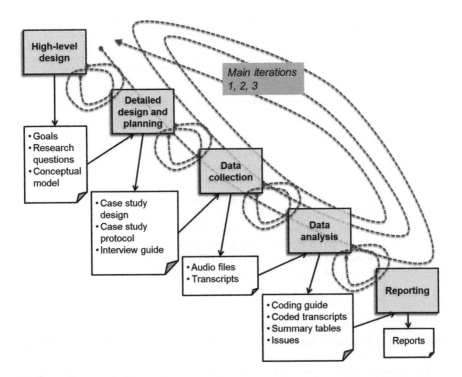

FIGURE 14.3 Overview of the steps that were carried out in both minor iterations and backtracks, as well as in three main iterations.

1. High-level design.
2. Detailed design and planning.
3. Data collection.
4. Data analysis.
5. Reporting.

The high-level design resulted in goals and research question that were negotiated in workshops, over e-mail and phone conversations. The conceptual model was particularly helpful as a vehicle of shared understanding of the scope of the study among the many stakeholders involved.

The detailed design and planning involved several difficult decisions on what to document and to what level of detail. The larger the case study scale, the more the information produced and the more vital the shared understanding among researchers of what is going on.

14.3.1 Methods of Data Collection

The main source of information in this study is the semistructured interviews that we performed with the selected practitioners in the case study companies. To help the

TABLE 14.2   Steps and Topics of the Interview Guide in the REVV Study

Steps	Main Topic
1	The consent information letter is shown, explained, and handed out to the interviewee.
2	Introduction: discussion of the interviewee work situation.
3	The interviewers briefly present the high-level goals of the project. The interviewers ask about the interviewee's view of the RE–V&V alignment.
4	The interviewers presents the initial research view of the RE–V&V alignment phenomenon defined by the conceptual model and asks the interviewee to map this picture to the interviewee's company.
5	General questions about requirements and testing.
6	Questions on quality and functional requirements evaluation.
7	Questions on requirements testing alignment.
8	Questions on change management-related questions.
9	Questions on feedback gathering and measurement.
10	The interviewers ask about possible solutions and ideas.
11	Conclusions.
12	Final remarks.

interviewer to check that the research questions were covered and keep the interview semistructured, we designed an interview guide with question areas.

The interview guide generated in the REVV study design phase was a document containing 30 questions to be asked during the interviews divided in 12 steps. As can be observed in Table 14.2, the interview guide includes 11 steps, although these can be executed at the will of the interviewer in line with the semistructured approach. An interview may start with delivering a consent information letter, which states that the information is confidential and the interviewee is not constraint in participate in the interview. Thereafter, there is a set of warming-up questions, that is, questions on the interviewee work situation. These are followed by a step where the conceptual model is shown, which is used by researchers to explain the topic and terminology. In steps 5–10, there are questions designed to explore the domain in detail, for example, questions about the artifacts, quality requirements, and alignment between requirements and testing. These steps contain questions on key performance indicators and scenarios to be shown to the interviewees. The interview guide ends with two final steps, where questions about possible solutions and ideas and conclusive questions are asked. The interview guide had no constraints regarding the order nor the specific phrasing of the questions. Instead, it was adapted to the specific interview event and the specific dialogue with the interviewee.

The interview guide is summarized in Tables 14.2 and 14.3. The complete interview guide is given in Appendix C.

14.3.2   Case Selection Strategy

One strategy in choosing the companies in the study context is maximum variation sampling in order to have a context where the results can be generalized. Another

TABLE 14.3 Overview of Specific Questions in the Interview Guide

Question Area	Question Subareas
Software requirements	Handling of functional and quality requirements, customer involvement.
Software testing	Handling of testing artifacts, customer involvement, testing of functional and quality requirements.
Alignment between requirements and verification processes	Alignment importance, current alignment method (documents, processes, methods, tools, principles, practices, etc.), alignment responsible, problems and challenges, improvement ideas and expected benefits.
Measurements and feedback gathering	Alignment-related measurements, performance indicators, customer satisfaction evaluation.
Product line engineering	Handling of requirements and testing, maintaining alignment, outsourcing maintaining alignment in case of outsourcing.

strategy is convenience sampling, that is, choosing companies from the industrial collaboration network that the research can gain access to, based on mutual trust. In this study, we chose a combination of both strategies, aiming at a variety of companies with respect to size, type of process, application domain, and type of product. A brainstorming session was held in order to discuss the kind of companies that could be suitable to involve in order to reach our research goals and the possible roles to be interviewed.

14.3.3 Selection of Data

During the execution of the REVV study, we had two strategies of finding interviewees. One strategy was based on discussing with our main contacts at each case company that might be relevant to interview. Another strategy was snowball sampling [162]. The snowball sampling techniques were applied in that by the end of each interview, interviewees were asked if they knew a person or a role in a company whom we could interview with knowledge of the areas of interest. Afterward, we mapped these roles to our conceptual model to see which processes and artifacts they were working with. Our goal was to select interviewees in order to achieve wide coverage of processes and artifacts we were interested in.

14.3.4 Case Study Protocol

The case study protocol is used as a repository to keep all information relating to the design and execution of the study. This includes, for example, the procedures and instruments for the interviews, events such as research meetings, and decisions and actions taken. The protocol is also used to guide the data collection and, therefore, ensure that the intended data are collected. The main sections of the case study protocol are shown in Table 14.4. This document is being updated continuously during the course of the REVV study.

TABLE 14.4   Overview of the Main Sections of the REVV Case Study Protocol

Case Study Protocol	Description
Preamble	Description of the purpose of the protocol, guidelines for data and document storage, and publication plan.
General Procedures	Overview of the research project and the research method. Description of the procedures for conducting each case, including details on contacts and timing.
Research instruments	Interview guides, questionnaires, and so on to be used to ensure consistent data collection.
Data analysis guidelines	Detailed description of data analysis procedures, including data schema, *a priori* codes, and so on.
References	Reference list.
Appendix	Template letter to invite participants, letter of obligations, and case study checklists.

This protocol was inspired by Pervan and Maimbo [135]. An alternative protocol based on Brereton et al.'s work [28] can be found in Table 3.3.

14.3.5 Ethical Considerations

REVV case study project was subject to a nondisclosure agreement between the companies and the Universities. There were long delays in the process of contract signing as one particular partner company had requests on clauses that other companies could not accept. The issues were finally resolved by creating a separate, detached project with a tailored contract.

It was crucial to ensure the secrecy of the interview records and transcripts, and our trust and honor as researchers are at stake if our promise on confidentiality is not kept. In the REVV study, all audio records and transcripts were encrypted, and the names of interviewees were removed from the transcripts before data analysis. All files were stored on a server that required secure network access and encrypted authentication. This was sometimes tedious and induced extra work and technical problems that unexpectedly gave long lead times at several occasions.

In the beginning of each interview, we obtained individual consent from each interviewee through a consent letter that is given in Appendix E. No interviewee expressed concerns after understanding the implication of the consent letter. We believe that the trust that interviewees showed us largely depend on the ethical reputation of the involved research groups and the individual researchers' credibility.

14.4 DATA COLLECTION

REVV study applied a semistructured interview strategy, where the interview guide acted as a checklist to ensure that all important topics were covered. Interviews lasted for about 90 min. Two to three researchers interviewed one practitioner. One of the interviewers led the interview, while the other(s) followed the interview guide, took notes, and asked additional questions.

The entire interviews were transcribed word by word. The only step that was not transcribed was step 1 of the interview guide (see Table 14.2; the complete interview guide is given in Appendix C).

In the transcripts, we added comments that could describe the mood of the interviewee, for example, if the interviewee was annoyed by the question or was laughing. We also added information about the interview (location, participants, date, and place). This activity required long time, each interview (on average 90 min long) required about 15 h of work to be transcribed.

The main artifacts of the data collection phase were interview audio files and transcripts. In the REVV study, the interviews lasted for about 90 min, and the size of audio files (in moderately compressed format) was around 100 MB, thus entailing around 3 GB of audio data for 30 interviews.

The transcripts produced in the REVV study followed predefined rules for denoting questions, answers, and interpretations of the interviewee. For example, we placed everything that was said by the interviewer within square brackets. The interviews were transcribed almost literally, although pauses, sighs, and passages that were obviously out of scope of the interview were not transcribed.

14.5 DATA ANALYSIS

The data analysis in the REVV study was carried out in several rounds in an iterative manner. The main three iterations, as depicted in Figure 14.3, were related to the following achievements:

First main iteration: Creating the coding scheme. The creative process of developing a coding scheme involved several trials and many discussions among researchers. We arrived at a multilevel coding scheme exemplified in Figure 14.4.

Second main iteration: Creating the multilevel coding. This round involved a large part of the effort spent in the data analysis. The coding practices were aligned among the coders through several workshops.

Text	High - and Medium - Level Coding				Comments: Low-Level Coding
	High Level Research Question (1–3)	Medium Level		Group 2 (Cat. A–D)	
		Group I (Cat. 1–13)			
		Primary	Secondary		
A: Yes we tried to have testers in the requirements reviews, so they are there to kind of see, is this requirement testable?	B — experienced and expected benefits	PQ — product quality aspects			Current alignment practice: testers participating in requirements review
A. Variability should be more explicit on a detailed requirements level. A lot of times you have to be very explicit about the things which should be able to vary or not. Traditionally, it has been an area of concern as well. But it should be explicit in detailed requirements.	P — Problems, challenges	RQ — Requirements		PL — Product lines engineering	Variability is not explicitly defined

FIGURE 14.4 Example of how the REVV coding scheme was applied. The multilevel coding was done in a spreadsheet program, enabling sorting and filtering of the data through the codes.

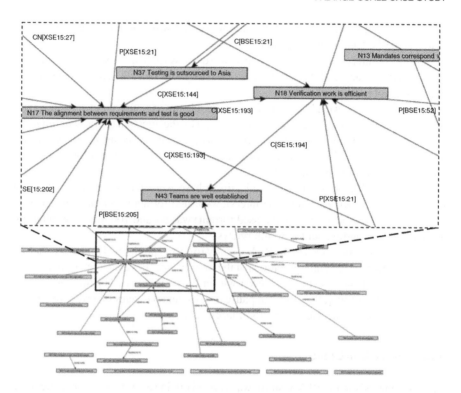

FIGURE 14.5 Example of how the REVV analysis applied graphs to investigate relations between proposition nodes. The figure shows a magnification of a small part of a large proposition network. Propositions were hypothesized based on quotes from interviews that were then grouped by the analyzers. During this creative process, the multilevel coding acted as an indispensable index for navigating among all the numerous quotes that were stored in a spreadsheet. The proposition network diagram was generated from the analysis spreadsheet through a script that was developed to produce an xml file that could be read by a graph layout program.

Third main iteration: Creating proposition nodes and their relations. This round also involved large effort and required a lead time of over 5 months, partly due to an ambitious peer-review approach in order to align the proposition node and relation definitions among the analyzers. An example of a graph of propositions and their relations for one of the interviews is given in Figure 14.5. The graph includes nodes that represent propositions related to RE and V&V alignment that may or may not be true. The edges in the analysis graphs represent relations among propositions to indicate, for example, if the fact that one proposition is true or false might negatively or positively contribute to the truth value of another proposition. The large-scale nature of the study implies a challenge in combining partial analysis with a comprehensive picture, and we foresee that the graph analysis can provide a common set of cross-analysis concepts.

Future iterations: Drawing conclusions from the analysis. This round is by the time of writing in a planning stage for the entire data set. However, partial analysis, conclusion drawing, and reporting are made for a subset of the data [172].

The data analysis was an extensive process that involved a great deal of creativity as well as mutual learning and experience exchange among the involved researchers. The large amount of data as well as the complexity of the phenomena under study means that not one single person can be expert on all transcripts and analysis results. Each involved researcher became over time specialized in parts of the data material, while learning general aspects of the entire data set through knowledge exchange with the other analyzers. This process was sometimes effort-intensive and tedious, but the resulting knowledge and experience gained are rewarding.

14.6 LESSONS LEARNED

14.6.1 Effort Estimation Lessons

A major lesson learned from this large-scale case study is that it is easy to underestimate the effort needed to pull such a large endeavor through. Table 14.5 presents a rough estimate of the hours spent on some of the activities in the REVV study. The interviewing cost also includes traveling.

The numbers in the "Total for study" column of Table 14.5 are obtained by multiplying the number of hours in column "Per interview" by 30, the total number of interviews. As can be seen from Table 14.5 the most labor-intensive activity was the transcription, amounting to approximately 33% of the total cost. Available estimates claim that it takes 6 h to transcribe 1 h of interview [118]. In our case, the interviews were on average 1.5 h long and the transcription was done by nonexperienced transcribers in most of the cases, hence the longer time needed. It is not unreasonable to estimate at up to 10 h for transcribing 1 h of interview. Even though the highest cost is the transcription effort (almost 30%), the total cost of the data analysis phase is also high (24%).

There are several reasons for the high effort needed in the analysis:

1. The high complexity of analyzing large amounts of textual data.
2. The many steps necessary to be taken in order to reducing the data into manageable pieces.
3. The complexity of drawing conclusions from these pieces.

The overall effort so far of the REVV study was approximated to almost 1700 h. The number is a rough approximation and costs related to the communication with companies, arrangement of meetings, and reporting are not included in the table and in the overall cost. Some other activities, such as the design of the research questions

TABLE 14.5   A Partial, Approximate Effort Analysis of Hours Spent by Researchers in the REVV Study

Phase	Activity	Cost		Total cost (%)
		Per interview (h)	Total for study (h)	
Case study design and planning	Design interview guide		150	9
	Validation interview guide		40	2
	Writing case study documentation (design and plan)		100	6
Data collecton	Interviewing	5	150	9
	Transcribing	15	450	27
Analysis and interpretation	Definition of coding scheme		150	9
	Validation of coding scheme		100	6
	Coding	5	150	9
	Coding validation		100	6
	Data extraction and abstraction to issues	5	150	9
	Validation of results	5	150	9
Total		35	1690	100

and the selection of subjects, are also not included in the estimate, as these are very much dependent on the situation.

14.6.2 Design and Planning Lessons

The following lessons learned summarize our main experiences with the definition phase of this large-scale case study:

Scoping of research questions. During the course of the REVV project, the re-searchers involved in the definition phase were many, with different expertise and experiences; this affected the choice of the research questions. The study had a wide scope and as a consequence many research questions and subques-tions were defined. The main challenge in this phase was to find an agreement among the researchers on the research questions and the level of details of them.

Multiple viewpoint benefit. The benefit of having several researchers was to define goals and research questions from many different points of view, reducing the subjectivity of the study.

Conceptual model create shared understanding. The conceptual model itself (Figure 14.2) and, in particular, the discussions needed to create it were key to create a shared understanding among the involved researchers. Researchers typically have a rich and specific knowledge and it is central that they determine and limit the scope of the study and have the same view of that scope. After some initial resistance in establishing common terminology, agreeing on the conceptual model helped focus the subsequent efforts. With many researchers involved, we would have risked that each one would focus on their respective interest, at least subconsciously, instead of the goals of the study. Neither the goals nor the research questions had this limiting and focusing effect; the conceptual model was essential.

Iteration in long and short cycles. The goals and research questions usually evolve during the study and were narrowed to specific research questions during the course of the project after several iterations. We went through the cycle all the way to preliminary analysis of some aspects, when realizing that some research questions needed to be elaborated or reconsidered.

Finding interviewees through organizational understanding. When selecting the context of the study, the roles, and the subjects to be interviewed, it was difficult to know how many roles related to requirements and verification there were and to create a complete list of possible roles to interview. This was due to the complex and wide structure of the companies with many different organizational departments and units. A lesson learned is to investigate the structure of the companies under study during the planning and design phase.

Stable case study protocol. The writing and updating of the case study protocol was challenging. Many events happened during the study and frequent versions of the instruments were produced. The events and the information about the study were spread across all the researchers and it was difficult to keep track of all the events and update the protocol consequently.

Creating shared awareness. To keep all the researchers update of all events and information was challenging. For example, some of the researchers missed informing the researchers geographically located in other universities because the information was judged not complete or not relevant. Therefore, it is important that the researchers have frequent meetings and do cross-checking of all the documents produced in order to have a shared understanding.

14.6.3 Data Collection Lessons

The following lessons learned summarizes our experiences from large-scale data collection:

Combining narrow and wide interests. During interviews, the particular researcher who is leading the interview and asking questions may tend to focus more on the topics she/he is personally interested in, rather than the bigger objectives of the large-scale study. In the REVV study, 2–3 researchers were participating in each interview, and we minimized this threat in the following ways: (a) All applicable questions from the interview guide had to be asked during the interview. (b) Researchers who were attending the interview but not leading it contributed by keeping track of the interview guide coverage to check that no applicable questions were forgotten.

Transcription effort trade-off. It is laborious and tedious to transcribe interviews (see effort estimates in Table 14.5). However, there is a great advantage of having both participated in the interview and produced the transcript, as the in-depth understanding of the text increases along the time spent with the material. When conducting a large-scale study, there is a trade-off between outsourcing the transcription at a lower cost and the lost opportunity of internalizing the data set.

Transcription consistency. When several researchers are involved in the study, it is important that all transcripts follow the same format and include all necessary information regarding interview (place and date), participants, interviewer's questions, and interviewee's answers. The notation used in transcripts should be discussed and agreed upon. It should be easy to distinguish between questions and answers in the transcript. In addition, it is advisable to record the time stamp of each question in the audio file to make it easy to trace transcript sections back to the audio file.

14.6.4 Data Analysis Lessons

The following lessons learned summarizes our experiences from the large-scale data analysis:

Structure and flexibility trade-off. Due to multiple researchers involved as well as the geographical distribution of the researchers, a well-defined process and the supporting artifacts were central in achieving a coherent and consistent analysis results. Very early in the study, it became apparent that we would not pull this through without synchronizing our work using a committed and shared view of our ways of working, analogous to the need of synchronization and commitment needed in large-scale software development. Albeit if a well-defined process is adhered to, it is vital that the process enables flexibility in terms of allowing large and small iterations. An exploratory, qualitative research effort needs flexible ways of working, while a large-scale research in a distributed setting requires structure to be efficient, so this is a delicate trade-off.

Benefit of concrete examples. We found it beneficial to the progress that we used concrete examples when seeking consensus, shared understanding, and making decision. For example, pilot coding of interview transcripts were used by researchers who then came together in synchronization and agreement meetings where differences were analyzed and discussed. This resulted in refinements to the process and artifacts based on real examples rather than abstract argumentation.

Coding consistency. The name of the codes in the coding scheme is not enough; coding guidelines and example codings need to be established to help keep the coding consistent among researchers. The need for coding advice is emphasized as the number of researcher increases.

14.6.5 Reporting Lessons

Some preliminary lessons have also been made in the ongoing REVV study regarding how to conduct the reporting activities in a large-scale case study, although the project has not yet manifested itself in research publications.

Cross-company learning and benchmarking opportunities. By reporting to industry partners in facilitated workshop sessions, we have been able to create appreciated cross-company learning among our industry partners in the REVV project. We also see great potential in opportunities of future benchmarking activities that are enabled, thanks to the comprehensive scope of this project.

Balancing general and personal interests in publication strategies. It is important to establish a research publication strategy that takes into account the special difficulties in a multiresearcher study. In the REVV project, we established a publication strategy to first publish partial results on one case to make a focused and early delivery in line with our first iterations. We then focus in parallel on two types of publications: (1) journal-grade publications with cross-cutting analysis of the entire data set, and (2) the focused publications based on deep cuts into the data to the benefit of the individual thesis projects of the involved doctoral candidates, respectively. We have also agreed upon a set of ethics on the authorship and order of authors on future publications, where all involved researchers can go ahead in parallel and publish based on this data set, but must at any publication instance invite the others to participate. All researchers in the REVV then have the opportunity to either contribute to the text if they want to and be included in the author list or else if they prefer not to contribute to the text or feel that their general contribution to the results are insignificant, they can be in the acknowledgments section.

14.6.6 A General Lesson

The REVV project is ongoing at the time of writing, and the results are still to be published. But even if we have not yet seen the final outcome of this research, all involved researchers have learned many lessons in relation to a large-scale case study research methodology. A general lesson learned is the importance of continuously being aware of the balance of efforts spent, so that investments in laborious tasks, such as transcription and coding, do not take too much of the total research budget in order to save enough resources for the (even) more creative parts related to analysis, theory creation, and taking the results into action in the real world.

EPILOGUE

Wenn jemand eine Reise tut, so kann er was erzählen.[1]

Learning about case study research and also undertaking case study research has been a journey for the authors of this book; a journey now into its second decade. We have not traveled everywhere and of course we have not learned all there is to learn about case study research in software engineering. But as a result of our journey we believe that we have experiences that may be of value to others, and we willingly share those experiences with the empirical software engineering research community.

The learning and maturation of a research community is also a journey. For example, the value of flexibility in study design and the importance of qualitative data may be hard to appreciate and to therefore accept, particularly for those whose approach to research is built on the foundations of the natural sciences, where randomization and quantification are gold standards. It takes time to appreciate the unique and valuable contribution of case study research and, as a result, it understandably takes time to learn to distinguish between, for example, a biased experiment and a stringent case study.

We have "Learn(ed) to do by knowing and to know by doing" according to Dewey's pedagogy[2]. For case study research in software engineering, we now offer practical

---

[1] When somebody makes a journey, he has something to tell. Mattias Claudius, *Urians Reise um die Weld* (1786).
[2] John Dewey, 1859–1952.

Case Study Research in Software Engineering: Guidelines and Examples, First Edition.
Per Runeson, Martin Höst, Austen Rainer, and Björn Regnell.
© 2012 John Wiley & Sons, Inc. Published 2012 by John Wiley & Sons, Inc.

knowledge to those who seek to undertake case study in software engineering, and also to those who seek to learn from the results of others' case studies of software engineering.

As the research discipline of software engineering matures through the research community's development of its own effective research methodology, we hope to see developments in four main directions: (i) Replication studies, whether literal or theoretical, are essential contributors to a comprehensive body of knowledge. We hope that these studies will receive their proper recognition in the community, in the way that original studies are recognized. (ii) Case studies can be an effective approach for technology or methodology evaluation and transfer into industrial practice. We hope that case studies may help researchers and practitioners to "buy into" the broad philosophy and practice of evidence-based software engineering. (iii) Larger and more comprehensive case studies better mirror the large-scale and complexity of real software engineering. We hope to see large-scale studies capable of investigating large scale, complex software engineering phenomena. Such large-scale studies are most likely to be achieved through joint efforts from multiple researchers and research groups. We hope to see an increase in these joint efforts. (iv) Further development of the case study research strategy to fit the particular requirements of software engineering research. We hope to see software engineering case studies that, for example, fully exploit the wide range of types of data available in software engineering.

We welcome you to the journey and hope that you find it as rewarding as we have!

APPENDIX A

CHECKLISTS FOR READING AND REVIEWING CASE STUDIES

A.1 DESIGN OF THE CASE STUDY

1. What is the case and its units of analysis?
2. Are clear objectives, preliminary research questions, hypotheses (if any) defined in advance?
3. Is the theoretical basis—relation to existing literature or other cases—defined?
4. Are the authors? intentions with the research made clear?
5. Is the case adequately defined (size, domain, process, subjects?)?
6. Is a cause–effect relation under study? If yes, is it possible to distinguish the cause from other factors using the proposed design?
7. Does the design involve data from multiple sources (data triangulation), using multiple methods (method triangulation)?
8. Is there a rationale behind the selection of subjects, roles, artifacts, viewpoints, and so on?
9. Is the specified case relevant to validly address the research questions (construct validity)?
10. Is the integrity of individuals/organizations taken into account?

Case Study Research in Software Engineering: Guidelines and Examples, First Edition.
Per Runeson, Martin Höst, Austen Rainer, and Björn Regnell.
© 2012 John Wiley & Sons, Inc. Published 2012 by John Wiley & Sons, Inc.

A.2 DATA COLLECTION

11. Is a case study protocol for data collection and analysis derived (what, why, how, when)? Are procedures for its update defined?

12. Are multiple data sources and collection methods planned (triangulation)?

13. Are measurement instruments and procedures well defined (measurement definitions, interview questions)?

14. Are the planned methods and measurements sufficient to fulfill the objective of the study?

15. Is the study design approved by a review board, and has informed consent obtained from individuals and organizations?

16. Is data collected according to the case study protocol?

17. Is the observed phenomenon correctly implemented (e.g., to what extent is a design method under study actually used)?

18. Is data recorded to enable further analysis?

19. Are sensitive results identified (for individuals, the organization or the project)?

20. Are the data collection procedures well traceable?

21. Does the collected data provide ability to address the research question?

A.3 DATA ANALYSIS AND INTERPRETATION

22. Is the analysis methodology defined, including roles and review procedures?

23. Is a chain of evidence shown with traceable inferences from data to research questions and existing theory?

24. Are alternative perspectives and explanations used in the analysis?

25. Is a cause–effect relation under study? If yes, is it possible to distinguish the cause from other factors in the analysis?

26. Are there clear conclusions from the analysis, including recommendations for practice/further research?

27. Are threats to the validity analyzed in a systematic way and countermeasures taken? (Construct, internal, external, reliability)

A.4 REPORTING AND DISSEMINATION

28. Are the case and its units of analysis adequately presented?

29. Are the objective, the research questions and corresponding answers reported?

30. Are related theory and hypotheses clearly reported?

31. Are the data collection procedures presented, with relevant motivation?

32. Is sufficient raw data presented (e.g., real-life examples, quotations)?
33. Are the analysis procedures clearly reported?
34. Are threats to validity analyses reported along with countermeasures taken to reduce threats?
35. Are ethical issues reported openly (personal intentions, integrity issues, confidentiality)
36. Does the report contain conclusions, implications for practice, and future research?
37. Does the report give a realistic and credible impression?
38. Is the report suitable for its audience, easy to read, and well structured?

A.5 READER'S CHECKLIST

39. Are the objective, research questions, and hypotheses (if applicable) clear and relevant? 1, 2, 5, 29, 30
40. Are the case and its units of analysis well defined? 1, 5, 28
41. Is the suitability of the case to address the research questions clearly motivated? 8, 9, 14
42. Is the case study based on theory or linked to existing literature? 3
43. Are the data collection procedures sufficient for the purpose of the case study (data sources, collection, validation)? 11, 13, 16, 18, 21, 31
44. Is sufficient raw data presented to provide understanding of the case and the analysis? 32
45. Are the analysis procedures sufficient for the purpose of the case study (repeatable, transparent)? 22, 33
46. Is a clear chain of evidence established from observations to conclusions? 6, 17, 20, 23, 25
47. Are threats to validity analyses conducted in a systematic way and are countermeasures taken to reduce threats? 27, 34, 37
48. Is triangulation applied (multiple collection and analysis methods, multiple authors, multiple theories)? 7, 12, 22, 24
49. Are ethical issues properly addressed (personal intentions, integrity, confidentiality, consent, review board approval)? 4, 10, 15, 19, 35
50. Are conclusions, implications for practice and future research, suitably reported for its audience? 26, 29, 36, 37, 38

APPENDIX B

EXAMPLE INTERVIEW INSTRUMENT (XP)

This appendix gives an example of an interview instrument. The instrument was used in the XP case study, which is described in Chapter 10.

General (~10 min)

- Explain about the study, what we are looking for, how they will benefit from the results and that they will be anonymous.
- Subjects personal history in the company (keep short)
- Describe how this project fits into the overall organization structure and product portfolio.

Gate Model (~10 min)

- About the corporate gate model (ask for any documents that can be provided)
- What is required as exit criteria from tollgate 3?
- Which documents are used at tollgate 3?
- How is the tollgate 3 decision taken?

Case Study Research in Software Engineering: Guidelines and Examples, First Edition.
Per Runeson, Martin Höst, Austen Rainer, and Björn Regnell.
© 2012 John Wiley & Sons, Inc. Published 2012 by John Wiley & Sons, Inc.

XP (~15 min)

- XP introduction, how was this performed?
- XP generally, how did it work, describe the most significant aspects.
- What worked well?
- What did not work as well?
- XP experiences compared to your previous way of working.
- Did you adapt XP to fit the gate model?

Adjustments to Gate Model (~20 min)

- How was the tollgate 3 decision affected by you using XP?
- Describe any adaptations of the gate model in general.
- Any adaptations specifically due to XP?
- How was it apparent to people outside your team that you were using XP?
- How did you work with the documents required by the gate model?
- Did you use the software product as a form of communication in itself?
- How did the planning game affect your project?
- How did you perform time estimation?
- Could you start development at a different stage than in your previous projects?
- How was the project affected by working on the most important feature first?
- How did the automatic unit testing affect your project status reporting?
- How was your delivery certainty versus the gate model affected?
- What are the advantages and disadvantages of the gate model?
- What are the advantages and disadvantages of the XP methodology?

Ending (~5 min)

- Other observations? Anything we have not covered?
- Any relevant observations with regards to your specific perspective in the project?

Finish with a brief summary, thank the subject, and confirm that it is ok to come back to the subject with questions in retrospect. Inform about the feedback procedure.

APPENDIX C

EXAMPLE INTERVIEW INSTRUMENT (REVV)

This appendix gives an example of an interview instrument. The instrument was used in the REVV case study, which is described in Chapter 14. This interview instrument was used to guide a pair of interviewers when conducting a semistructured interview. The items where used as checklist items, not imposing a specific order. Instead the interviewers adapted the sequence of interactions to what topics where brought up by the interviewee's. At regular intervals the interviewee checked if there were questions relevant to the interviewee's competence that remained unanswered and, in that case devoted some interview time to those questions. It is an important skill of an interviewer to be able to balance control of with adaption to the current line of interaction. It requires some practice and experience to obtain this skill.

Interview Guide

Version 1.3, Last Changed: Thursday, 20 August 2009

Step 1. The consent information letter is shown, explained, and handed out to the interviewee. [The consent letter is given in Appendix E.]

Step 2. Introduction: discussion of the interviewee's work situation.

Case Study Research in Software Engineering: Guidelines and Examples, First Edition.
Per Runeson, Martin Höst, Austen Rainer, and Björn Regnell.
© 2012 John Wiley & Sons, Inc. Published 2012 by John Wiley & Sons, Inc.

Q1: Tell us about your work.
- Role.
- Daily tasks.
- Responsibility.

Q2: Which roles/other persons do you cooperate the most with in your daily work? How?

Step 3. The interviewer presents the goals of the project.

Q3: Can you tell us your views of RE and V&V alignment?

Q4: What do you see are the challenges in RE and V&V alignment; can you perhaps give some examples?

Step 4. The interviewers present the conceptual model (Figure C.1) and explain their view of RE and V&V alignment.

Q5: How does the conceptual model map to your company?

Step 5. General questions about requirements and testing.

Q6: Which organizational processes, units and roles are involved in requirements management? How are functional and quality requirements artifacts managed?
- Identified.
- Changed.

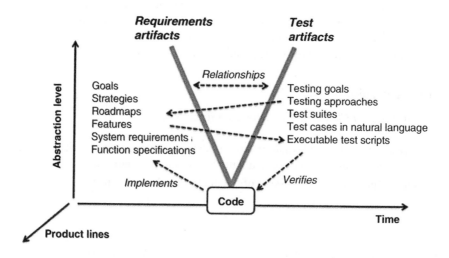

FIGURE C.1 Conceptual model presented to the interviewee in Step 4.

- Measured.
- Prioritized.
- Validated.

Q7: Which organizational processes, units, and roles are involved in testing? How are testing artifacts managed?
- Identified.
- Changed.
- Measured.
- Prioritized.
- Validated.

Q8. Is there a difference between testing functional and quality requirements?

Q9. How is the customer involved in the requirements and testing phases?

Q10. Product line engineering (PLE) questions:
- In a product line engineering context, is there a difference between domain and application engineering with respect to roles and processes?
- How is commonality and variability identified and classified?

Step 6. Questions on quality and functional requirements evaluation.

Q11: What quality requirements are the most important in your work?
- Efficiency/performance/capacity.
- Reliability.
- Safety, security.
- Maintainability, usability.
- Others.

Q12: In which development phases are quality requirements evaluated? How (through measurement, reviews, testing, etc.)?

Q13: What are the pros and cons of working with quality requirements?

Q14: PLE: How are the domain and application quality and functional requirements evaluated?

Step 7. Questions on requirements and testing alignment.

Q15: What is used now to align requirements and testing?
- Documents.
- Processes, methods.
- Tools.
- Principles and practices.

Q16: Who is responsible for alignment (organizational processes, units, and roles)?

Q17: Are testers participating in requirements validation?

Q18: Is the test strategy based on requirement documents?

Q19: Is there a difference between functional and quality requirements with respect to alignment?

Q20: What are the current problems/challenges in terms of alignment? (What does not work now?)

Q21: How is the alignment maintained in case of testing outsourcing?

Q22: PLE: How is the alignment handled if product line engineering?

APPENDIX D

EXAMPLE OF A CODING GUIDE

This appendix include an example of a coding guide from the REVV large-scale case study described in Chapter 14. The coding guide was used to help align the work among 11 involved researchers to minimize the validity threat of inconsistent coding application. The choice of the example included in the coding guide (Table D.5) was important in this alignment process.

D.1 CODING INSTRUCTIONS

- Code as much of the transcript as possible, even if you think that the text is not very relevant to "alignment."[1] Since interviews are focused on alignment, everything said during interview could be useful for further analysis. Code questions as well.
- Codes are prioritized. Please use the priorities in the following way:
  - High level codes—assign the code with highest priority.
  - Medium level codes—choose the code that fits best. Since 2 columns are used for coding ("Primary code" and "Secondary code"), use the "Primary

---

[1] *Definition of alignment.* Alignment between requirements and V&V is how methods, tools, processes, artifacts, measures, roles, practices, and so on, are used in companies in order to coordinate requirements and V&V. It also includes reviews, such as requirements reviews by testers in order to check requirements testability and/or coverage by test cases.

Case Study Research in Software Engineering: Guidelines and Examples, First Edition.
Per Runeson, Martin Höst, Austen Rainer, and Björn Regnell.
© 2012 John Wiley & Sons, Inc. Published 2012 by John Wiley & Sons, Inc.

code" column for the code that fits best, and the "Secondary code" column for second best fitting code. If more than two codes are applicable—write it in "Comments" field.

- Use "Comments" field as much as possible. It can be used for
  - describing additional code categories (if code category is not in the list but you think it is important to have it);
  - listing other applicable codes;
  - explanations of "why" you chose particular code;
  - your interpretations of the text;
  - advices you may have for further analysis.

D.2 CODES

Transcripts should be coded using three levels of codes:

1. *High* abstraction level codes, based on research questions.
2. *Medium* level codes, based on code grouping—code categories.
3. *Low* level code is your interpretation of the text (in the Comments field), which is a statement summary.

D.2.1 High Level Codes: Research Questions

Priority range: 1 (highest)–3 (lowest), see Table D.1.

If several research questions are applicable to the same text statement in a transcript, it should be coded by using the code with the highest priority. The other codes should be mentioned in "Comments" column. Try to use "P" and "B" codes as much as possible.

TABLE D.1   High Level Codes: Research Questions

Prio	Research Question	Description
1	P—problems, challenges	Problems and challenges related to alignment, or absence of alignment. Also includes "bad" practices.
2	B—experienced and expected benefits	Suggestions on the way to improve alignment and expected benefits to be achieved by it. Also, current "good" alignment practices and their benefits.
3	C—current alignment practices	Current practices—the description on how the alignment between requirements and V&V is handled. If a person mentions difficulties or problems related to current practices, then it should be coded as "P—problems, challenges". If the text is about good current practices and their benefits, it should be coded "B—experienced and expected Benefits."

TABLE D.2   Medium Level Codes: Categories

No.	Category Name	Description
1.	TR—traceability	Requirements–testing traceability. Includes not only traceability between requirements and test artifacts, but also traceability among requirements artifacts at different abstraction level, and among testing artifacts, as well as the traceability to code or source.
2.	IC—interactions, communication, people	Anything related to people or units interaction. Also includes interactions with vendors, suppliers. Communication barriers and lack of communication should be assigned this category as well.
3.	FG—feedback gathering	Feedback gathering related information, for example, lessons learnt. Includes information on how feedback from project participants is being gathered and used within organization. This code particularly regards the information on how the interviewees receive feedback about their work. Also includes feedback from postmortem analysis and from process assessments.
4.	OP—organization, processes	Anything related to organization structure, roles, processes, stakeholders. Also includes information regarding organizational change or process change.
5.	CM—configuration management	Information related to configuration management. Includes change management, change control, and so on. Also includes the attitude toward changes. Does not include organization change—organizational or process changes should be assigned "Organization, processes" category.
6.	PQ—product quality aspects	Anything related to product quality. Could include quality requirements, reviews, as well as any quality related issues, such as importance of quality, lack of quality, tradeoffs between quality and functional requirements, system architecture and costs, and so on. Process quality should be assigned "Organization, processes" category.
7.	ME—measurements	Any information about measurements related to artifacts, products, processes, and so on. Includes key performance indicators, measurement needs, and so on.
8.	DE—decisions	Anything related to decision making and distribution. If a particular role is in charge of it, please assign it to the "Organization, processes" category, otherwise use this category. This category is useful for coding information "between chairs"—things that cannot be clearly assigned to a role.

TABLE D.3   Medium Level Codes: Categories—Continued

No.	Category Name	Description
9.	TL—tools	Includes information regarding tools, also presence or absence of tools.
10.	RQ—requirements	Anything related to requirements, excluding change management, process, quality requirements and tools, since these are separate categories.
11.	TE—testing	Anything related to testing, excluding change management, process, and tools.
12.	AR—artifacts	Information about artifacts—all but requirements and testing. Includes architectural, design artifacts, code, and so on.
13.	OT—other	Category that is not among 1–12 categories, but you consider it important. Please describe it in the "Comments" column.

TABLE D.4   Extra Categories

No.	Extra Category Name	Description
A	PL—product lines engineering	Product lines engineering related information—anything regarding variability or product delta or domain (platform, generic components) or application (configurations, customized, unique end products) engineering.
B	OU—outsourcing	Outsourcing related information.
C	OS—open source	Open source related information.
D	AG—agile	Agile software development related information.

D.2.2 Medium Level Codes: Categories

Text should be assigned one or two of the following categories. Text is coded in two columns—"Primary code" and "Secondary code":

- If only one code is applicable—write it down in the "Primary code" column.
- If more than one code is applicable—write the best fitting code into "Primary code" column, and the second best suitable into the "Secondary code" column.
- If more than two codes are applicable—write it in "Comments" field.

If the category you want to assign is not among 1–12 categories in Tables D.2 and D.3, please use the 13th category "Other" and describe it in the "Comments" column.

Furthermore, when applicable, text should be assigned one of these extra categories, see Table D.4. Use these codes only in cases when it is clear that information falls into these categories.

D.2.3 Coding Example

A part of a coding example is presented in Table D.5

TABLE D.5 Coding Example

Text	High Level — Research Question (1-3)	Medium Level — Group 1 (cat. 1–13) Primary	Medium Level — Group 1 (cat. 1–13) Secondary	Medium Level — Group 2 (cat. A–D)	Comments: Low Level Coding
A: Yes we tried to have testers in the requirements reviews, so they are there to kind of see, is this requirement testable?	B—experienced and expected benefits	PQ—product quality aspects			Current alignment practice: testers participating in requirements review
A. Variability should be more explicit on a detailed requirements level. A lot of times you have to be very explicit about the things that should be able to vary or not. Traditionally, it has been an area of concern as well. But it should be explicit in detailed requirements.	P—problems, challenges	RQ—requirements		PL—product lines engineering	Variability is not explicitly defined

217

APPENDIX E

EXAMPLE OF A CONSENT
INFORMATION LETTER

This appendix gives an example of a consent information letter that can be tailored to other case studies. A consent letter is handed out to interview subjects in a case study in order to make explicit and clear the ethical principles that is committed by the researchers. After handing over the signed letter, explicit consent is obtained from the interviewee. This enables researchers to use the data gathered in the interview in a responsible manner, for example, while protecting the anonymity of the interviewee, as stated in the consent letter. This consent letter was used in the REVV case study, which is described in Chapter 14.

Information to Interviewees

This interview is conducted within the EASE industrial excellence center. EASE is a consortium between Lund University, Blekinge Institute of Technology, and <List of industry partners>.

A contract is established that the Official Secrets Act under Swedish Law (1980:100) shall apply, meaning that information stated to be confidential is kept as such.

Prof. Per Runeson is the Director of the center and can be contacted at per.runeson@cs.lth.se; +46 46 222 93 25.

Case Study Research in Software Engineering: Guidelines and Examples, First Edition.
Per Runeson, Martin Höst, Austen Rainer, and Björn Regnell.
© 2012 John Wiley & Sons, Inc. Published 2012 by John Wiley & Sons, Inc.

We would like to emphasize that

- your participation is entirely voluntary;
- you are free to refuse to answer any question;
- you are free to withdraw at any time.

The interview will be kept strictly confidential and will be made available only to members of the research team of the study, or in case external quality assessment takes place, to assessors under the same confidentiality conditions. Excerpts from the interview may be part of a final research report, but under no circumstances will your name or any identifying characteristic be included in the report.

Lund, May 13, 2009

<Signature>
Per Runeson
Director

REFERENCES

1 ISO/IEC 15939: Software Engineering—Software Measurement Process. Technical Report, International Organization for Standardization, 2001.

2 L. M. Abdullah and J. M. Verner. Outsourced strategic it systems development risk. In *Proceedings of the Third International Conference on Research Challenges in Information Science*, 2009, pp. 275–286.

3 H. Alexander and B. Potter. Case study: the use of formal specification and rapid prototyping to establish product feasibility. *Information and Software Technology*, 29(7): 388–394, 1987.

4 J. W. Anastas and M. L. MacDonald. *Research Design for the Social Work and the Human Services*. Lexington, New York, 1994.

5 C. Andersson. A replicated empirical study of a selection method for software reliability growth models. *Empirical Software Engineering*, 12(2):161–182, 2007.

6 C. Andersson and P. Runeson. A replicated quantitative analysis of fault distributions in complex software systems. *IEEE Transactions on Software Engineering*, 33(5):273–286, 2007.

7 C. Andersson and P. Runeson. A spiral process model for case studies on software quality monitoring—method and metrics. *Software Process: Improvement and Practice*, 12(2):125–140, 2007.

8 A. A. Andrews and A. S. Pradhan. Ethical issues in empirical software engineering: the limits of policy. *Empirical Software Engineering*, 6(2):105–110, 2001.

Case Study Research in Software Engineering: Guidelines and Examples, First Edition.
Per Runeson, Martin Höst, Austen Rainer, and Björn Regnell.
© 2012 John Wiley & Sons, Inc. Published 2012 by John Wiley & Sons, Inc.

9   A. Aurum, H. Petersson, and C. Wohlin. State-of-the-art: software inspections after 25 years. *Software Testing, Verification and Reliability*, 12(3):1099–1689, 2001.

10   D. Avison, R. Baskerville, and M. Myers. Controlling action research projects. *Information Technology & People*, 14(1):28–45, 2001.

11   N. Baddoo and T. Hall. Motivators of software process improvement: an analysis of practitioners' views. *Journal of Systems and Software*, 62(2):85–96, 2002.

12   N. Baddoo and T. Hall. De-motivators of software process improvement: an analysis of practitioners' views. *Journal of Systems and Software*, 66(1):23–22, 2003.

13   V. R. Basili and F. Shull. Evolving defect "folklore": a cross-study analysis of software defect behavior. In M. Li, B. Boehm, and L. Osterweil, editors, *Software Process Workshop*, Number 3840 in *LNCS*. Springer-Verlag, 2005, pp. 1–9.

14   V. R. Basili, F. Shull, and F. Lanubile. Building knowledge through families of experiments. *IEEE Transactions on Software Engineering*, 25(4):456–473, 1999.

15   V. R. Basili and D. M. Weiss. A methodology for collecting valid software engineering data. *IEEE Transactions on Software Engineering*, 10(6):728–737, 1984.

16   R. L. Baskerville and A. T. Wood-Harper. A critical perspective on action research as a method for information systems research. *Journal of Information Technology*, 11(3):235–246, 1996.

17   K. Beck. Embracing change with extreme programming. *Computer*, 32(10):70–77, 1999.

18   U. Becker-Kornstaedt. Descriptive software process modeling—how to deal with sensitive process information. *Empirical Software Engineering*, 6:353–367, 2001.

19   I. Benbasat, D. K. Goldstein, and M. Mead. The case research strategy in studies of information systems. *MIS Quarterly*, 11(3):369, 1987.

20   T. Berling, C. Andersson, M. Höst, and C. Nyberg. Adaptation of a system dynamics model template for code development and testing to an industrial project. In *Proceedings of the Software Process Simulation Modeling Workshop*, Portland, OR, USA, 2003.

21   E. Bjarnason, K. Wnuk, and B. Regnell. Overscoping: reasons and consequences—a case study on decision making in software product management. In *4th International Workshop on Software Product Management*. IEEE, Sydney, Australia, September 2010.

22   B. W. Boehm. A spiral model of software development and enhancement. *Computer*, 21(5):61–72, 1988.

23   B. W. Boehm and R. Ross. Theory-w software project management: a case study. In *Proceedings of the 10th International Conference on Software Engineering*, 1988, pp. 30–40.

24   H. Bouwman and E. Faber. Case Study Protocol B4U. Technical Report TI/RS/2003/008, Telematica Instituut, Technische Universiteit Delft, February 2003.

25   M. G. Bradac, D. E. Perry, and L. G. Votta. Prototyping a process monitoring experiment. In *Proceedings of the 15th International Conference on Software Engineering*. IEEE Computer Society Press, 1993, pp. 155–165.

26   M. G. Bradac, D. E. Perry, and L. G. Votta. Prototyping a process monitoring experiment. *IEEE Transactions on Software Engineering*, 20(10):774–784, 1994.

27   L. Bratthall and M. Jørgensen. Can you trust a single data source exploratory software engineering case study? *Empirical Software Engineering*, 7(1):9–26, 2002.

28   P. Brereton, B. A. Kitchenham, and D. Budgen. Using a protocol template for case study planning. In *Proceedings of the 12th International Conference on Evaluation and Assessment in Software Engineering*, University of Bari, Italy, 2008.

29   P. Brereton, B. A. Kitchenham, D. Budgen, M. Turner, and M. Khalil. Lessons from applying the systematic literature review process within the software engineering domain. *Journal of Systems and Software*, 80(4):571–583, 2007.

30   L. C. Briand, J. Wüst, S. V. Ikonomovski, and H. Lounis. Investigating quality factors in object-oriented designs: an industrial case study. In *Proceedings of the 21st International Conference on Software Engineering*. IEEE Computer Society, 1999, p. 345.

31   J. P. Campbell, R. L. Daft, and C. L. Hulin. *What to study: generating and developing research questions*, 1st edition. Sage, 1982.

32   T. D. Cook and D. T. Campbell. *Quasi-Experimentation. Design & Analysis Issues for Field Studies*. Houghton Mifflin Company, 1979.

33   R. G. Cooper. *Winning at New Products: Accelerating the Process from Idea to Launch*, 3rd edition. Perseus, 2001.

34   J. Corbin and C. Strauss. *Basics of Qualitative Research*, 3rd edition. Sage, 2008.

35   P. B. Corcoran. Case studies, make-your-case studies, and case stories: a critique of case-study methodology in sustainability in higher education. *Environmental Education Research*, 10(1):7–21, 2004.

36   D. S. Cruzes and T. Dybå. Research synthesis in software engineering: a tertiary study. *Information and Software Technology*, 53(5):440–455, 2011.

37   B. Curtis, H. Krasner, and N. Iscoe. A field study of the software design process for large systems. *Communications of the ACM*, 31(11):1268–1287, 1988.

38   N. Dalkey and O. Helmer. An experimental application of the delphi method to the use of experts. *Management Science*, 9(3):458–467, 1963.

39   D. Damian and J. Chisan. An empirical study of the complex relationships between requirements engineering processes and other processes that lead to payoffs in productivity, quality, and risk management. *IEEE Transactions on Software Engineering*, 32(7):433–453, 2006.

40   K. Deng and S. G. MacDonell. Maximizing data retention from the ISBSG repository. In *Proceedings of the 12th International Conference on Evaluation and Assessment in Software Engineering*, University of Bari, Italy, 2008.

41   O. Dieste, A. Grimán, and N. Juristo. Developing search strategies for detecting relevant experiments. *Empirical Software Engineering*, 14:513–539, 2009.

42   T. Dingsøyr and N. B. Moe. The impact of employee participation on the use of an electronic process guide: a longitudinal case study. *IEEE Transactions on Software Engineering*, 34(2):212–225, 2008.

43   Y. Dittrich, M. John, J. Singer, and B. Tessem. For the special issue on qualitative software engineering research. *Information and Software Technology*, 49(6):531–539, 2007.

44   Y. Dittrich, K. Rönkkö, J. Eriksson, C. Hansson, and O. Lindeberg. Cooperative method development. *Empirical Software Engineering*, 13(3):231–260, 2007.

45   M. Dixon-Woods, A. Booth, and A. J. Sutton. Synthesizing qualitative research: a review of published reports. *Qualitative Research*, 7(3):375–422, 2007.

46   T. Dybå and T. Dingsøyr. Empirical studies of agile software development: a systematic review. *Information and Software Technology*, 50(9-10):833–859, 2008.

47   S. Easterbrook, J. Singer, M.-A. Storey, and D. Damian. Selecting empirical methods for software engineering research. In F. Shull, J. Singer, and D. I. Sjøberg, editors, *Guide to Advanced Empirical Software Engineering*. Springer-Verlag, London, 2008.

48   K. M. Eisenhardt. Building theories from case study research. *The Academy of Management Review*, 14(4):532, 1989.

49   K. El-Emam. Ethics and open source. *Empirical Software Engineering*, 6:291–292, 2001.

50   E. Engström and P. Runeson. Software product line testing—a systematic mapping study. *Information and Software Technology*, 53(1):2–13, 2011.

51   E. Engström, P. Runeson, and M. Skoglund. A systematic review on regression test selection techniques. *Information and Software Technology*, 52(1):14–30, 2010.

52   L. Esterhuizen. Doing Case Studies for the Refugee Sector; A DIY Handbook for Agencies and Practitioners. Technical Report, The Information Centre about Asylum and Refugees in the UK (ICAR), International Policy Institute, King's College London, 2004.

53   N. Fenton and N. Ohlsson. Quantitative analysis of faults and failures in a complex software system. *IEEE Transactions on Software Engineering*, 26(8):797–814, 2000.

54   N. Fenton and S. L. Pfleeger. *Software Metrics: A Rigorous and Practical Approach*, 2nd (revised printing) edition. PWS Publishing Company, London, 1997.

55   B. Flynn. Empirical research methods in operations management. *Journal of Operations Management*, 9(2):250–284, 1990.

56   B. Flyvbjerg. Five misunderstandings about case-study research. In *Qualitative Research Practice*, concise paperback edition. Sage, 2007, pp. 390–404.

57   S. Freudenberg and H. Sharp. The top 10 burning research questions from practitioners. *IEEE Software*, 27(5):8–9, 2010.

58   B. G. Glaser and A. Strauss. *Discovery of Grounded Theory. Strategies for Qualitative Research*. Sociology Press, 1967.

59   R. L. Glass, V. Ramesh, and I. Vessey. An analysis of research in computing disciplines. *Communications of the ACM*, 47(6):89–94, 2004.

60   R. L. Glass, I. Vessey, and S. A. Conger. Software tasks: intellectual or clerical? *Information and Management*, 23(4):183–191, 1992.

61   R. L. Glass, I. Vessey, and V. Ramesh. Research in software engineering: an analysis of the literature. *Information and Software Technology*, 44:491–506, 2001.

62   M. W. Godfrey and Q. Tu. Evolution in open source software: a case study. In *Proceedings on the International Conference on Software Maintenance*, 2000, pp. 131–142.

63   O. S. Gómez, N. Juristo, and S. Vegas. Replications types in experimental disciplines. In *Proceeding of the 4th International Symposium on Empirical Software Engineering and Measurement*, 2010.

64   T. Gorschek, P. Garre, S. Larsson, and C. Wohlin. A model for technology transfer in practice. *IEEE Software*, 23(6):88–95, 2006.

65   D. Gotterbarn. Ethics in qualitative studies of commercial software enterprises ethical analysis. *Empirical Software Engineering*, 6:301–304, 2001. 10.1023/A:1011970531432.

66   T. Hall and V. Flynn. Ethical issues in software engineering research: a survey of current practice. *Empirical Software Engineering*, 6:305–317, 2001.

67   T. Hall, A. W. Rainer, N. Baddoo, and S. Beecham. An empirical study of maintenance issues within process improvement programmes in the software industry. In *Proceedings of the IEEE International Conference on Software Maintenance*, 2001, pp. 422–430.

68   J. Hannay, D. Sjøberg, and T. Dybå. A systematic review of theory use in software engineering experiments. *IEEE Transactions on Software Engineering*, 33(2):87–107, 2007.

69   W. Hayes. Research synthesis in software engineering: a case for meta-analysis. In *Proceedings of the 6th International Software Metrics Symposium*, 1999, pp. 143–151.

70   P. Herceg. Defining Useful Technology Evaluations. Technical Report MTR070061R1, MITRE Corporation, September 2007.

71   A. R. Hevner, S. T. March, J. Park, and S. Ram. Design science in information systems research. *MIS Quarterly*, 28(1):75–105, 2004.

72   N. E. Holt. A systematic review of case studies in software engineering. Master's thesis, University of Oslo, Department of Informatics, May 2006.

73   M. Höst and P. Runeson. Checklists for software engineering case study research. In *Proceedings of the 1st International Symposium on Empirical Software Engineering and Measurement*, 2007, pp. 479–481.

74   S. Hove and B. Anda. Experiences from conducting semi-structured interviews in empirical software engineering research. In *Proceedings of the 11th IEEE International Software Metrics Symposium*, 2005, pp. 1–10.

75   J. H. Iversen, L. Mathiassen, and P. A. Nielsen. Managing risk in software process improvement: an action research approach. *MIS Quarterly*, 28(3):395–433, 2004.

76   A. S. Jadhav and R. M. Sonar. Evaluating and selecting software packages: a review. *Information and Software Technology*, 51:555–563, 2009.

77   A. Jedlitschka and D. Pfahl. Reporting guidelines for controlled experiments in software engineering. In *Proceedings of the International Symposium on Empirical Software Engineering*, 2005.

78   P. M. Johnson, H. Kou, M. Paulding, Q. Zhang, A. Kagawa, and T. Yamashita. Improving software development management through software project telemetry. *IEEE Software*, 22(4):76–85, 2005.

79   N. Juristo and S. Vegas. Using differences among replications of software engineering experiments to gain knowledge. In *Proceeding of the 3rd International Symposium on Empirical Software Engineering and Measurement*, 2009, pp. 356–366.

80   S. H. Kan. *Metrics and Models in Software Quality Engineering*. Addison Wesley, 2003.

81   A. Karahasanović, B. Anda, E. Arisholm, S. E. Hove, M. Jørgensen, D. Sjøberg, and R. Welland. Collecting feedback during software engineering experiments. *Empirical Software Engineering*, 10(2):113–147, 2005.

82   L. Karlsson, B. Regnell, and T. Thelin. Case studies in process improvement through retrospective analysis of release planning decisions. *International Journal of Software Engineering and Knowledge Engineering (IJSEKE)*, 16(6):885–916, 2006.

83   D. Karlström. Integrating management and engineering processes in software product development. PhD thesis, Lund University, 2004.

84   D. Karlström and P. Runeson. Decision support for extreme programming introduction and practice selection. In *Proceedings of the 14th International Conference on Software Engineering and Knowledge Engineering*, 2002, pp. 835–841.

85   D. Karlström and P. Runeson. Combining agile methods with stage–gate project management. *IEEE Software*, 22(3):43–49, 2005.

86   D. Karlström and P. Runeson. Integrating agile software development into stage–gate managed product development. *Empirical Software Engineering*, 11(2):203–225, 2006.

87   J. Kasurinen, O. Taipale, and K. Smolander. Test case selection and prioritization: risk-based or design-based? In *Proceedings of the 4th International Symposium on Empirical Software Engineering and Measurement*, ESEM '10, 2010, pp. 10:1–10:10.

88   I. M. Kellner, J. R. Madachy, and M. D. Raffo. Software process simulation modeling: why? what? how? *Journal of Systems and Software*, 46(2–3):91–105, 1999.

89   B. A. Kitchenham. DESMET: A Method for Evaluating Software Engineering Methods and Tools. Technical Report TR96-09, Keele University, UK, August 1996.

90   B. A. Kitchenham. Evaluating software engineering methods and tools, part 1: the evaluation context and evaluation methods. *SIGSOFT Software Engineering Notes*, 21(1): 11–14, 1996.

91   B. A. Kitchenham. Evaluating software engineering methods and tools, part 2: selecting an appropriate evaluation method—technical criteria. *SIGSOFT Software Engineering Notes*, 21(2):11–15, 1996.

92   B. A. Kitchenham. Evaluating software engineering methods and tools, part 3: selecting an appropriate evaluation method—practical issues. *SIGSOFT Software Engineering Notes*, 21(4):9–12, 1996.

93   B. A. Kitchenham. Evaluating software engineering methods and tools, part 7: planning feature analysis evaluation. *SIGSOFT Software Engineering Notes*, 22(4):21–24, 1997.

94   B. A. Kitchenham. The role of replications in empirical software engineering—a word of warning. *Empirical Software Engineering*, 13:219–221, 2008. 10.1007/s10664-008-9061-0.

95   B. A. Kitchenham, H. Al-Khilidar, M. A. Babar, M. Berry, K. Cox, J. Keung, F. Kurniawati, M. Staples, H. Zhang, and L. Zhu. Evaluating guidelines for reporting empirical software engineering studies. *Empirical Software Engineering*, 13(1):97–121, 2007.

96   B. A. Kitchenham, D. Budgen, and P. Brereton. Using mapping studies as the basis for further research—a participant–observer case study. *Information and Software Technology*, 53(6):638–651, 2011.

97   B. A. Kitchenham and S. Charters. Guidelines for Performing Systematic Literature Reviews in Software Engineering (version 2.3). Technical Report EBSE, Technical Report EBSE-2007-01, Keele University and Durham University, July 2007.

98   B. A. Kitchenham, T. Dybå, and M. Jørgensen. Evidence-based software engineering. In *Proceedings of the 26th International Conference on Software Engineering*. Edinburgh, Scotland, UK, 2004, pp. 273–281.

99   B. A. Kitchenham, R. T. Hughes, and S. G. Linkman. Modeling software measurement data. *IEEE Transactions on Software Engineering*, 27(9):788–804, 2001.

100   B. A. Kitchenham, D. R. Jeffery, and C. Connaughton. Misleading metrics and unsound analyses. *IEEE Software*, 24:73–78, 2007.

101   B. A. Kitchenham and L. Jones. Evaluating software engineering methods and tools, part 5: the influence of human factors. *SIGSOFT Software Engineering Notes*, 22(1):13–15, 1997.

102 B. A. Kitchenham and L. Jones. Evaluating software engineering methods and tools, part 6: identifying and scoring features. *SIGSOFT Software Engineering Notes*, 22(2):16–18, 1997.

103 B. A. Kitchenham and L. Jones. Evaluating software engineering methods and tools, part 8: analysing a feature analysis evaluation. *SIGSOFT Software Engineering Notes*, 22(5):10–12, 1997.

104 B. A. Kitchenham, S. G. Linkman, and D. Law. DESMET: a methodology for evaluating software engineering methods and tools. *Computing and Control Engineering Journal*, 8(3):120–126, 1997.

105 B. A. Kitchenham, S. L. Pfleeger, L. M. Pickard, P. W. Jones, D. Hoaglin, K. El Emam, and J. Rosenberg. Preliminary guidelines for empirical research in software engineering. *IEEE Transactions on Software Engineering*, 28(8):721–734, 2002.

106 B. A. Kitchenham and L. M. Pickard. Evaluating software engineering methods and tools, part 10: designing and running a quantitative case study. *SIGSOFT Software Engineering Notes*, 23(3):20–22, 1998.

107 B. A. Kitchenham and L. M. Pickard. Evaluating software engineering methods and tools, part 11: analysing quantitative case studies. *SIGSOFT Software Engineering Notes*, 23(4):18–20, 1998.

108 B. A. Kitchenham and L. M. Pickard. Evaluating software engineering methods and tools, part 9: quantitative case study methodology. *SIGSOFT Software Engineering Notes*, 23(1):24–26, 1998.

109 B. A. Kitchenham, L. M. Pickard, and S. Pfleeger. Case studies for method and tool evaluation. *IEEE Software*, 12(4):52–62, 1995.

110 B. A. Kitchenham, R. Pretorius, D. Budgen, P. Brereton, M. Turner, M. Niazi, and S. Linkman. Systematic literature reviews in software engineering—a tertiary study. *Information and Software Technology*, 52(8):792–805, 2010.

111 H. K. Klein and M. D. Myers. A set of principles for conducting and evaluating interpretive field studies in information systems. *MIS Quarterly*, 23(1):67, 1999.

112 J. Kontio, J. Bragge, and L. Lehtola. The focus group method as an empirical tool in software engineering. In F. Shull, J. Singer, and D. Sjøberg, editors, *Guide to Advanced Empirical Software Engineering*. Springer, 2008.

113 R. Kyburz-Graber. Does case-study methodology lack rigour? The need for quality criteria for sound case-study research, as illustrated by a recent case in secondary and higher education. *Environmental Education Research*, 10(1):53–65, 2004.

114 R. Larsson. Case survey methodology: Quantitative analysis of patterns across case studies. *The Academy of Management Journal*, 36(6):1515–1546, 1993.

115 A. S. Lee. A scientific methodology for MIS case studies. *MIS Quarterly*, 13(1):33, 1989.

116 L. Lehtola, M. Kauppinen, and S. Kujala. Requirements prioritization challenges in practice. In *Product Focused Software Process Improvement*, Number 3009 in *LNCS*, Springer-Verlag, 2004, pp. 497–508.

117 T. C. Lethbridge. Mixing software engineering research and development—what needs ethical review and what does not? *Empirical Software Engineering*, 6:319–321, 2001.

118 T. C. Lethbridge, S. E. Sim, and J. Singer. Studying software engineers: data collection techniques for software field studies. *Empirical Software Engineering*, 10:311–341, 2005.

119 K. Lewin. Action research and minority problems. *Journal of Social Issues*, 2:34–2:36, 1946.

120 J. Li, N. B. Moe, and T. Dybå. Transition from a plan-driven process to scrum: a longitudinal case study on software quality. In *Proceedings of the 2010 ACM-IEEE International Symposium on Empirical Software Engineering and Measurement*, ESEM '10. ACM, New York, NY, USA, 2010, pp. 1–13.

121 M. Lindvall, D. Muthig, A. Dagnino, C. Wallin, M. Stupperich, D. Kiefer, J. May, and T. Kahkonen. Agile software development in large organizations. *Computer*, 37(12): 26–34, 2004.

122 J. Lonchamp. A structured conceptual and terminological framework for software process engineering. In *Proceedings of 2nd International Conference on Software Process: Continuous Software Process Improvement*. IEEE Computer Society Press, Berlin, Germany, 1993, pp. 41–53.

123 W. A. Lucas. The Case Survey Method: Aggregating Case Experience. Technical Report R-1515-RC, The Rand Corporation, Santa Monica, CA, 1974.

124 D. Martin, J. Rooksby, M. Rouncefield, and I. Sommerville. 'Good' organisational reasons for 'bad' software testing: an ethnographic study of testing in a small software company. In *Proceedings of the 29th International Conference on Software Engineering*, 2007, pp. 602–611.

125 R. Matulevičius. Validating an evaluation framework for requirements engineering tools. In *Information Modeling Methods and Methodologies*, Idea Group Publishing, 2005, pp. 148–174.

126 L. McLeod, S. MacDonell, and B. Doolin. Qualitative research on software development: a longitudinal case study methodology. *Empirical Software Engineering*, 16(4):430–459, 2011.

127 J. Miller. Applying meta-analytical procedures to software engineering experiments. *Journal of Systems and Software*, 54(1):29–39, 2000.

128 J. Miller. Statistical significance testing: a panacea for software technology experiments? *Journal of Systems and Software*, 73:183–192, October 2004.

129 J. Miller. Replicating software engineering experiments: a poisoned chalice or the holy grail. *Information and Software Technology*, 47(4):233–244, 2005.

130 D. C. Montgomery. *Design and Analysis of Experiments*, 3rd edition. Wiley, 1991.

131 W. J. Orlikowski. Case tools as organizational change: investigating incremental and radical changes in systems development. *MIS Quarterly*, 17(3):309–340, 1993.

132 A. Oručević-Alagić and M. Höst. Analysis of software transition from proprietary to open source. In *Proceedings of OSS 2010—International Conference on Open Source Systems*, 2010.

133 S. Owen, P. Brereton, and D. Budgen. Protocol analysis: a neglected practice. *Communications of the ACM*, 49(2):117–122, 2006.

134 D. E. Perry, S. E. Sim, and S. Easterbrook. Case studies for software engineers. In *29th Annual IEEE/NASA Software Engineering Workshop—Tutorial Notes*, 2005, pp. 96–159.

135 G. Pervan and H. Maimbo. Designing a case study protocol for application in is research. In *Proceedings of the 9th Pacific Conference on Information Systems*, 2005, pp. 1281–1292.

136 K. Petersen, R. Feldt, S. Mujtaba, and M. Mattsson. Systematic mapping studies in software engineering. In *Proceeding of the 12th International Conference on Evaluation and Assessment in Software Engineering*, University of Bari, Italy, 2008.

137 K. Petersen and C. Wohlin. A comparison of issues and advantages in agile and incremental development between state of the art and an industrial case. *Journal of Systems and Software*, 82(9):1479–1490, 2009.

138 K. Petersen and C. Wohlin. Context in industrial software engineering research. In *Proceeding of the 3rd International Symposium on Empirical Software Engineering and Measurement*, 2009, pp. 401–404.

139 S. L. Pfleeger. Understanding and improving technology transfer in software engineering. *Journal of Systems and Software*, 47:111–124, 1999.

140 L. Pickard, B. A. Kitchenham, and P. Jones. Combining empirical results in software engineering. *Information and Software Technology*, 40(14):811–821, 1998.

141 F. Pino, F. García, and M. Piattini. Software process improvement in small and medium software enterprises: a systematic review. *Software Quality Journal*, 16:237–261, 2008.

142 H. Post, C. Sinz, F. Merz, T. Gorges, and T. Kropf. Linking functional requirements and software verification. In *17th IEEE International Conference on Requirements Engineering*. IEEE Computer Society, 2009, pp. 295–302.

143 A. Rainer, T. Hall and N. Baddoo, Persuading Developers to 'Buy into' Software Process Improvement: Local Opinion and Empirical Evidence, International Symposium on Empirical Software Engineering, 2003, pp. 326–335.

144 A. W. Rainer. *An Empirical Investigation of Software Project Schedule Behaviour*. Doctoral thesis, Bournemouth University, 1999.

145 A. W. Rainer. An empirical investigation of software project schedule behaviour. *Empirical Software Engineering*, 5(1):75–77, 2000.

146 A. W. Rainer. Representing the behaviour of software projects using multi-dimensional timelines. *Information and Software Technology*, 52(11):1217–1228, 2010.

147 A. W. Rainer. The longitudinal, chronological case study research strategy: a definition and an example from IBM Hursley Park. *Information and Software Technology*, 53(7):730–746, 2011.

148 A. W. Rainer and S. Beecham. A follow-up empirical evaluation of evidence based software engineering by undergraduate students. In *Proceeding of the 12th International Conference on Evaluation and Assessment in Software Engineering*, University of Bari, Italy, 2008.

149 A. W. Rainer, S. Beecham, and C. Sanderson. An assessment of published evaluations of requirements management tools. In *Proceedings of the 13th International Conference on Evaluation and Assessment in Software Engineering*, Durham, UK, 2009.

150 A. W. Rainer and S. Gale. Evaluating the quality and quantity of data on open source software projects. In *Proceedings of the 1st International Conference on Open Source Systems*, Genova, Italy, 2005.

151 A. W. Rainer and T. Hall. An analysis of some 'core studies' of software process improvement. *Software Process: Improvement and Practice*, 6(4):169–187, 2001.

152 A. W. Rainer and T. Hall. Identifying the causes of poor progress in software projects. In *Proceedings of the 10th International Symposium on Software Metrics*, 2004.

153 A. W. Rainer, T. Hall, N. Baddoo, and D. Wilson. An overview of the practitioners, processes and products project. In *Proceedings of the 6th Annual Conference of the U.K. Academy of Information Sciences*, Portsmouth, UK, 2001.

154 A. W. Rainer and M. J. Shepperd. Investigating software project schedule behaviour. In *Proceedings of the 2nd International Conference on Empirical Assessment and Evaluation in Software Engineering*, Keele, UK, 1998.

155   A. W. Rainer and M. J. Shepperd. Re-planning for a successful project. In *Proceedings of the 6th International Software Metrics Symposium*, Boca Raton, Florida, 1999.

156   B. Regnell, P. Beremark, and O. Eklundh. A market-driven requirements engineering process—results from an industrial improvement programme. *Requirements Engineering*, 3(2):121–129, 1998.

157   B. Regnell, R. Berntsson Svensson, and K. Wnuk. Can we beat the complexity of very large-scale requirements engineering? In B. Paech and C. Rolland, editors, *Requirements Engineering: Foundation for Software Quality*, Volume 5025 of *Lecture Notes in Computer Science*. Springer, Berlin/Heidelberg, 2008, pp. 123–128.

158   B. Regnell, M. Höst, J. Natt och Dag, P. Beremark, and T. Hjelm. An industrial case study on distributed prioritisation in Market-Driven requirements engineering for packaged software. *Requirements Engineering*, 6(1):51–62, 2001.

159   B. Regnell, M. Höst, F. Nilsson, and H. Bengtsson. A measurement framework for team level assessment of innovation capability in early requirements engineering. In W. Aalst, J. Mylopoulos, N. M. Sadeh, M. J. Shaw, C. Szyperski, F. Bomarius, M. Oivo, P. Jaring, and P. Abrahamsson, editors, *Product-Focused Software Process Improvement*, Volume 32 of *Lecture Notes in Business Information Processing*. Springer, Berlin/Heidelberg, 2009, pp. 71–86.

160   C. K. Riemenschneider, B. C. Hardgrave, and F. D. Davis. Explaining software developer acceptance of methodologies: a comparison of five theoretical models. *IEEE Transactions on Software Engineering*, 28(12):1135–1145, 2002.

161   H. Robinson, J. Segal, and H. Sharp. Ethnographically-informed empirical studies of software practice. *Information and Software Technology*, 49(6):540–551, 2007.

162   C. Robson. *Real world research* 2nd edition. Blackwell, 2002.

163   M. Rodgers, A. Sowden, M. Petticrew, L. Arai, H. Roberts, N. Britten, and J. Popay. Testing methodological guidance on the conduct of narrative synthesis in systematic reviews: effectiveness of interventions to promote smoke alarm ownership and function. *Evaluation*, 15(1):49–73, 2009.

164   M. Rosemann and I. Vessey. Linking theory and practice: performing a reality check on a model of is success. In *Proceedings of the European Conference on Information Systems*, 2005, pp. 854–865.

165   M. Rosemann and I. Vessey. Toward improving the relevance of information systems research to practice: the role of applicability checks. *MIS Quarterly*, 32(1):1–22, 2008.

166   W. W. Royce. Managing the development of large software systems. In *Proceedings of IEEE WESCON 26*, 1970, pp. 1–9.

167   P. Runeson. A survey of unit testing practices. *IEEE Software*, 23(4):22–29, 2006.

168   P. Runeson, C. Andersson, T. Thelin, A. A. Andrews, and T. Berling. What do we know about defect detection methods? *IEEE Software*, 23(3):82–90, 2006.

169   P. Runeson, P. Beremark, B. Larsson, and B. Lundh. Spin-syd—a non-profit exchange network. In *1st International Workshop on Software Engineering Networking Experiences*, Joensuu, Finland, 2006.

170   P. Runeson and M. Höst. Guidelines for conducting and reporting case study research in software engineering. *Empirical Software Engineering*, 14(2):131–164, 2009.

171   P. Runeson and M. Skoglund. Reference-based search strategies on systematic literature reviews. In *Proceedings of the International Conference on Evaluation and Assessment in Software Engineering*, Durham, UK, 2009.

172 G. Sabaliauskaite, A. Loconsole, E. Engström, M. Unterkalmsteiner, B. Regnell, P. Runeson, T. Gorschek, and R. Feldt. Challenges in aligning requirements engineering and verification in a large-scale industrial context. In *Proceedings of the 16th International Working Conference Requirements Engineering: Foundation for Software Quality*, 2010, pp. 128–142.

173 C. Sadler and B. A. Kitchenham. Evaluating software engineering methods and tool, part 4: the influence of human factors. *SIGSOFT Software Engineering Notes*, 21(5):11–13, 1996.

174 O. Salo and P. Abrahamsson. Empirical evaluation of agile software development: The controlled case study approach. In F. Bomarius and H. Iida, editors, *Proceedings of the 5th International Conference Product Focused Software Process Improvement*, Number 3009 in *LNCS*, Springer-Verlag, 2004, pp. 408–423.

175 C. Sanderson. A DESMET-based evaluation of commercial requirements management tools in an industrial setting. Master's project, University of Hertfordshire, School of Computer Science, 2009.

176 C. B. Seaman. Qualitative methods in empirical studies of software engineering. *IEEE Transactions on Software Engineering*, 25(4):557–572, 1999.

177 C. B. Seaman. Ethics in qualitative studies of commercial software enterprises: case description. *Empirical Software Engineering*, 6:299–300, 2001.

178 C. B. Seaman and V. R. Basili. Communication and organization: an empirical study of discussion in inspection meetings. *IEEE Transactions on Software Engineering*, 24(7):559–572, 1998.

179 G. Shanks. Guidelines for conducting positivist case study research in information systems. *Australasian Journal of Information Systems*, 10(1):76–85, 2002.

180 H. Sharp and H. Robinson. An ethnographic study of XP practice. *Empirical Software Engineering*, 9(4):353–375, 2004.

181 A. J. Shenhar, D. Dvir, O. Levy, and A. C. Maltz. Project success: A multidimensional strategic concept. *Long Range Planning*, 34(6):699–725, 2001.

182 F. Shull, V. R. Basili, J. Carver, J. C. Maldonado, G. H. Travassos, M. Mendonca, and S. Fabbri. Replicating software engineering experiments: addressing the tacit knowledge problem. In *Proceedings of the International Symposium Empirical Software Engineering*, 2002, pp. 7–16.

183 F. Shull, J. Carver, S. Vegas, and N. Juristo. The role of replications in empirical software engineering. *Empirical Software Engineering*, 13:211–218, 2008.

184 F. Shull and R. L. Feldman. Building theories from multiple evidence sources. In F. Shull, J. Singer, and D. Sjøberg, editors, *Guide to Advanced Empirical Software Engineering*. Springer-Verlag, London, 2008.

185 F. Shull, M. G. Mendoncça, V. R. Basili, J. Carver, J. C. Maldonado, S. Fabbri, G. H. Travassos, and M. C. Ferreira. Knowledge-sharing issues in experimental software engineering. *Empirical Software Engineering*, 9:111–137, 2004.

186 F. Shull, J. Singer, and D. Sjøberg, editors. *Guide to Advanced Empirical Software Engineering*. Springer-Verlag, London, 2008.

187 J. E. Sieber. Not your ordinary research. *Empirical Software Engineering*, 6:323–327, 2001.

188 S. Siegel and N. J. Castellan. *Nonparametric Statistics for the Behavioral Sciences*, 2nd edition. McGraw-Hill, 1988.

189 S. E. Sim, J. Singer, and M.-A. Storey. Beg, borrow, or steal: Using multidisciplinary approaches in empirical software engineering. *Empirical Software Engineering*, 6:85–93, 2001.

190 J. Singer, T. C. Lethbridge, N. G. Vinson, and N. Anquetil. An examination of software engineering work practices. In *CASCON First Decade High Impact Papers*, CASCON '10. ACM, New York, NY, USA, 2010, pp. 174–188.

191 J. Singer and N. G. Vinson. Why and how research ethics matters to you. Yes, you! *Empirical Software Engineering*, 6:287–290, 2001.

192 J. Singer and N. G. Vinson. Ethical issues in empirical studies of software engineering. *IEEE Transactions on Software Engineering*, 28(12):1171–1180, 2002.

193 D. Sjøberg, T. Dybå, B. Anda, and J. E. Hannay. Building theories in software engineering. In F. Shull, J. Singer, and D. Sjøberg, editors, *Guide to Advanced Empirical Software Engineering*. Springer-Verlag, London, 2008.

194 D. Sjøberg, T. Dybå, and M. Jørgensen. The future of empirical methods in software engineering research. In L. Briand and A. Wolf, editors, *Future of Software Engineering (FOSE'07)*, 2007, pp. 358–378.

195 D. Sjøberg, J. E. Hannay, O. Hansen, V. B. Kampenes, A. Karahasanovic, N.-K. Liborg, and A. Rekdal. A survey of controlled experiments in software engineering. *IEEE Transactions on Software Engineering*, 31(9):733–753, 2005.

196 R. E. Stake. *The Art of Case Study Research*. SAGE Publications, 1995.

197 M.-A. Storey, J. Ryall, J. Singer, D. Myers, L.-T. Cheng, and M. Muller. How software developers use tagging to support reminding and refinding. *IEEE Transactions on Software Engineering*, 35(4):470–483, 2009.

198 C. Stringfellow and A. A. Andrews. An empirical method for selecting software reliability growth models. *Empirical Software Engineering*, 7(4):319–343, 2002.

199 E. B. Swanson and C. M. Beath. The use of case study data in software management research. *Journal of Systems and Software*, 8(1):63 – 71, 1988.

200 O. Taipale, K. Smolander, and H. Kalviainen. Finding and ranking research directions for software testing. In I. Richardson, P. Abrahamsson, and R. Messnarz, editors, *Software Process Improvement*, Volume 3792 of *LNCS*. Springer-Verlag, 2005, pp. 39–48.

201 H. E. Thomson and P. Mayhew. Approaches to software process improvement. *Software Process: Improvement and Practice*, 3(1):3–17, 1997.

202 W. F. Tichy. Hints for reviewing empirical work in software engineering. *Empirical Software Engineering*, 5:309–312, 2000.

203 E. J. Uusitalo, M. Komssi, M. Kauppinen, and A. M. Davis. Linking requirements and testing in practice. In *Proceedings of the 16th IEEE International Requirements Engineering Conference*. IEEE Computer Society, 2008, pp. 265–270.

204 M. van Genuchten. Why is software late? An empirical study of reasons for delay in software development. *IEEE Transactions on Software Engineering*, 17(6):582–590, 1991.

205 J. C. van Niekerk and J. D. Roode. Glaserian and Straussian grounded theory: similar or completely different? In *Proceedings of the 2009 Annual Research Conference of the South African Institute of Computer Scientists and Information Technologists*. ACM, New York, NY, USA, 2009, pp. 96–103.

206   R. van Solingen and E. Berghout. *The Goal/Question/Metric Method. A Practical Guide for Quality Improvement of Software Development.* McGraw-Hill, 1999.

207   A. M. Vans, A. von Mayrhauser, and G. Somlo. Program understanding behavior during corrective maintenance of large-scale software. *International Journal of Human-Computer Studies,* 51:31–70, 1999.

208   J. M. Verner, J. Sampson, V. Tosic, N. A. Abu Bakar, and B. A. Kitchenham. Guidelines for industrially-based multiple case studies in software engineering. In *Third International Conference on Research Challenges in Information Science,* Fez, Morocco, 2009, pp. 313–324.

209   N. G. Vinson and J. Singer. Getting to the source of ethical issues. *Empirical Software Engineering,* 6:293–297, 2001.

210   C. Wallace, C. Cook, J. Summet, and M. Burnett. Human centric computing languages and environments. In *Proceeding Symposia on Human Centric Computing Languages and Environments,* 2002, pp. 63–65.

211   C. Wallin, F. Ekdahl, and S. Larsson. Integrating business and software development models. *IEEE Software,* 19(6):28–33, 2002.

212   D. B. Walz, J. J. Elam, and B. Curtis. Inside a software design team: knowledge acquisition, sharing, and integration. *Communications of the ACM,* 36(10):63–77, 1993.

213   C. Wohlin, A. Gustavsson, M. Höst, and C. Mattsson. A framework for technology introduction in software organizations. In *Proceedings of the Software Process Improvement Conference,* Brighton, UK, 1996, pp. 167–176.

214   C. Wohlin, K. Henningsson, and M. Höst. Empirical research methods in software engineering. In R. Conradi and A. Wang, editors, *Empirical Methods and Studies in Software Engineering—Experiences from ESERNET.* Springer, 2003.

215   C. Wohlin, M. Höst, M. C. Ohlsson, B. Regnell, P. Runeson, and A. Wesslén. *Experimentation in Software Engineering: An Introduction.* International Series in Software Engineering. Kluwer Academic Publishers, 2000.

216   A. L. Wolf and D. S. Rosenblum. A study in software process data capture and analysis. In *Proceedings of the 2nd International Conference on the Software Process,* Berlin, Germany, February 25–26, 1993, pp. 115–124.

217   R. K. Yin. *Case Study Research: Design and Methods,* 3rd edition. SAGE Publications, 2003.

218   M. V. Zelkowitz and D. R. Wallace. Experimental models for validating technology. *Computer,* 31(5):23–31, 1998.

219   M. V. Zelkowitz, D. R. Wallace, and D. Binkley. The culture clash in software engineering technology transfer. In *Proceedings of the 23rd NASA/GSFC Software Engineering Workshop,* Greenbelt, MD, 1998.

Index

Case Study Research in Software Engineering: Guidelines and Examples, First Edition.
Per Runeson, Martin Höst, Austen Rainer, and Björn Regnell.
© 2012 John Wiley & Sons, Inc. Published 2012 by John Wiley & Sons, Inc.

Printed and bound by CPI Group (UK) Ltd, Croydon, CR0 4YY

09/06/2025

14685901-0001